Monopoly, Big Business, and Welfare
in the Postwar United States

Monopoly, Big Business, and Welfare in the Postwar United States

by

DEAN A. WORCESTER, JR.

HD
2785
.W6

UNIVERSITY OF WASHINGTON PRESS

SEATTLE AND LONDON

To Joy

Preface

IN RECENT YEARS there has been increased interest in the use of alleged monopoly power on the part of oligopolistic business and labor unions in a way that initiates or sustains inflation, increases unemployment, squeezes the disadvantaged firm, or mis-allocates resources. Data such as those assembled and published by the Bureau of the Census are used to determine the degree of oligopolistic power, and decisions to allow or disallow mergers, to bring governmental pressure to bear in collective bargaining negotiations, and to include understandings concerning price changes in those negotiations are made upon such determinations.

Some years ago I was surprised by scattered evidence that came to my attention which suggested that the degree of concentration called oligopolistic was typical of much American industry generally considered to be essentially competitive. Then cost studies made for industries regarded as classical examples of oligopoly often revealed no economies of scale that would make them invulnerable to entry. Finally, various studies appeared which seemingly showed only negligible effects of oligopoly and monopoly in the American economy.

This book brings evidence and analysis to bear on the extent and importance of oligopoly in the United States economy. My intention has been to cast all of the analysis in a form that is consistent with the empirical data presently available. As far as possible, implicit theorizing has been avoided, and the propositions advanced are subject, at least in principle, to empirical test; although in some cases more emphasis must be placed on the "at least in principle" than I would wish.

This study would not have been possible without the aid of the Ford Foundation. The aid took the form of a grant for the academic year 1960-61 and indirectly supplied summer grants upon two other occasions.

A number of people have assisted me. Professor Joe S. Bain called my attention to a basic source of data and W. Walter Williams, former Undersecretary of Commerce, helped me to a good start in Washington. At the Bureau of the Census I was given much assistance and counsel by Maxwell R. Conklin, Irving Rottenberg, and Jack Gottsegen. In addition, I received useful suggestions from Simon S. Whitney at the Federal Trade Commission, Frank J. Kottke, now at Washington State University, from David N. Cohen at the Business Defense Services Administration, and from Dr. Paul E. Nelson, Jr. of the Agricultural Marketing Service of the Department of Agriculture. Professors John E. Floyd, Donald F. Gordon, and Kenneth M. McCaffree read portions of the manuscript and offered valuable suggestions. I, of course, remain responsible for all errors of omission and commission that remain.

Department of Commerce materials, predominately census materials, provide the only new compilations of data. It is unfortunate that limitations of time and money made it necessary to take only a sample of one year's data. All census data which appear in this book were processed exclusively by Census agents in the Census offices; and only the totals have been taken from the premises, and those only after it was determined that no disclosure is involved. I am grateful for the assistance rendered.

It is hoped that enough has been done to stimulate a more useful tabulation of available raw data in the future. It is possible to use census data to construct product classes that approach economically meaningful categories far more exactly than ever before. These classes can be grouped in such a way as to avoid disclosure while serving to open up "industry" economics to objective scrutiny virtually for the first time. If this book stimulates such a study, I shall count it a success whether or not my particular findings, or the models which are related to them, are accepted.

Portions of certain chapters are taken from articles that appeared previously. A portion of my article, "Product Differentiation as an Alternative to Monopoly" (Proceedings of the 34th Annual Conference of the Western Economic Association, 1959) appears in Chapter II, and about half of "Monopoly and Income Distribution" (Proceedings of the Western Economic Association, 1956) in Chapter IX.

I also wish to record my indebtedness to Wendy Walker and Carol Haertel who uncomplainingly struggled with successive versions of difficult rough drafts, to Barbara Gervenack who helped with the final preparation of the manuscript, and to Marion Olson Dunsmore for her careful, skillful editorial assistance.

DEAN A. WORCESTER, JR.

Contents

List of Tables

Monopoly, Big Business, and Welfare
in the Postwar United States

Chapter I

Principal Findings and Procedures

THIS BOOK develops the thesis that highly concentrated industries which are composed by both great firms and small can be expected to approximate competitive criteria for performance. It does not identify optimal performance with competitive performance.

The principal tool of analysis is the independent maximization hypothesis, deduced from a simple economic game which rests upon somewhat novel postulates. They include economic rationality, less-than-perfect knowledge, and information available only at a cost. Collusive agreements are possible, but they also have costs, and may be broken. More novel is the assumption that firms are typically multiproduct, and that each product is initially the output of a monopolist who faces entry from firms which are of potentially equal efficiency.

The independent maximization hypothesis is applied to price, output, sales expense, and research and development. The less objective the decision-criteria, the stronger is the hypothesis when viewed a priori. As applied to price-quantity, it forecasts higher profits for an innovating firm if it neither expands output (and lowers price) sufficiently to prevent the appearance of rivals nor colludes with rivals when they do appear, but rather establishes a monopoly position in the first period and accepts price reductions commensurate with holding approximately its initial output as rivals appear. The firm may adjust its output, but only modestly, if the demand function for the product is stable, but will expand it, perhaps substantially, if the demand moves rightward.

Alternative policies are possible, if not optimal; and the two alternative policies mentioned above are assumed to have been followed by a number of firms. It turns out that a different size distribution of firms is predicted for each of the market strategies—highly unequal if innovating firms follow a large-output, limit-price strategy; log-normal if they follow the independent maximization hypothesis; and approximately equal if they follow a collusive policy. The statistical materials which I have been able to gather tend to support the independent maximization hypothesis.

Few data are available which reveal the relative size of the leading firms. This is particularly true of data related to well-defined products as opposed to the conglomerate size of firms in the sum total of their product markets. Special studies of Census of Manufactures data, Federal Trade Commission and Department of Justice complaints, and analyses of indexes of disparity computed by the Federal Trade Commission and Herfindahl indexes presented in Ralph L. Nelson's study of concentration provide a modest basis for analysis. It is argued that product definitions appropriate to monopoly power are typically narrower than those generally used in past studies, and that data collected using such definitions would provide a clearer test of the hypothesis.

Product competition and sales expense raise interesting logical problems. A good may be enhanced in value in the eyes of the consumer by many devices which attach a product to a want in fictitious or misleading ways. If products are to be distinguished by the action of consumers, and if the test of separateness is the observed differences in price when consumers have a choice, different brands of the "same" drug or differently packaged "identical" bobby pins, and the like, must be considered different products. Likewise, if physically different goods are regarded as equivalent by consumers, as shown by the fact that whenever they are offered a choice they always take the cheaper, the goods are economically the same. By this test any product change, however trivial, and any sales effort, however "irrelevant" or misleading, that leads consumers to attach different values to certain units of supply is value-creating and as productive as any other activity that produces an equal value. By this test, the greatest producers of all time are those who have by means of religious and national symbolism led people to sacrifice their very lives and those of their loved ones for the products they offered: "truth," "independence," "freedom," "safety," "honor," "duty," and other abstractions the meanings of which are enshrouded by philosophical problems.

The subjective test for the identification of product is, like all other tests, arbitrary. It has the advantage of consistency in the sense that the end of economic activity is taken as satisfaction of the consumer's wants and his judgment is therefore final. The subjective test has the disadvantage of distinguishing such a multitude of ephemeral products as to vitiate statistical investigation of market structure and performance. Many of the microeconomic manufactured products must be combined before they can be reduced to the 7000 or so 7-digit products of the Census of Manufactures which are regarded by students of industry structure as too narrowly defined and too numerous.

The subjective test also outrages the sensibilities of those who are convinced that "false" values are created by sales expense and product differentiation. Here is a slippery field indeed. It is traversed in Chapter II. The point to be made here is that any welfare failures which flow from product differentiation and sales expense, as well as errors that arise because of improper combination of products into statistical aggregations, are as chargeable against competitive industries as against oligopolies and monopolies. For that reason, failures to optimize found below are not necessarily associated with oligopoly.

The plan of this book is as follows. Chapter II attempts to relate the subjective microeconomic definition of product to a statistically meaningful one. It finds a point of contact in the theory of discrimination and introduces the concepts of subproducts and variants which are combined into generic products. The latter are statistically operational.

An important thesis of this book is that the actual degree of concentration in product markets is substantially higher in the United States than shown in previous studies. Understatement of the degree of concentration rests, in part, upon the definition of product classes chosen for earlier empirical studies. Too much attention is given to policy considerations in such studies, with the result that the economic importance of the groups has carried undue weight in defining the boundaries of a product. The result is a tendency to find high concentration in industries which ship a high volume of goods, and competition in industries that ship small volumes, with too little regard paid to the microeconomic tests for monopoly.

Chapter III defines oligopoly in an operational way. In formal microeconomic analysis, oligopoly exists when there is interdependence that makes the position of an individual firm's demand curve dependent upon some action taken by a rival firm. Technically, cross elasticities of demand and supply can measure the amount of influence. This test is operational in principle, but statistical determination requires many accurate data and independent action by the firms. It can, therefore, be used only occasionally. Performance tests are also used by some students to define industry structures. Because alternative structures can produce similar performance, performance is here regarded as a consequence of structure and not as its definition. Empirical work is usually based upon concentration ratios. It is assumed that when a few firms produce the lion's share of the output of some product, interdependence of demand must exist. For purposes of the present study, concentration is chosen as the definition best suited to operational analysis.

Chapter IV attempts to show why former studies understate the degree of oligopoly according to the concentration test. A sample of data collected from the 1954 Census of Manufacturers is then presented which shows much higher degrees of concentration. The sample is taken from the two extremes of concentration for 5-digit products and does not provide a proper basis for a new estimate of the incidence of oligopoly in the economy as a whole. But the substantial concentration found in the least concentrated group leaves the general conclusion in little doubt. The findings are buttressed by analysis of studies made of 4- and 5-digit products by Ralph L. Nelson.

The independent maximization hypothesis as applied to price and output is presented in Chapter V. It provides an explanation for the great disparity of firm sizes found in empirical studies of which very little cognizance has been taken by those who look upon firms as maximizing organizations. The effects of collusion, leadership, and spontaneous coordination upon relative size are examined. A critical analysis of some oligopoly models which postulate management preoccupation with the price variable is part of this analysis.

Data from various sources which reveal the disparity of firm size by product are presented in Chapter VI. They tend to confirm the independent maximization hypothesis. The sample of census data suggests a typical progression of firm size, in which the largest firm produces twice that of the second and the second twice that of the third. Both greater and lesser disparity are found. Various cost and demand characteristics are examined, but none account for the different disparity of firm sizes. Consequently, alternative policies on the part of the leading firms are hypothesized as causative of the different rates of progression of firm size.

Because the sample of census data covers only about 4 per cent of the 5- and 7-digit products, the 1950 Federal Trade Commission's study of the 1000 largest firms is examined in some detail. Although confined to the largest firms, it covers over 400 of the 1000 5-digit products. Many of those not included were omitted because they had regional markets. This study supports the general conclusion that the disparity of firm size among the leading producers of a given product is typically great. So does the evidence from the complaints of the Federal Trade Commission and the Department of Justice gathered for the prosecution of the 1951 anti-merger amendment to the Clayton Act, Section 7. The disparity of firm size found in these complaints is somewhat less than that found for business as a whole.

Chapter VII applies the independent maximization hypothesis to sales expense and product differentiation in a formal way. It is presented separately rather than included in Chapter V because neither is relevant to the size distribution of firms and because the analysis is a priori. Independent maximization does gain some support from the data of Chapter VI, and, as pointed out above, there is more reason to suppose that firms will act independently in these areas than there is for price and output. The analysis suggests that the same mechanisms that produce lower prices and larger output under the pressure of rivalry and entry also produce larger selling expense and a wider variety of subproducts.

Chapter VIII examines the proposition that absolutely large firms have an advantage in research. The advantages that the large firm may enjoy in research are not necessarily associated with particular products. Instead, its advantage may lie primarily in the broad range of products to which one or another of its research findings may contribute. Analysis of research activity is, therefore, better related to the firm as a whole rather than to concentration in particular product markets. In this sense, size rather than oligopoly is basic, and the firm may be monopolistic, oligopolistic, or competitive in its various product lines. Nevertheless, the amount of research that one large firm finds it profitable to undertake depends in part upon the amount done by other firms. Different types of research are distinguished. A review of the literature establishes no clear advantage of large scale. When analysis similar to that which produced the independent maximization hypothesis is applied to research on the assumption that research is just another avenue toward the maximization of profits it is again found that more developmental research will be undertaken where rivalry and entry exist, as compared to the monopoly or the collusive position. It will also tend to be carried to the place where the marginal return is equal to that of alternative business expenditures. Fundamental research, on the other hand, will be neglected in favor of developmental research. Monopoly or collusion produces more fundamental research and less developmental. This is a move toward an optimal level in the former, and away from it in the latter case, although the former remains suboptimal.

Chapter IX falls into four divisions. The nature of the welfare test supplied by welfare economics is considered, and a tripartite test more readily capable of operational determination is advanced as a surrogate. The tests are growth, distribution of income, and welfare loss as shown by costs, prices and profits. The second section attempts to relate oligopoly in the American economy to income distribution. It does not find any important distortion. It is noted that this may be a consequence of a distortion of costs from production into sales and subproduct differentiation which may contribute little to welfare. The extent of distortion is examined in connection with an analysis of the extent of the welfare loss as computed by Harberger and Schwartzman in their separate studies of this matter. Their data employ broad definitions of industries and are subject to a number of objections, most of which imply a higher estimate of welfare loss than theirs.

The final section of Chapter IX summarizes the conclusions of the book as they relate to the significance of oligopoly in the American economy. In general, the economy is found to be suboptimal in its performance, but less so than one would suppose probable in the light of the high concentration and the great disparity of firm size in most industries. Nor can it be said that less concentration would improve matters much.

The conclusions rest to a considerable extent upon models which have faced, at best, only implicit tests. They are consistent with a considerable body of statistical data reported or summarized herein.

It is hoped that a major study can be mounted which would construct more meaningful products from the 7-digit data collected by the census—products that would be similar with respect to the degree of interrelationship among its subproducts. If that were done, it would be possible to provide much more satisfactory tests for the hypotheses advanced here and elsewhere.

Chapter II

Definition of Products

THE PRODUCTS of formal microeconomic theory differ enormously from those used in statistical studies. While this is inevitable and desirable in many instances because differing particular objectives of individual studies justify greater or lesser degrees of aggregation, judgments relating to the performance of branches of the economy or the economy as a whole are obscured or invalidated because of the lack of correspondence of the products of welfare theory to those for which statistical data are assembled. The purpose of this chapter is to provide a rationale that relates microeconomic products, sometimes referred to hereafter as *elements,* to the statistical products of the census and of other statistical compilations.

Products are at once the output of firms and the inputs of final users. Because value is thought to flow from the satisfaction of consumer wants, the more fundamental basis for the definition of products is by type of final use. We follow this practice in defining products.

The products of microeconomic theory are elemental, in the sense that products are classified separately if users regard them as different, however trivial the difference, and indicate this by a willingness to pay different prices. This definition is well suited to welfare analysis, because it is a logical deduction from the postulate that value as recognized by the consumer is the ultimate test of value. There is, however, an extremely large number of such elementary products, a large proportion of which are short lived. Elemental products are often good substitutes for others in final use. Virtually every product significant enough to be considered worthy of analysis is a collection of microeconomic products, and is referred to here as a *generic* product.

The primary function of this chapter is an attempt to associate elements into generic products in a way which connects the products of microeconomic theory to statistically useful constructs. The problem is to establish principles where subsets called generic products are formed out of the universal set of elementary products.

Basically, our procedure is to group elements which are substitutes in consumption. It is argued that this is not only more convenient but is also more appropriate for welfare economics than is separate treatment of each element. The argument is based on the idea that consumer surplus may be tapped by product variety, raising total revenues to the industry above what they would be with a single product without a corresponding increase in total consumer satisfaction. In contrast, larger numbers of independent products make a full contribution to consumer surplus, offset, partially, only by the income effect.

Satisfactory definition of generic products is prerequisite to analysis of industry performance and of industry structure, but the problems of definition and analysis are separate and should not be confused. It is tempting to consolidate products on the basis of high cross elasticity of supply. Just as monopoly power based upon the production of an element can be partially or fully eliminated by the presence of other elements of a generic product, apparent monopoly of a generic product may be partially or fully eliminated by high cross elasticities of supply with other generic products.

"Monopoly" power may indeed be small if entry is possible at small cost. But if entry at small cost were ubiquitous, *all* products, regardless of use, would be classified as one by the cross elasticity of supply test. This would vitiate the basic problems associated with the allocation of resources.

We prefer, therefore, to *define* products in terms of end use, and to *define* industry structure in terms of the number of firms engaged actively in the individual product markets. *Analysis* of the significance of the industry structure rests importantly upon cross elasticities of supply and ease of entry.

It is possible to infer something about the number and importance of potential entrants from existing industry structure. Firms are of two general types, normal and conglomerate. A normal firm produces a single set of elementary products which are complementary in production. A conglomerate firm produces two or more such sets. If a particular set of elements is always produced by a normal firm, it is reasonable to infer that diseconomies are involved in its inclusion in a conglomerate structure. Where elements of a generic product are produced by a conglomerate firm, it is probable that barriers to entry are weak because other conglomerate firms can add such elements if profits appear. This is not certain, because economies of scale may be enjoyed by firms that combine certain groups of complementary products. Low barriers to entry become a virtual certainty when elements of a generic product are produced by both normal firms and conglomerate firms.[1]

The reader who is willing to accept the idea that dissimilar products can be appropriately combined into census-type products may find it better to skip this chapter and proceed directly to Chapter III. There a

[1] It may be helpful to define these relationships more precisely and to visualize them. *Elements* constitute a universal set, E, each element of which may be visualized as a point in two dimensions or a line in three dimensions. A *normal firm,* n, produces a single subset, N, of elements. Each firm may be visualized as a triangle containing one or more points. If two or more firms produce a given element, this may be visualized by arranging the firms in space and allowing elemental lines to pass through the firms. Each firm is conceived as occupying a single plane. A *conglomerate firm*, c, also occupies a single plane. It may be represented as a rectangle which surrounds two or more triangles and includes subset C of the universal set. A generic product is a subset U of elements that provide similar values in end use. It may be visualized as a smooth figure that circumscribes the elemental points or lines. Generally a subset U will have multiple intersections with N and C subsets.

The adjacent Figure 2-A shows five firms, one conglomerate, which together produce six elements which make up four generic products which are designated A, B, C, D, as shown on the product plane at the right hand side. There are three N subsets, two of which form one C subset. Product A is a classical monopoly. A single firm produces a single elementary product. The classical competitive industry would exist if there were many firms producing only A. B is produced by three firms, one of which is conglomerate. It is complementary in production with two other elements. Good C includes the other two complements to B plus an element from another N subset. It is produced by the three firms that produce B and also by another firm. The conglomerate firm produces some of this generic product, which includes three elements, two from one group of production complements and one from the other. D is produced by two firms.

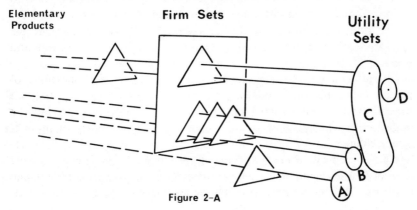

Elementary Products   **Firm Sets**   **Utility Sets**

Figure 2-A

choice is made from among the standard definitions of oligopolistic structure after consideration of their characteristics.

The remainder of this chapter is divided into three parts. Section A relates the differentiation of physically identical products to the theory of price discrimination and, in so doing, casts doubt upon the welfare gains that may be associated with the multiplication of micro-products. These conclusions are reviewed in Chapter IX. Section B deals with nonidentical elements of a generic product, and offers an objective device whereby elements can be combined into generic products., It shows why firms tend to produce more than one element related to a generic product. The formal models of product competition are treated in Chapter VII. This initial treatment is the minimum required to advance the argument which underlies the combination of a number of micro-products into statistically operational aggregates. Section C offers some examples of price structures and illustrates several "effective generic demand curves."

Although analysis and examples normally associated with monopoly or oligopoly are used in this chapter, the task at hand is the definition of a product and the combination of similar products as they are understood in microeconomic theory into census-type products, regardless of industry structure. As will become evident, a structure of subproducts may exist in industries now generally considered to be unconcentrated and essentially competitive as well as in those generally regarded as oligopolistic or monopolistic. Definition of oligopolistic structure must await the definition of product classes. This is done in Chapter III. Analysis of the relative performance of oligopolies follows in Chapters V, VII, VIII, and IX.

A. Theoretical Problems

1. Shortcomings of the Microeconomic Definition of a Product

The principal theses of Section A are that adherence to the principle that products should be regarded as different if they sell for different prices (1) virtually destroys contact between economic analysis and empirical evidence about market behavior by making the logically valid units small, ephemeral, and fundamentally subjective; and (2) fails to provide a sure guide to the maximization of consumer welfare. The latter applies directly only to consumer goods, upon which attention is centered here.

Pigou's analysis of price discrimination offers an access to the necessary analytical distinctions that permit a valid combination of elemental products into generic products. He defined three degrees of price discrimination:[2] discrimination of the first degree, based upon individual units of the commodity; discrimination of the second degree, based upon price groups; and of the third degree, based upon groupings of customers. In the latter, buyers are in one or more separate markets and cannot resell to each other, thus making the products entirely independent from the consumer's viewpoint. Thus third-degree discrimination exists when physicians use a different scale of charges for rich and poor patients, or railroads charge different rates for carrying products in different classifications. Second-degree discrimination exists when the "same" product is sold at different prices to consumers who can choose to buy at either price. No commonly accepted example can be given at this point, but the sale of a specific drug of given potency and quantity but under different brand names at different prices may stand in lieu of such an example for the time being. First-degree discrimination exists in those markets where each sale is an occasion for higgling and each buyer is induced to pay his maximum price for each unit. It is formally equivalent to a market where each buyer must negotiate an all-or-nothing bargain with the sole supplier.

The traditional definition of price discrimination, whether it be of the first, second, or third degree, involves the sale of a homogeneous product at different prices. As theory has become more sophisticated, the definition of a particular product has come to depend upon the attitude of the customer, not upon the physical characteristics of the product. The concept of a homogeneous product is thereby lost and, with it, the basis upon which the theory of discrimination rests, because when some units are sold at a higher price they may be regarded as superior by a snobbish or uninformed buyer for that reason alone. To avoid this problem, price discrimination is sometimes defined as occurring when the ratio of marginal cost (including selling costs?) of a product produced by a given firm bears a different relationship to its price than to those of its "other" products.[3] Standing by itself, this definition is so broad as to include almost any monopolistic or monopsonistic deviation from pure competition by a multi-product firm. In that case, either discrimination is swallowed up in monopoly or monopoly is swallowed up into discrimination, and indeed Professor Coase, one of the discussants of Machlup's paper, declared himself in favor of viewing interactions among the various products (and the various factors

[2] A. C. Pigou, *The Economics of Welfare* (1st ed.; London: MacMillan, 1904).
[3] Fritz Machlup, *Business Concentration and Price Policy* (Princeton, N.J.: Princeton University Press for National Bureau of Economic Research, 1955), pp. 397-98.

of production in factor markets) as accomplishing the absorption of the theory of discrimination into the general field of monopoly pricing. If not already established, this position at least threatens the traditional one. The traditional position is favored for purposes of this book.

a. First-Degree Discrimination: One Product or Many?

The crucial distinctions are brought out most clearly in first-degree discrimination. Suppose that the output of an economy consists of a finite number of physically homogeneous products which are available for sale in each time period in specific quantities. Let there be constant physical returns to scale so that marginal and average variable costs are constant in the production of each product and let any deviation in entrepreneurial return transfer manpower between the entrepreneurial group and the employee group so that long-run price is equal to average and marginal cost in each industry with the entrepreneurial return included. Total cost = Total expenditures = Total receipts.

What is implied by a negatively sloped demand curve for any one of the products? The textbook analysis of the law of demand offers four determinants: (1) decreasing marginal utility as larger quantities are taken; (2) the inclusion of additional buyers with weaker effective demands for the product at lower prices; (3) income effects that follow from a change of the product's price; and (4) substitution relationships between this product and others which depend upon changes of relative prices.

Attention is focused on the first determinant. It is clear that if a person will buy two units of a product at a particular price, but only one at a higher price, the second item is not subjectively identical to the first in the mind of the buyer when income and substitution effects are negligible.[4]

The idea of consumer surplus, and the basis for the ability to raise total revenue by the imposition of all-or-nothing bargains, rest on the fact that when a buyer purchases more than one unit of a good, one is usually put to a more important use than the others. This is to say that, microeconomically speaking, they are different products. The peculiarity is that they are such good substitutes that either can fulfill either use. Thus total utility depends solely upon the number of units consumed, not upon their identity.

---

[4] Abba P. Lerner seems to point this out in the "strictest of micro-economic views," for he says that consumer surplus must then be zero because MC = P for each unit. "Consumer Surplus and Micro-Macro," *Journal of Political Economy,* LXXI (February, 1963), 81.

One can conceive the higgler who attempts to achieve first-degree price discrimination to be an expert entrepreneur who adds to his costs by taking time to carefully ration supply and to use his wits to point out the use of each item so as to make each item exactly fit the particular purpose that the potential customer already had for each of the units purchased. Under these special conditions the consumer's utility functions do not shift as a result of the entrepreneurial activity. If each transaction is carried out under ideal circumstances, the marginal costs of the seller on each sale (his time being his principal variable cost) will equal the price obtained. If one takes the modern microeconomic position, a firm operating under first-degree price discrimination sells not "a product" at "numerous prices" but instead offers many products (that happen to be physically identical) each at a single price.

As long as any consumer demand curve has slope for reason 1, the product involved serves more than one type of want, so that a wider range of products or qualities is potentially profitable. Sellers may find it profitable to "differentiate the product" (if costs of differentiation are low enough) to sell to each at his maximum price. This may be regarded alternatively as first-degree discrimination, as the ultimate in third-degree discrimination, or as the application of simple monopoly power to each of a large number of products.

However one may classify this phenomenon, it is evident that welfare is not increased. The additional effort has absorbed what Marshall called the consumer surplus. Total revenues and total costs are larger, since the added entrepreneurial effort receives its marginal returns; but the added effort contributes neither to physical output nor to the utility derived from it, and such effort amounts to a transfer from the consumers to the "differentiators." If the entrepreneurs are thought of as being outside of the system, the increased expenditures of the consumers of the monopolized product not only lose consumer surplus in that market but also suffer shrinking demand curves because of an adverse income effect.

The welfare loss from differentiation can be more clearly seen with the aid of a simple equilibrium model. It is convenient to postulate measurement in utility and disutility units and utilize them in a model which devotes labor time to leisure, and to the production of good A and good B. These goods are considered to be independent in consumption. We distinguish between (1) the effects of new processes that lower the disutility costs required per unit of utility; (2) the effects of the introduction of a new independent product; (3) the effects of differentiation which does not involve product innovation; and (4) the effects of differentiation which does include such effects. For simplicity, all costs are disutility costs and are supplied from or absorbed by leisure at constant disutility cost.

Figure 2-1 illustrates the effect of new processes which reduce the disutility cost per unit of both commodities A and B by equal amounts.

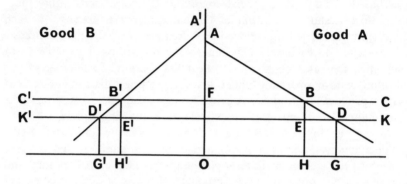

Figure 2-1

Output of good A rises as one moves from point O to the right, and output of good B rises as one moves leftward from point O. Marginal disutility is equal to marginal utility using old processes at points B and B'. The net gain from production is AFB + A'FB'.

The new processes reduce the disutility cost of production of both products to that shown by line K'K yielding the total net gain of ADD'A', an increase of D'DBB'. It should be noted that in this instance the total amount of disutility declines because the total elasticity of demand for the goods is less than -1.0. This is shown by the fact that the area D'G'GD is less than B'H'HB. It is a result of a reduction of the work week and of increased leisure.

A second step toward the demonstration of the appropriateness of combining different microeconomic products is illustrated with Figure 2-2, to evaluate the welfare effect of a new product. Suppose that initially all production is devoted to good B. Work involving disutility of B'H'OF is expended to achieve a net gain of B'FA'. When good A is introduced, additional work is performed at the expense of leisure at a disutility cost of FOHB, but additional new utility is gained in the amount AFB. A net gain is recorded as a result of the new product.

A third step is illustrated by Figure 2-3, where an existing product is improved. The essence of product improvement is a higher marginal

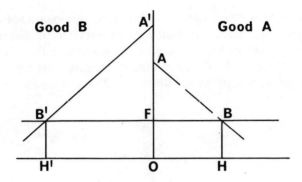

Figure 2-2

utility function. It is similar to the introduction of a new product and calls for a greater expenditure of labor to acquire a larger supply of the better product. If the product is improved only in durability it is better regarded as a process improvement because it simply offers the same total utility as before but for a smaller expenditure of work.

In Figure 2-3, the quality of good A is improved so that it comes to yield A″ABB″ more net utility than before, calling forth additional work equal to HGB″B in disutility.

We can now take the critical step and consider the effect of introducing substitute goods. If the uses to which different units of a good are put are somewhat different, it is probable that a somewhat different product will more exactly satisfy each use. Figure 2-4 illustrates a situa-

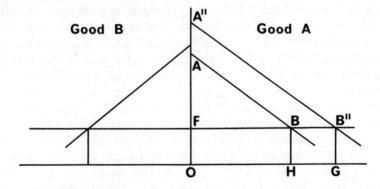

Figure 2-3

tion where costs are undertaken to differentiate a homogeneous product so as to make each unit appropriate for each use. One of the new series of products is superior for each use, so the marginal utility schedule for composite good A is A″B″ higher than the schedule appropriate to the undifferentiated product by A″ABB″.

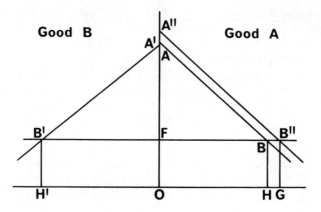

Figure 2-4

According to the microeconomic definition, a very large number of separate microeconomic goods exists in place of former good A. Technically speaking, there is a separate market for each. The marginal equality between marginal cost and price may prevail everywhere, and entry or exit may hold profits to competitive levels. If we consolidate the myriad of substitute products by arraying them in descending order of prices and making a cumulative sum of their quantities, we find that total utility is increased by only A″ABHGB″ while total costs are increased by A″FBHGB″. The prime effect of the added costs has been to absorb the consumer surplus, although some expansion of utility has also occurred.

The effect shown in Figure 2-4 is the limiting case where perfection of differentiation and discrimination is achieved and where the added resources are available at constant costs. But the result is not as preposterous as it may seem. Each step toward differentiation yields a business profit by the ordinary standards. Investment to improve the product meets the test of market acceptance. Each change improves real GNP if the usual test is applied. The added resources earn a normal return, and the monetary or fiscal authorities are only doing their duty when they support the increase of spending sufficient to finance the added productive effort of the expanding companies producing A goods. Nevertheless, the gain in total utility is small and the loss of welfare substantial, unless employment is regarded as superior to leisure per se.

The present purpose is not to raise the question of welfare loss from differentiation. It is to question the validity of insisting upon the separation of products according to the usual microeconomic principle. What is desired is acceptance of the concept of defining products according to whether or not they expand the utility frontier. The new products described by Figure 2-2 do achieve this end. So does the introduction of a superior homogeneous product that substitutes for the former product in all of its uses as illustrated by Figure 2-3. The substitution of a product or a series of products for some or all of the uses of an existing product may contract the utility frontier rather than expand it. Figure 2-4 illustrates an extreme instance of this. It is important to note that this does *not* necessarily involve the exercise of monopoly power.

In this extreme case, the increase in the marginal utility schedule is small, and the success of the entrepreneurs in capturing the consumers' surplus is complete. Introduction of a range of substitute products often produces a substantial shift in the utility schedule. Differentiation is never achieved in such exquisite perfection.

2. The Generic Demand Curve

We may call a demand curve for a group of products, such as curve A″B″ in Figure 2-4, a "generic" demand curve. The products need not be physically identical but are so considered in this section. It will reflect the Marshallian demand curve, which encompasses all consumer satisfaction, only when the differentiated subproducts are so numerous and so priced as to leave each buyer indifferent between making the purchase and doing without any of the generic product. Cross elasticity relationships, the need to offer a finite number of products, and the lack of information prevent any close approximation to the Marshallian demand curve by a generic product in practice. These matters are examined in Section B. Here we assume that elements do not differ in a physical sense, and that skill in differentiation and in discrimination holds cross elasticity to zero.

Figure 2-5 illustrates the relationships that may exist between a generic product and two approximations to it. The demand for the generic product is that which would exist if a full range of differentiated subproducts were available. It is shown as line AB. If only one optimum element of the possible range of similar elements is produced,

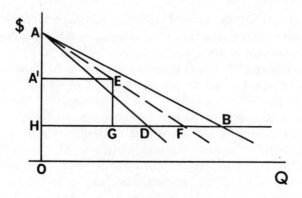

Figure 2-5

the marginal utility function is lower, say AD, and price and quantity are indicated by point D. The availability of two elements of this product can be expected to increase the total usefulness of the product. Thus line AEF is appropriate, with prices at E and F. With only one price, the location of the effective marginal utility curve, hypothesized as AD in Figure 2-5, is not known. With two prices, however, one can surmise that the generic curve lies above A′EF, and probably considerably above it, as will be shown in Section B of this chapter. The line A′EGF is called the *effective generic demand function* because it denotes the limit presently achieved in the industry. The surplus of satisfaction remaining for the consumers is no less than the area above A′EGF and below AEF.

In general, the higher the cross elasticity of demand between two products (or, what amounts to the same thing, the greater the effort made to separate and differentiate two subproducts from each other so as to reduce the cross elasticity) the more reasonable it is to regard them as serving the same want and therefore to classify them as part of the same generic product. But, by the same token, competition between them is more likely to reduce the price difference between them and thereby leave more of the consumer surplus in the hands of the consumers.

a. Second-Degree Discrimination

The two prices of Figure 2-5 illustrate the combination of two microeconomic products into a single generic product which is to second-degree price discrimination what a full range of products is to first-degree discrimination.

The cost of securing the maximum price for each unit of a physically identical good has proved to be greater than the gain from higgling. This is, perhaps, the clearest lesson learned by modern retailing. As goods become more abundant, and as the hourly wages of salesmen rise, a one-price policy attracts so large a volume of sales as to virtually eliminate higgling. Nevertheless, a number of price lines often exist for physically identical goods over long periods of time in locations which are easily accessible to the same buyers. Thus a given brand of toothpaste sells at more than 25 per cent variation in different stores in the same shopping district, and a wide variety of identical goods sells for substantially less in the "bargain basements" of department stores. In addition, different price-quality lines are typically sold side by side. Each market is open to all buyers. But they are separated by inconvenience, difference of services, ignorance, and misinformation.

One way to look at such price differences is to consider them as the measure of the value of the convenience, the difference of services or the cost of overcoming the ignorance or misinformation. Another way to look at the same phenomenon is as a measure of success in transferring a portion of the consumer surplus to the producers, albeit most or all of it is being absorbed in the cost of the achievement. The former is more appropriate when differences are associated with services, the latter when differences are associated with misinformation or ignorance.

b. Products, Subproducts and Variants

To simplify discussion, the word "product" is used henceforth to denote a generic product . Each is composed of one or more elements which sell for different prices. An element which is produced by a specific firm is called a *variant*. When a firm innovates a new element that falls inside a generic product, it may be referred to as a *subproduct*.

In general, the expectation is that the generation of subproducts, as distinguished from new products, will leave the consumer's utility frontier unchanged or will contract it. Although it is possible that the expansion of the area under the utility function will rise faster than the cost of differentiation, no guarantee of this is offered by setting marginal cost to equal price. In practice it is quite possible for a new element to have genuine uniqueness that expands the utility frontier for some buyers, and at the same time to contract the utility frontier for others. Nevertheless, the distinction is clear in principle. A product for our purposes is regarded as a collection of elements and/or subproducts.

Unfortunately, no method exists by which one can measure changes in the utility frontier directly, and no indirect measure is likely to be convincing to all observers. The distinction between differentiation of old and innovation of new products sometimes rests upon ignorance and misinformation. It also arises from rational business policies which capitalize on these conditions. It sometimes rests on monopoly power and collusive oligopoly power. In the latter cases, differentiation does not depend on consumer ignorance or misinformation.

No definite per se list of criteria can be given that will distinguish between separate products and subproducts, but the following are symptomatic of subproducts: (1) high cross elasticity coefficients in those cases where relative prices change; (2) persistent, well-defined price lines; (3) emphasis on striking, but minor, product differences; (4) heavy sales costs, particularly when emphasis is on minor or seemingly irrelevant matters; (5) insistence on the provision of accompanying services by the seller; (6) credit services that tend to tie the customer to an institution; (7) failure of the quantity sold of the group of products to expand by as much as the output of the new subproduct.[5]

[5] The logic behind this approximation can be illustrated with Figure 2-B in the following way. Let the summed marginal utilities of the community be AB with one subproduct, and AFC for two subproducts whose prices are OE and OD. The functions being straight lines, the added consumer surplus is ABC minus EDBF. Since these areas are equal, no change has occurred in the net community utility frontier. More work is done, it earns its marginal return, but the return adds nothing to net consumer surplus. A net addition would be recorded had AFC lain to the right, a net subtraction had it lain to the left of the position shown.

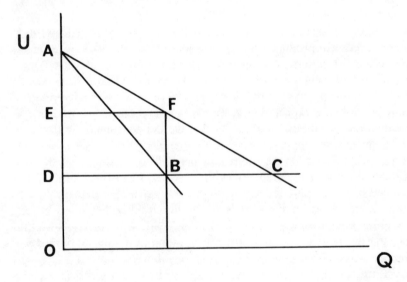

Figure 2-B

Differentiated products are not found exclusively in markets dominated by large oligopolistic or monopolistic enterprise. Indeed, many small businessmen and professional men have an exquisite touch for discrimination. Mass merchandising which utilizes hired sales personnel to sell branded, quality controlled, mass-produced commodities is not well suited to discrimination. Nevertheless, many market phenomena seem to offer examples not only of differentiation, but of second-degree price discrimination.

Summary

An attempt is made to find an analytical principle which permits the combining of products found on the market into a smaller number of generic products suitable for empirical work. The watershed between the microeconomic definitions and those used in empirical work is found in the theory of discrimination which can alternatively be thought of as involving either a given product selling at different prices or a group of related products.

By relating the definition of the product to its effect on aggregate welfare it is possible to distinguish between the introduction of new products, which expand welfare, and new elements of a generic product—subproducts—which do not, or at least may not. The division is not entirely satisfactory, because subproducts may contain an element of newness that expands the utility frontier. Microeconomic products are regarded as subproducts if one or more of the seven criteria listed at the end of the preceding section are met. The introduction of a new subproduct is considered as subtracting from consumer welfare, unless the output of the generic product rises by at least as much as that of the new subproduct. Otherwise, the presumption is that the producers' gains, most or all of which may be absorbed in costs, are taken from the consumer's surplus. In the Section B, the combining of elements which are not physically identical is investigated. The analysis proceeds on the assumption that differentiation does not expand the utility frontier.

B. Principles for Combining Subproducts

Section A presents a basic theoretical argument for treating physically identical products which sell for different prices as members of the same product although they are put to somewhat different uses and although they differ in the minds of the buyers. The root of the theoretical argument is that the difference of prices rests upon discriminating monopoly power, perhaps acquired by high selling cost, and that the consumers' utility frontiers are not expanded by the introduction of such subproducts.

The analysis in Section A implies cross elasticities of zero among subproducts. They represent the ultimate in the separation of sub-products. This section attempts to develop principles according to which physically dissimilar microeconomic products may be combined into generic products. Entrepreneurs are not regarded as capable of achieving maximum total revenues by the equivalent of optimal all or nothing bargains with each buyer. Instead, cross elasticity among subproducts may be high. The higher the cross elasticity, the more appropriate it is to consider various products to be members of the same generic product. But the lesson of Section A is not forgotten. In principle, market control can separate subproducts so as to eliminate statistically measurable cross elasticity relationships without making invalid their combination into a common generic product. Hence cross elasticity alone is not suffi-cient for classification. Indeed, the greater the success of differentiation (and, therefore, the more probable that price discrimination shrinks the utility frontier) the lower the statistically measurable cross elasticity will be. Successful differentiation involves characteristic business activity. Hence a second test, as noted above, classifies products together if they meet some or all of the seven symptomatic tests listed in section A.

To summarize, products may be classified together if they are associated *either* by high cross elasticity *or* by costs that tend to reduce cross elasticity. Homogeneity is not required.

Products that differ greatly in physical characteristics may satisfy a particular type of want. Physical differentiation must usually shift the generic demand curve somewhat to the right. We define the generic demand curve as that relevant to an optimal range of differentiated products. Thus, in many cases, the generic demand curve can be approached only if a substantial range of physically different subproducts is produced. This phenomenon is neglected here.

1. Distinguishing Among Different Generic Products

The argument thus far has attempted to find a logical basis for combining microeconomic products into larger aggregates. But it does not offer a guide for the separation of different generic products. The basic problem from a statistical viewpoint is to find *objectively defined* products that serve reasonably distinct wants. One difficulty in defining a generic product is the tendency for some elements of such a product to have positive cross elasticities with products outside of the group. For example, luxury cars may be in sharper competition with foreign travel than they are with Rambler Americans. Virtually everything may be tied in somewhere in the chain mail of substitutes.

The following procedure provides an avenue out of this dilemma which will produce a finite number of operationally defined products.

Variants of different elements may be chosen as "centers" such that zero cross elasticities, and costs designed to separate such centers from each other, prevail. All other variants that relate to a given center according to the two tests given above will then be counted as elements of that group or product. Trial and error, or possibly some efficient type of factor analysis, can be used to discover the minimum number of "centers" which would cover the maximum number of products with minimum overlap. No doubt some variants fall in no group. If so, they are monopolies by this test. Others fall in two or more groups. It is not clear that such overlap is inappropriate, but it is not neat. Some of the "monopolies" might well be limited by many poor substitutes which render its monopoly power trivial.

This procedure has the advantage of being operational. It has the further advantage of finding breaks in the chain of substitutes, because each relationship is measured in terms of a particular variant. It has the disadvantages of rather arbitrary choices of the "centers" and of requiring many accurate data.

This approach is not pursued further at this time. Census definitions are unavoidable for most of the empirical work in subsequent chapters.[6]

2. Producer Goods and Consumer Goods

The principles whereby unlike products may be combined into generic products and an effective generic demand curve found is stated in terms of consumer goods and utility functions. Utility functions are not directly related to producer goods, but this is not fundamental to the relationship between subproducts and generic products. A generic curve exists for producer goods as well as for consumer goods. There is a surplus that may be tapped if an all-or-nothing bargain can, as compared to the market price, extract a larger revenue for the same quantity of input. Different qualities and prices often provide a continuum of prices, and the related quantities can be summed to find an effective generic demand function.

3. Cross Elasticity and the Effective Generic Demand Curve

When differentiation fails to fully separate elemental products, cross elasticities rise above zero. This limits the ability of firms to appropriate

[6] This matter is discussed further in connection with the definition of oligopoly in Chapter III.

consumers' surpluses. The effects are illustrated in Figure 2-6. Let the generic product reflecting the maximum utility derivable from a maximum range of subproducts be A_nC_n and the proximate generic product with a single element with unit costs of Q_1C_1 be A_1C_1. Suppose that a subproduct which is superior for some uses is introduced which has unit costs of OE. The utility from the generic product rises to A_2C_2, increasing total utility by $A_1A_2C_2Q_2Q_1C_1$.

Suppose further that a cross elasticity relationship with the original product exists such that it loses sales to the original product at the rate of three units for each dollar that its price is above that of the original product. Thus its demand becomes B_2C_2 if the price of the original subproduct remains at OE'.

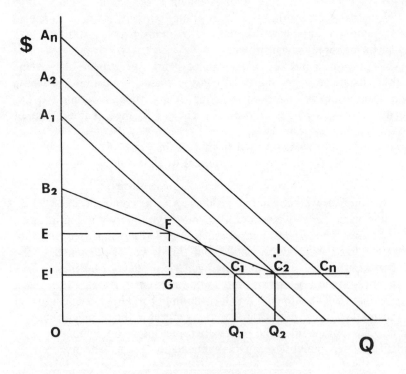

Figure 2-6

If competitive pressures exist, both products will come to be produced, quantity EF at price OE and quantity GC_2 at price OE'. Total physical production rises in this example, by Q_1Q_2, but sales in value terms rise by EFGE′ plus $Q_1C_1C_2Q_2$. A normal firm is virtually compelled to produce both elements if they are complementary in production.

There is no very satisfactory objective way, in general, to determine whether or not the welfare gain to the consumer is greater than his added costs. In this case the added costs, EFGE′ plus $Q_1C_1C_2Q_2$, appear to be somewhat less than the added utility, $A_1A_2C_2C_1$, but it is evident that the net change could be in either direction. The lower the effective cross elasticity, the greater the probability of reduced consumer surplus. The fact that the quantity sold rises from Q_1 to Q_2, or that sales rise from $OQ_1C_1E′$ to OQ_2C_2GFE, provides no guarantee that welfare is expanded as a result of the innovation.

Some examples are given in Section C which raise this question in a practical way.

Whatever may happen to welfare, it makes some sense to speak of the broken line $EFGC_2$ as an "effective generic demand curve" for the composite commodity illustrated in Figure 2-6. There is no reason why additional subproducts cannot be included.

One should note that an index price, I, associated with the output OQ_2 would provide an exaggerated estimate of the demand for the generic product with two subproducts. Any average price weighted by physical quantities will lie to the right of the generic demand curve. Point I is appropriate for the two prices OE and OE′.

C. Examples of Second- and Third-Degree Price Discrimination

The following pages present a few examples that are suggestive of the appropriateness of second- and third-degree discrimination as a basis for the classification of subproducts into products. The examples include both consumer and producer goods.

1. Calculating Machines

Electric calculating machines come in a number of models and price ranges. They differ primarily in the complexity of the calculations of which they are capable. Many users must have wondered if concentration upon a single highly sophisticated model would not so reduce costs as to enable all users to purchase the complex machine at the same cost, or nearly the same cost, as the simpler machine.

The Burroughs Corporation faced this problem. Their vice-president of product planning reports :

> Custom in our industry has placed certain relative values on features, and people are prepared to pay more for machines with these features than they would for machines without them. Yet the additional manufacturing

cost of these features is practically nil. To keep the cost of the basic machine down by building all alike, manufacturing proposed a single model to sell at the minimum feature price. If we sold at this price, they argued, the prospective buyer of the minimum feature machine would be happy because he got more machine for the same money and the prospective buyer of the maximum-feature machine would be happy because he got his machine for less money. The argument proved to be faulty (1) because it violates a fundamental sales precept that the buyer always should have a choice, and (2) because it traded a small cost saving for the larger profit obtained through the higher price possible on the more heavily featured machine. This larger profit greatly exceeded the additional manufacturing cost. . . .[7]

One cannot be certain that users of the simpler machines would be equally content with the more heavily featured machines at the same price, but it is possible that the proposal made by the manufacturing department is correct. There is, no doubt, something to the "fundamental sales precept" cited by Mr. Mengle, but in the same article he reported with approval the company's decision to market a new line of machines with quality and features "equal" to the existing lines which were to be restyled. It is possible, and less costly, to give consumers a choice without providing two full lines of features and price differentials to match. Consequently, attention centers upon the second reason given, namely that larger profits on the more highly featured machines would be sacrificed to achieve small gains in cost.

It is probable, but not inevitable, that marginal cost bears a different relationship to price for each line. Suppose, however, that the additional cost of adding features, advertising them, and selling the products makes marginal costs equal, not merely to marginal revenue, but to price in each price line. Would we wish to regard this result as approximating

---

[7] Milton E. Mengle, *Getting the Most from Product Research and Development* (New York: American Management Association; Special Report No. 6, 1955), pp. 117-18. Mengle noted that the courses of action open to top management for the expansion of business were the following: (1) modification of the product; (2) adjustment of price or, alternatively, of the quality of the product; (3) alteration of the number of models or of their features and price relationships; (4) discovery of new applications of the products; (5) alteration of the method of distribution; (6) alteration of advertising themes and media, sales promotion, or discount structure; (7) addition of entirely new lines of products. It is noteworthy that the adherence to rigid price lines is apparently rejected in the same article that lays such stress on the maintenance of a line of features which offer disproportionate profit in certain lines. Mengle also asserts that one cannot simply match the products of rival companies in this line of products because of the five years required to develop a new line. Because of this, he asserts that information on the present share of the market is not useful in long-term planning. Rather, production is directed to "exactly what the market needs."

the competitive result, with each of a number of firms producing a number of different virtually homogeneous products? Or is the view of the manufacturing department more nearly correct, with its implication that the more highly featured machine is a near-perfect substitute for the others, so that the various price lines are subproducts of a generic group? If the latter, and if the better machine is virtually no more costly to manufacture, the large profit margins (or, perhaps, the high product development and marketing costs) associated with the highly featured machines reflect discrimination that reduces users' surpluses.

If one attempts, as is done here, to support the latter point of view, one must face the fact that there are a number of companies producing similar machines, that each has made approximately the decision made by Burroughs Corporation, and that in spite of considerable pressure to expand markets, no firm has pressed so large a supply of the more profitable machines upon the market as to bring about a merging of the various price lines. In particular it would seem profitable for one of the firms to monopolize the market by bringing out its best model at the low price. Its profits would rise, although total industry revenues and profits would fall. But this is not attempted. One reason for this may be the great risk involved in such a large, supra-incremental decision. The alternative theoretical position must somehow explain why it is that competitive pressures have made margins and profits low for the cheaper machines while the same companies have been able to maintain more profitable price-cost relationships for the more expensive machines.

The demand for calculating machines seems to be differentiated at the upper level and undifferentiated at the lower, in the sense that some people require the expensive machine but the others can use either. Some, who do not require expensive machines, may purchase them for prestige purposes or in the expectation of future need, but most will, presumably, choose the cheaper machine if it meets their needs. Thus, it is relatively easy to maintain several price lines. The nature of the cost function and the substitutability of the more expensive machine for the cheaper argue for the application of the secondary price discrimination model to this situation.

Thus there is reason to suppose that Mr. Mengle is correct in stating, "Custom in our industry has placed certain relative values on features, and people are prepared to pay more for machines with these features than they would for machines without them." This suggests that approximate price matching has become established, and that firms sell as much as they can at these prices, but not enough to break the price structure.[8] A company may attempt to find a new niche with a machine of "equal quality and features but without frills," which, they think, "will not take sales away" from their other models. This, in effect, adds an additional series of subproducts and enhances the firm's ability to approximate first-degree discrimination. Companies may compete in many other ways, but each refrains from challenging the basic price-quality differentials. Attempts to exploit the more lucrative markets with improved (or at least changed) designs, sales costs, and customer service gradually tend to build up costs and reduce profits. In time, the price structure may break down and something approximating the universal machine may emerge. But "custom" and "fundamental sales precepts" carry weight, and the price-quality structure persists.

2. "Plexiglass": Third-Degree Discrimination Between Separate Products

"Lucite," also known as "Plexiglass," provides a superficially similar example which requires a different interpretation. Professor Kahn quotes Professors Stocking and Watkins that the substance is sold for $22 an ounce to dentists but at 85 cents an ounce, or about 1/26th as much, for commercial molding purposes. Apparently the product is identical except for packaging and sales channel, because it is further reported that the producer contemplated, and perhaps went to the additional expense of contaminating the lower-priced material used for commercial molding so as to prevent its use in dentures.[9]

From this information one infers that the two "subproducts" are substantially the same from a technical and manufacturing point of view. The products are so separated in final use, however, that one confidently expects cross elasticities of demand between them to be zero without intervention by the sellers. Nevertheless, the price differential can be maintained only by some system of control to prevent diversion of the plastic from commercial to dental users. While "customary" price maintenance policy may be said to separate the markets, this situation is essentially different from that exemplified by calculating machines. It is different because seller activity is directed to the separation of two unrelated uses. There is no continuum of subproducts sold in the same market and consequently no interstices that justify the term "price lines" or qualities devoted to very similar satisfactions. Conse-

---

[8] The rationality of this procedure is examined in Chapter V, where the independent maximization hypothesis is developed.

[9] Walter Adams (ed.) *Structure of American Industry* (New York: MacMillan, 1950), p. 218.

quently, this case is more appropriately regarded as a classical example of third-degree discrimination. The same physical substance serves very different wants and forms two different products. It closely fits Pigou's division according to classes of customers and is not complicated by interrelationships of demand. Although the buyers are not in the same market, the sellers are in both, and third parties could profit from the differential prices; therefore, some kind of a barrier is needed to preserve them. A price differential in this case does connote the existence of monopoly power and a loss of welfare more evidently than do price differentials between subproducts.

3. Gasoline

These two principles become entangled with each other when the economically important case of petroleum products is considered, because of the great variety of uses to which petroleum products are put. Many products are sold to two or more virtually unrelated types of buyers. But second-degree discrimination characterizes gasoline sales to private motorists. The firms' demand curve for gasoline is much flatter than that for the generic product. Most companies market two lines of gasoline, and some market three. In addition, somewhat different price policies are followed by different producing companies, and many individual filling stations are by no means completely controlled by their suppliers. There is substantial competition for volume, and price wars often occur.

At one extreme are companies like the Standard Oil Company of California, which engages in exploration, crude production, refining, transportation, research, and other operations, in addition to selling through a complex retailing system that attempts to participate in most of the markets of the western United States and, increasingly, in other United States and foreign markets. Attention is here confined to the market in the western United States.

The company markets through three dealer systems: Standard stations which are owned and operated by the wholly-owned subsidiary assigned the western region; Chevron stations which are owned and operated by owner-operators, but which retail Standard's product lines under Standard's brand names and generally follow the policies, including the price policies, laid down for the Standard stations; and Signal stations which are also owner-operated, but which handle Standard products under the Signal brand and have their own separate distribution system and price and service policies. Signal prices, service, and general service are just a cut below those of the other stations. Company officials declare that a different class of customers patronizes the Signal stations. For example, their cars average two years older.

Standard's belief, based upon long and successful experience, is that purchasers of gasoline can be divided into at least two major categories: those who will pay a little more, by as much as two cents a gallon, for good products accompanied by excellent service, smart, courteous attendants, and scrupulously clean premises; and those who will accept lower standards in order to secure lower prices. In the long run, the cost of providing the full range of service, cleanliness, and so on, may absorb the increased revenues due to their presence. Nevertheless, a continuous effort to maintain market segments goes on. Performance of products, extension of credit, location of outlet, access to outlet, and concessions from market price to certain classes of trade are among the devices used. The distinction between major and minor brands is, of course, a major device. Cassady and Jones declare the practice of the major California companies to be a "good example of market segmentation." The practice referred to is the sale of as much gasoline as possible at the higher major-brand price, and the disposal of the rest to independents to be sold under other brands. It is noteworthy that they declare that the quality of regular gasoline, with rare exceptions, is essentially homogeneous, and that the same thing may be said of premium gasolines.[10]

A similar observation holds true for the distinction between premium and regular gasoline sold by each station. Cassady and Jones find that at the time of their study, premium-grade gasoline "is not at all necessary" for most motors but that nevertheless approximately 60 per cent of the families in the area used it.[11] While it is true that premium-grade gasoline is physically different from regular gasoline and that some motors perform very much better when it is used while none performs less well, the maintenance of a price differential at all times, coupled with advertising directed primarily toward extolling changes in the premium product, tends to differentiate those consumers who wish to use the "best" from those who are more easily satisfied or, in some cases, from those who are better informed.

As previously noted, the Standard Oil Company of California attempts to do within its own organization what other firms do by sales to independents, although Standard Oil still supplies some independents.

[10] Ralph Cassady, Jr. and Wylie L. Jones, *The Nature of Competition in Gasoline Distribution at the Retail Level* (Berkeley, Calif.: University of California Press, 1951), p. 215; also Chapter V, p. 55.

[11] *Ibid.*, p. 59.

Other major refiners on the West Coast approach Standard's differentiation, but Standard of California apparently is the most finely adjusted. Minor brands and retail outlets can share only in the differentials that can be encompassed within a single type of station and may be expected to be less profitable. At the same time some of the independents can be expected to innovate high-volume, low-cost, limited-service outlets that make low-margin gasoline profitable. They are the natural innovators in this type of development, because they emphasize the price appeal. In doing so, these independents set the base price above which the others establish their price lines.

Figure 2-7 is a very crude illustration of the kind of relationship that is discussed here. It uses dollars-and-cents gasoline prices found by Livingston and Levitt in a study of six midwestern metropolitan areas on a single day and relative outputs based on Cassady and Jones' finding that 60 per cent of gasoline sold in the Los Angeles area is premium grade.[12] The metropolitan areas range in population from 110,000 to 5,500,000. Examination of the price patterns suggests that a greater variety of service-station outlets may be available in the larger cities because the overlap of price is longer and there is a tendency toward a larger number of price modes in the distribution of prices.

Figure 2-7 is based upon the major mode for the regular gasoline sold by each major type of service station in each of the six cities, designated by the letter A through F. Gasoline is sold by two types of outlet: Group I which will "sell large-refiner brands that are advertised on a national or regional basis," which tend to be full-service stations and which do not rely on price appeal; and Group II stations which typically sell non-refiner brands, may not offer full service, and do emphasize price appeal. There were 6,044 Group I outlets, and 1,190 Group II outlets, but the latter accounted for over 25 per cent of gasoline sales.

Livingston and Levitt also published the smallest, the typical, and the largest difference between the prices charged for the regular grade and the premium grade gasoline from Group I and Group II stations in each city. There is no way to ascertain quantities sold from Livingston and Levitt's study, although they do indicate the percentage of outlets selling at each price level. What is done here is to allocate total sales 75 per cent to the major brands and 25 per cent to the others, and to suppose that in both cases 60 per cent of total sales are of premium grade. The key price for each city is that at the major mode for regular gasoline. Other prices are found by adding the price differentials typical

[12] S. L. Livingston and Theodore Levitt, "Competition and Retail Gasoline Prices," *Review of Economics and Statistics,* XLI (May, 1959), 119-22.

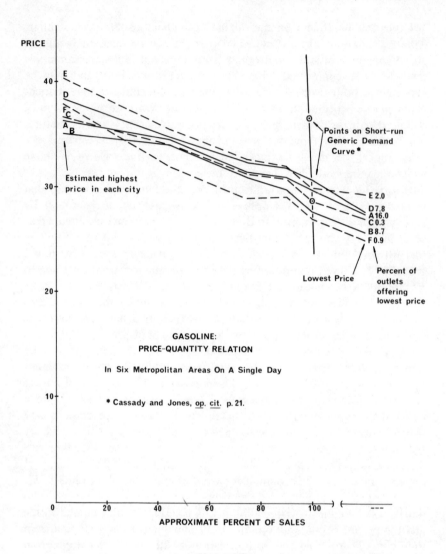

Figure 2-7

for the city. These data are presented in cumulative fashion, with percentage of sales at the highest price (always 45 per cent according to our assumptions) forming the base to which sales at the next lower price are added, and so on until 100 per cent is reached.

The ends of the lines are extended to the lowest price found in each city on one hand, and to the highest calculated price, on the other. While the former is accurate, the latter is probably exaggerated because it is found by adding to the highest price at which regular gasoline was sold the largest differential found for premium gasoline. In all cases, the highest prices were found for a very small number of stations, so the high prices are plotted very close to the ordinate. The lowest prices were sometimes offered by a significant number of outlets, but the nature of Figure 2-7 made the "quantity" at which they were plotted arbitrary, so no significance can be attached to the slope of the lines beyond 100 per cent. The results are comparable to the "effective generic demand curve" shown in Figure 2-6. Consumers probably lose some consumer surplus, but cross elasticity protects the bulk of it.

The circled dots at the 99 per cent and 100 per cent outputs indicate the price-quantity relationship that some investigators find relevant to the generic product, "gasoline." If correct, the marginal revenue to the industry demand curve must be far below zero, and industry profits would be maximized at much higher price levels. If, on the other hand, 29 cents is taken as the basic price of gasoline and it is assumed that costs of a good-quality regular grade of gasoline are covered at that price, the amount added to revenues by differentiation of outlet and product is substantial, and no mean achievement.

The price premiums are not secured without costs. Nevertheless, if management weighs the additional costs against the additional returns in each case, the profit position of those who serve the full range of submarkets must be enhanced. This conclusion is supported by the fact that the minor-brand companies, which typically are unable to serve the whole quality range and which tend to be confined to the less attractive portions of the market, nevertheless exist and expand.

4. Flatirons

The Civilian Production Administration's Bureau of Demobilization attempted controlled resumption of production of domestic flatirons during World War II.[13] The successful resistance to a standardized victory iron to be sold at a uniform low price constitutes eloquent implicit testimony to the producer estimate of the profitability of price lines and of distinguishing features. Skeleton data for the "normal" prewar year, 1940, are given in the report and are reproduced in Table 2-1. If the quantities are cumulated from the most to the least expensive irons, Figure 2-8 is produced. None of the points can be plotted accurately, and the highest one is the most uncertain because of the

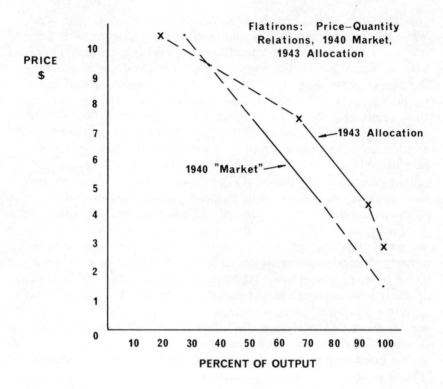

Figure 2-8

open-ended nature of the "over $9.00 price class." The others are
arbitrarily plotted at the midpoints of the appropriate price range. The
kinked line indicates the allocations made by the Civilian Production
Administration in 1943.[14] A more complete picture is given on page
111 of the monograph, where the allocation to each company is given,
along with a description of the iron and the allowed price. Automatic
1000-watt irons ranged in price from $11.70 down to $6.95 and in
allocation from 35,000 units to 321,000 units. Automatic and nonauto-
matic irons of lesser wattage ranged in price from $7.60 to $5.30 and
in allocation from 2,000 irons to 175,000 irons.

[13] Drummond Jones and Maryclair McCauley, *Resumption of Production of
Domestic Flatirons, April 1943, August 1944*. (Historical Reports on War Administration: WPB Special Study No. 6.), available at the National Archives, Washington, D.C.

Table II-1

Relative Quantities of Flatirons Produced
By Price Class, 1940

Price Class $	Quantity Percentage	Cumulative Quantity Percentage
Over 9	27.5	27.5
6.01 - 9	25.4	52.9
3.01 - 6	24.6	77.5
0.00 - 3	22.6	100.1

Figure 2-9 summarizes these data in the same manner as Figures 2-7 and 2-8. The smooth line indicates the relationship if price ranges $9-12, $7-9, and $5-7 were substituted for the actual data, with the midpoint of the price interval plotted above the output. Had the Bureau of Demobilization's allocation resulted from the action of market forces, one might suspect that output and sales efforts directed to the price lines furthest to the left of the smooth line had been more remunerative than the others. Because this was a highly controlled situation, no such speculation is relevant here. Nevertheless, the fact that a price range extending from $6.95 to $11.70 for a "1000 watt automatic flatiron" was approved by a wartime agency provides evidence both of the strength of the marketing dictum that the consumer should be offered a choice and of the willingness of business to fight to protect the integrity of their product differences and price lines. One can imagine that their motive may have been fear of "spoiling the market" for "de luxe" irons, should consumers once used to the best have been forced to use the next best for lack of choice.

These data do not indicate as much tendency toward virtual price-matching of variants as might be expected. Two firms each are found at $9.40, and at $6.95. Three firms selling nearly one third of the total sold at prices ranging from $8.55 to $8.95. All told, these price lines account for 58 per cent of the total. The largest allocation, which may be presumed to bear some relationship to the peacetime norm, is about twice the size of the next largest, but the next four firms are of approximately the same size in this market. The four largest were allocated 64 per cent and the eight largest 92 per cent of production, which is not extraordinarily concentrated for narrowly defined products. The four-firm index of disparity is 3.75, which is low even at the 5-digit level.[15]

[15] The nature of the index of disparity is discussed in Chapter VI, where a considerable amount of data revealing the relative sizes of major producers is also presented. See pp. 120-21.

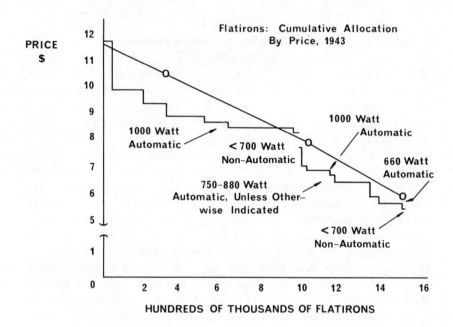

Figure 2-9

Three of the 15 firms produced two-product lines each. In each case the firm produced two lines of automatic irons, one a 1000-watt iron at prices ranging from $8.55 to $9.40, and the other of significantly less wattage (range 660-800) at a price range of $5.70 to $6.75. In this case the higher wattage sold at the higher price, and in each case the firm with the largest volume of sales asked the lowest prices and the firm with the smallest volume among the three asked the higher prices.

The price-quantity relationships suggest a demand curve of the type presented in Figure 2-7. Cross elasticities are undoubtedly sufficient to rotate the *ex ante* function downward from the marginal utility function for the generic product. If the marginal-utility function does not change, the variety of prices must reduce consumer surplus. But in this case the automatic feature and the higher wattage of the more expensive irons in all probability rotate the marginal-utility function upward, so that the effect on consumer surplus is in doubt. But the price range among the automatic irons of a given wattage is also considerable, and the nature of the ironing chore is not dramatically changed by the higher quality iron.

5. Automobiles

Similar representations may be made for automobiles. The statistical problems are complicated by the multiplicity of body styles and quality lines bearing the same brand name and by lack of data relating to these narrow product classes. Prices are particularly hard to handle because of the influence of trade-ins of used cars and the widespread practice of departing from list prices, especially during the latter part of the model years. Figure 2-10 cumulates the quantities sold at successively lower prices, relating total United States production by brand name to the list price of the lowest-priced four-door sedan of that brand, for the years 1925 and 1955.[16] Only 83 per cent of the total production given by the Statistical Abstract for 1925 is accounted for, but 96.1 per cent of 1955 production is included.

The outstanding difference between the two years is the range of prices. Cars sold at both higher and lower prices in 1925 than in 1955. If the lowest-priced car is taken as the base, the highest-priced brand has an index of 1810 in 1925 but of only 230 in 1955. If one attempts the rather arbitrary feat of dividing brands into high-, medium-, and low-priced groups, one finds price gaps such as those shown by the dotted lines on Figure 2-10.

In each case, the price lines are narrower in 1955 than in 1925. It also appears probable that the firms fail to secure the advantages of secondary discrimination because intermediate prices fall far below an envelope curve based upon the extremes of the distributions. But because the prices used are those for the cheapest 4-door sedan, Figure 2-10 vastly understates the effectiveness of the automobile companies to secure maximum revenues. The vertical distance between the broken flat lines and the diagonal line connecting the extremes of the distribution suggests that in 1955 some of the buyers of the low-priced cars might have been induced to pay in excess of $3,000 (rather than the $1,750 shown) for a more highly differentiated "low-priced" product. Some

---

[16] Prices prior to 1930 are taken from *Motor Service and Specifications Manual* (8th ed, Detroit, Mich.: Motor, 1931), pp. 2-5, and for later years from *Motors Handbook,* various editions from 1938 on. Output data are taken from *Automotive Industries* LVI (Philadelphia, Pa.: Chilton, February 19, 1927), 233, and the 1931, 1934, and 1937 editions, LXIV-LXV, LXX-LXXI, and LXVI-LXVII respectively. *Ward's Automobile Year Book* (Detroit, Mich.: Ward's Reports, Inc., 1947) and (Detroit, Mich.: Robert B. Powers, 1954) are used for the years 1938-1945, and *Automobile Facts and Figures* (Detroit, Mich.: National Automobile Association, 1959) is the source used for 1946-1959. The output data from the various sources are gathered on somewhat different bases, but agree approximately in the overlapping years, and are, perhaps, adequate for present purposes. It may be possible to use current model "blue book" values to avoid the use of list prices, which surely depart from market values, in a more elaborate study.

may have done so. Optional equipment, super-deluxe lines of the low-priced brands and credit costs have the effect of offering the consumer an almost infinitely varied product at a wide variety of prices. The same thing can be said of the medium-priced and the high-priced makes.

Another inference from Figure 2-10 is the apparent room for a line of cars which would have been lower priced and another line which would have been higher priced than anything available on the 1955

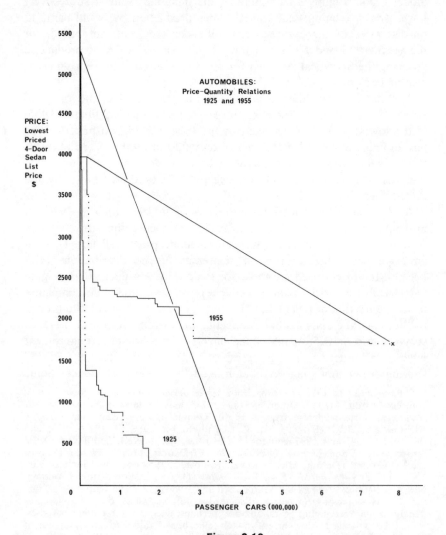

Figure 2-10

market. The recent development of the compact cars and the success of a number of inexpensive imports suggest that the automobile industry has recognized the need for greater product diversification and a wider range of prices if total revenues are to reach optimum levels. Very high-priced semi-sport luxury cars such as the Thunderbird, some models of Mercedes-Benz, Jaguar and Porsche have also found acceptance. The effect has been to push up the upper range of price while pushing down the lower range, although the range is still less than in the 1920's.

Figure 2-10 reveals a much tighter range of base prices among the lowest price lines as compared to the others. This suggests that the coefficients of cross elasticity among cars in the middle and upper price ranges are lower than in the lower price lines. Thus pure quantity competition is perhaps more characteristic of the standard cars, and somewhat more mixed with other elements for the higher price lines. There is a strong tendency for automobile producers in the United States to produce a full line of cars, although no other matches the range offered by General Motors. In any case, the overlap complicates the identification of subproducts.

So far automobiles have been treated as a single product composed of three subproducts each of which has a number of variants. The two or three General Motors or Chrysler brands that fall within each subproduct are treated as variants designed to increase the share of sales in that submarket. Cross elasticity among variants and between subproducts undoubtedly rotates the apparent demand curve below that for the generic product. On the other hand, as with the case of flatirons, the existence of many qualities, body styles, sizes, etc. in all probability has expanded the utility frontier somewhat. But unlike flatirons, this sort of innovation is more prominent within "quality" lines than between them. A wide range of body styles, high performance vs. economy, and other substantive differences appear within the two lower price lines. Durability, comfort, top speed, cruising speed, choice of transmissions, heating, cooling, and power options are generally duplicated for the standard models in all price brackets. One may imagine that the upward shift of any utility schedule or schedules associated with automobiles is related not so much to the introduction of new "quality" lines as to innovation of worthwhile features into all quality lines, and particularly into the lower price lines, over time.

Even these features may add relatively little to the satisfaction that accompanies ownership and use of an automobile. They may serve primarily as talking points in the competition for sales. But to the extent that they expand the utility frontier, they do so by improving the quality of the whole constellation of products. The old product drops from production and the degree of differentiation in any one year remains about the same.

D. Summary

Any comprehensive classification of products, such as that made in the Census of Manufactures, inevitably combines within each category products which are different from the standpoints of the consumer and of the individual firms. Microeconomic theory, by accepting price differences among similar products as conclusive evidence of true product differences in the mind of the consumer, opens the door to such a virtually infinite number of products as to defy empirically oriented analysis. This chapter attempts to establish a way of relating the concepts of microeconomic theory to empirically defined products.

Recourse is made to the concept of discriminating monopoly so that the introduction of "products" that expand the consumers' utility frontiers can be distinguished from those that fail to do so. While the distinction is clear in the limiting case, it presents difficulties in the others. The concept is advanced of a generic product composed of nonhomogeneous subproducts of which firms produce variants. An "effective generic demand curve" is described, with several prices reflecting the elasticity of the generic demand curve, cross elasticities among the subproducts and entrepreneurial action that reduces such cross elasticities.

A process for isolating identifiable statistical generic products is suggested, but not pursued. But concepts are illustrated by reference to the markets for calculating machines, plexiglass, gasoline, flatirons, and automobiles.

It may not be amiss to conclude that the rather simple demand relationship shown here for nonhomogeneous products can be used to throw some light on important problems of microanalysis and policy without the wealth of data and intricate cross elasticities required by a generalization of the theory of price which considers each element and variant separately. This approach is in harmony with the theory of discriminatory price and can be connected to the main body of economic analysis. By simplifying the formal structure, qualities of products are recognized, thereby acknowledging the usefulness of product groups and industries. The persistence of price lines, and competition of a type that protects the firms in the scramble to hold or to expand output shares of each element, are consistent with this concept.

Chapter III

Definition of Oligopoly

COMPETITION in general, and oligopolistic rivalry in particular, have many dimensions. Product competition and sales promotions are often secondary only to price and quantity competition. In some cases managements also vie to establish reputations for leadership in technology, partly to secure benefits in unrelated markets. In the next four chapters attention is focused on the rivalry of firms in particular product markets. This is appropriate for the basic economic problems associated with the optimal allocation of resources. The final two chapters take a somewhat broader view of optimal performance which is more suitable to research and development and other problems where conglomerate size may be more important than size in particular product markets.

If one wishes to make a statistical study of the allocative effects of market structure, it is necessary to combine the almost endless variety of products of microeconomic theory into a reasonably small number of products. The analysis and procedures suggested in Chapter II provide guidelines whereby this can be done without losing contact with microeconomic analysis and with minimal loss of meaning and detail.

Two additional steps remain to be taken before the economic effects of industry structure can be ascertained and relevant policy recommendations can be considered against an appropriate background of knowledge. The first of these is to define industry structure and the second is to establish the nature of interindustry relationships. Only then may one hazard reasonable a priori judgments that may be useful for policy making. The following pages develop a theory of structure. Current practice is then reviewed.

A. Theory of Industry Structure

One may conceive of a galaxy of elements which are capable of being grouped into product universes which serve definable end uses. This is the burden of Chapter II. In Figure 3-1 the 24 small letters stand for elements and the solid lines demark seven generic products which are designated by capital letters.

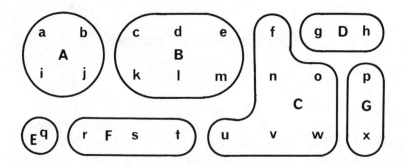

Figure 3-1

Most firms produce more than one element. If more than one is produced it is reasonable to assume that they are either neutral or complementary in production. If they are complementary in production the cost of each is lower because of the output of the others, and one may expect to find different firms producing very similar constellations of elements. Entry of new firms will then be inhibited by the need to reach adequate size to produce the group of elements if a competitive cost level is to be attained. If complementary relationships exist among a group of elements, but neutral relationships prevail among the production of the whole group and other groups, entry by larger firms which thereby become conglomerate is not inhibited.

If an element is a substitute in production for all others, it will be produced separately because costs are raised for each product if they are produced by the same firm. Elements which are substitutes in production will not be produced by conglomerate firms. Likewise, if a group of production complements is a substitute in its relation to other groups, it will not be produced by conglomerate firms. An element, or group of complements, may therefore be considered to be neutral if produced in conjunction with different constellations of other subproducts by various firms.

An element is neutral at a lower level if a firm producing other sub-products can commence its production without suffering higher (or lower) costs for its other products. An element is neutral at a higher level if, although it is part of a complementary group, the whole group can be added to the output of a firm without raising the cost of production of the other groups.

There is no reason in fact or theory that would lead one to expect particular groups of complements in production to also be substitutes in consumption. Thus the elements which are grouped into generic products in Figure 3-1 may be grouped quite differently as production complements. This is shown by Figure 3-2 which reproduces Figure 3-1 with firm boundaries added, as shown by heavier dashed lines. Nine firms are shown. Four are simple normal firms, numbered 4, 6, 7, and 9, which produce elements *q, v, w,* and *p* respectively. Of these only firm 7, producing element *w,* has a rival which produces the same element. But firm 9 must also compete with firm 8, and firm 6 must vie with firms 5, 7, 8, and 3 in their product markets.

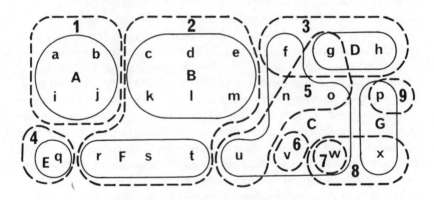

Figure 3-2

Three types of monopoly are shown. Firm 4 produces a "pure" product—the one-element product *E*—and has no rivals. This is the textbook monopoly case. Firm 1 is the sole producer of product *A* which is composed of four elements. Firm 1 is a differentiated normal firm. Firm 2 is an uncomplicated conglomerate firm which produces all of the elements composing each of two products, *B* and *F*. Firms 3, 5, and 8 are also conglomerate. Firm 3 produces three elements which include both of the elements of product D and one of the six elements that compose product C. Firms 5 and 8 are alike in that neither produces all of the elements of any product, and produces some of two. They differ in that firm 5 confronts four rivals, firms 3, 6, 7, and 8, one of them in two different product markets, while firm 8 confronts five rivals, firms 3, 5, 6, 7, and 9, each in a single product market.

Census data suggest that many firms are like firms 3, 5, and 8. The Bureau of the Census recognizes this and presents 4-, 5-, and 7-digit data on a product basis so that the output, or employment, of a firm need not be classified according to its principal industry. Product and firm data would be identical if all firms were like 1, 2, 4, 6, 7, or 9.

B. Structure and Market Power

We argue below that oligopoly structure is most usefully defined in terms of concentration. On that basis firms, 1, 2, and 4 are monopolies. Firms 3 and 5 are duopolists for product D, and firms 8 and 9 are duopolists for product G. Five firms produce the remaining product C. Firms produce the product mixes that they do because the component elements are complements in production, or are at least neutral.

What may be inferred from the relationships among firms 3, 5, 6, 7, 8, and 9? According to the analysis given above subproduct w is neither a substitute nor a complement. It is highly probable that the production of subproduct x is also neutral in production. If it were a complement, firm 7 would produce both w and x. If they were substitutes firm 8 would not produce both of them. Therefore, any market power that firm 8 may possess over subproduct x is restrained not only by firm 9 but also by firm 7. Beyond that, there is little to be added to what was said previously without considering the effect of additional firms, or the ability of firms to expand into new markets.

The thin lines encircle subproducts which are either neutral or are complements in production. If it is the latter, a firm such as 3 cannot commence production of a subproduct outside of its circle, such as o. But it may not preclude entry into a constellation of subproducts such as firm 5's set, $g, n, o, u,$ which includes subproduct o. Conglomerate expansion is as likely to follow complex production complement lines like this as the neat product lines illustrated by conglomerate firm 2. While firm 3 may have an advantage in attempting to expand into firm 5's territory since it is already producing $g,$ its ability to enter suggests that the barrier due to complementarity of production of g, n, o, u is not high, and that other firms with different constellations of products may be able to produce this group efficiently also.

Likewise, the circumstances that make it possible for one firm to add an additional set of complements to its product lines without diseconomies may well differ from those of other firms which, nevertheless, can add somewhat different sets without suffering diseconomies. Joint costs that are involved in each group of production complements prevent any satisfactory allocation of total costs to individual elements. Efficiency involves efficient production of the set. To the extent that complementary sets of firms overlap, competitive pressures exist which are not only difficult to disentangle but powerful because identity of interest among rival firms is thereby diminished.

For these reasons it is best to separate the structure of an industry from any immediate implication of market power.

The classification problem can be recapitulated in a more direct way by using set theory. Each elementary product that is produced and utilized as an end product can be considered as item in a universal set or galaxy of elements. These are classified into two major sets, each with its own subsets. One major set, which includes all elements, is composed of subsets which reflect similarity of final use. These are called generic products. The second major set, which also includes all elements, is composed of subsets of elements each of which includes a group of production complements. These are normal firm sets. A firm will enjoy some advantage if it produces the full group of production complements. Certain elements may be neutral and, therefore, are as economically produced in isolation as in company with others. Certain subsets of production complements taken as a group may also be neutral, and the subset may be produced as economically in company with other subsets as it is in isolation.

Subsets of products often do not coincide with subsets of production complements. The firm subsets may intersect the product sets in any manner. There may be many or few firms producing a given firm subset. The firm subset may not include the same elements for each firm because of special staff, resource market, or other conditions. Deviation of this type suggests low barriers to the invasion of a portion of a subset and, like conglomerateness, suggests a neutral relationship between elements or groups of elements.

Classification of industry structure involves both product and firm subsets. If an industry is competitive by the concentration test, the number of firms involved in the production of the elements that make up a product subset must be rather large and the largest firms must not dominate the market. This can be understood as a third subset that intersects the other two. If the possibility that firms may have different sets of production complements is neglected, one can visualize the number of firms as a third dimension added to Figure 3-2 with differing numbers of firms like 1, 2, 3, 4, 5, etc. If, for example, there are 100 firms like firm 4, all of about the same size, product q is produced under conditions of competition, not monopoly; and this becomes a textbook illustration of competition. If, on the other hand, there are only two firms, it is a textbook case of duopoly.

The definitional problems are not quite so clear cut if a large number of firms produces only one element of a product subset. For example, suppose that firm 8 is without rivals but that there are 100 firms like firm 9. By our definition, there are 101 firms producing product G, and it is competitive.

Because the elements and firm subsets may be neutral or near neutral, market power may be small even when industry structure is monopolistic when measured by numbers and firms. For that reason it is desirable to separate structure from performance. This is essentially a matter of how one prefers to define monopoly, oligopoly, and competition. We now give reasons for the stated preferences.

C. Four Definitions of Oligopoly

At least four modes of approach to the definition of oligopoly have been utilized since Chamberlin introduced the term. Two define oligopoly in terms of the additional parameter that faces decision-makers in firms which are not competitive or monopolistic. Oligopolists are those who when making decisions must consider the actions, reactions and strategies of rival entrepreneurs in addition to evaluating the impersonal market forces. One approach defines and attempts to measure inderdependence directly with cross elasticities and similar coefficients among the variants of the firms. The second approach infers interdependence from the degree of concentration and fewness of sellers.

But interdependence is not very interesting for its own sake. Interdependence and fewness are thought to produce monopoly-like performance. Studies of industries thought to be oligopolistic have failed to show any uniform pattern of performance, with the result that some have come to use a performance criterion rather than to rely on either interdependence or fewness to define oligopoly or monopoly. One performance test is price in excess of marginal cost. A second is failure to innovate, expand, adapt to changing opportunities or otherwise act with sufficient dynamism—tests a profit-maximizing monopoly should meet.

Performance tests are rejected here. Many different structures may yield similar results. If an industry composed of a small number of firms should perform well, it is unnecessarily confusing to then define the industry as being competitive. Likewise, it is incongruous to define an industry as being competitive just because marginal cost equals price if entry is limited, say by license, to 1000 firms of approximately equal size and large, monopolistic, quasi-rents are enjoyed.

The next section discusses the inadequacies of the proposed direct measures of interdependence. Their greatest flaw is their ambiguity. The fact that they cannot be used to isolate operationally-defined industries is an equally important reason for avoiding this approach to the definition and analysis of oligopoly.

Much interest exists in the activity and presumed power of larger firms which face relatively small firms in their markets. The belief that large firms tend to coordinate their policies to their private benefit is widespread. Data are available, and better data can be assembled, which can isolate objectively-defined industries according to the principles presented in the first section of this chapter. Since we have some information that implies that highly concentrated industries have higher profit rates than the others, an a priori basis exists for focusing analysis of this particular group of industries and the firms that operate in them. The word oligopoly has been closely associated with this group for many years, so in the interest of analytically unambiguous language other meanings of the word "oligopoly" are not implied in our usage in this book.

Oligopoly as defined here is without any implication of either optimal or suboptimal performance. Conjectural interdependence among oligopolistic firms may or may not exist. One object of analysis is to ascertain whether or not it does. Likewise, the quality of performance exhibited by oligopolies is an appropriate subject for analysis.

1. Interdependence of Demand

In principle, an operational definition should satisfy two conditions. It should be related to a significant phenomenon, and it should be capable of objective application. Cross elasticities and related measures of the degree of interdependence among firms meet the first criterion because the number and character of the variables about which the entrepreneurs must have policies are greater if there is interdependence which requires reaction. Application of cross elasticities and the like has, unfortunately, remained almost entirely subjective for reasons that follow. There is no substantial basis to suppose that it will be otherwise in the future.

Triffin was perhaps the first to develop the cross elasticity approach (1) in a systematic way.[1] Since that time a number of economists of the first rank have attempted to formulate criteria of interdependence so as to achieve a satisfactory basis for classification, but with indifferent success at best. Leaving aside, for the moment, all problems associated with the availability of data relating to specific products produced by or sold to specific firms, it is evident that even the pure theory of classification contains ambiguities.

A survey of the literature reveals the ambiguity in that various economists have advocated the use of such different devices as cross elasticity,[2,3] cross elasticity in an upward direction only,[4] the ratio between own elasticity and cross elasticity,[5] cross elasticity related to quantities,[6] and modified cross elasticities encompassing supply conditions,[7] each designed to measure the concept designated "fewness" or "interdependence" which relates to power over rival. The same writers have likewise urged own elasticity,[2,5] elasticity of substitution,[3] cross elasticity,[6,7] and cross elasticity in a downward direction only[4] as indexes of the other commonly recognized dimension of market structure: homogeneity of product.

It is noteworthy that, except for Triffin, entry is excluded from these definitions of industry structure. The others rest on the short-run considerations and, where cross elasticities are important, imply that consumers react promptly to changes of relative prices among similar products. As a consequence, producers are thought to be forced to

---

[1] Robert Triffin, *Monopolistic Competition and General Equilibrium* (Cambridge, Mass.: Harvard University Press, 1940), ch. iii.

[2] E. H. Chamberlin, "Elasticities, Cross Elasticities and Market Relationships: Comment," *American Economic Review,* XLIII, No. 5, Part I (December 1953); and E. H. Chamberlin (ed.), "Measuring the Degree of Monopoly and Competition," *Monopoly and Competition and Their Regulation* (London: Macmillan, 1954), p. 265.

[3] Sidney Weintraub, *Price Theory* (New York: Pitman, 1949), p. 99. The effort to classify with these coefficients is omitted in Weintraub's *Intermediate Price Theory* (Toronto: Chilton, 1964).

[4] William Fellner, "Elasticities, Cross Elasticities and Market Relationships; Comment," *American Economic Review,* XLIII, No. 5, Part I (December 1953).

[5] R. L. Bishop, "Elasticities, Cross Elasticities, and Market Relationships," *American Economic Review,* XLII, No. 5 (December 1952); and "Reply," *ibid.,* XLIII (December 1953).

[6] Triffin, *Monopolistic Competition,* pp. 99-108.

[7] A. Q. Papandreau, "Market Structures and Monopoly Power," *American Economic Review,* XXXIX, No. 5 (September 1949), 883-4. A careful survey of the literature and a highly refined system of classification based upon the variables which bear upon profit-maximization by the firm is presented by Fred C. Hung, "A Classification of Market Structures: Theory and Empirical Implications" (Ph.D. thesis, University of Washington, 1955).

consider the effects of their rivals' price, advertising, and product policies. This process is called "conjectural interdependence."

Longer-run considerations have again become more popular among economists in recent years. Entry is presently seen as a determinant of the ability of firms, whether oligopolistic or not, to exercise power over their rivals or their customers. Thus supply conditions are considered relevant to market power. A firm of great relative size in a market may be sharply limited either by high cross elasticities of demand among existing rivals, by a very flat demand curve for its product, or by the ability of potential rivals to undertake production of identical or substitute products. The latter flattens the firm's *ex ante* demand curve but not its statistical demand function.

But the situation is worse than this for those of us who wish to use interdependence as an objective definition. As Professors Stigler, Kaysen and Turner point out, a large number of poor substitutes may be as influential a restraint as a small number of good substitutes.[8] This rationalizes flat, high-elasticity demand curves confronting monopolistic industries whose statistical demand curves show low elasticities. The rival products may be very different in manufacture or location (foreign travel for a cabin cruiser, jewelry for furniture, bowling for fishing equipment). This fact makes the objective use of cross elasticities and related concepts virtually impossible, because weak interrelationships are lost in the maze of seasonal, cyclical, regional, and random movements. Kaysen and Turner are correct when they say that such relationships cannot be observed directly.

Professor Baumol goes further. On the basis of his work as a consultant to firms which one would expect to be much influenced by the policies of rival firms, he concludes that large, presumably oligopolistic firms actually pay very little attention to each others' policies and actions, except where critical long-range decisions are to be made.[9] Instead, lines of policy are laid out and followed for considerable periods of time. They are modified at intervals in the light of experience but not as a result of specific actions and anticipated reactions. If this observation is soundly based, there is no intricate pattern of interdependent stimulus and response of the tactical sort implied by the cross-elasticity concept and much of the literature of the theory of games that is related to it.

---

[8] G. J. Stigler, *Theory of Price* (New York: Macmillan, 1952), pp. 55-6. Carl Kaysen and Donald F. Turner, *Antitrust Policy, an Economic and Legal Analysis* (Cambridge, Mass.: Harvard University Press, 1959), pp. 295-6.

[9] William Baumol, *Business Behavior, Value and Growth* (New York: Macmillan, 1959), ch. iv.

Both the consumers' and the firms' response mechanisms are too sluggish to justify such efforts. Large firms that produce a substantial proportion of the market supply adjust directly to market phenomena and only indirectly to rivals' policies. Long-run cross elasticities should stand out all the more clearly because of this, but the longer the period of time considered and the wider the range of substitutes (including the more numerous poor ones) the more independent the apparent behavior of the "oligopolist." One piece of evidence supporting this view has earlier been cited in connection with calculating machines.

2. Concentration as an Indicator of Oligopoly

In the absence of direct measurement of interdependence, efforts to determine the prevalence and significance of oligopoly and monopoly in the United States have come to rest heavily upon deductions related to the degree of concentration in manufacturing industry as measured by shipments, employment, or assets. The proportion of production of the four, eight, or twenty largest firms, usually measured by value of shipments as defined by the Bureau of the Census, provides the principal source of information for these studies. The most commonly used concentration ratio is the percentage of total shipments originating from the four largest producers.[10]

Fewness is also a significant phenomenon. It is considered important in the structure of political and social organization as well as in economic organization. While it is by no means easy to apply in an objective as opposed to a subjective way, the analysis of the first section of this paper provides an objective basis for such an analysis which has been quite imperfectly utilized by past studies and which can be considerably improved using data already collected over a period of more than

---

[10] Census data are classified according to five levels of detail which are designated as 2-digit, 3-digit, 4-digit, 5-digit, and 7-digit. The first three are referred to as major industry groups, industry groups, and industries, respectively. Shipments in these groups are classified under the name of the principal product of each establishment (or plant) related to a firm. Five-digit data are referred to as product classes, and 7-digit data as products. Shipments of different products from a given establishment are isolated in these data. Four-digit data are also presented on a product basis in some tabulations and are referred to as product groups. Twenty 2-digit major industry groups, approximately 440 4-digit industries (and product groups), approximately one thousand 5-digit product classes, and approximately seven thousand 7-digit products are utilized in the Standard Industrial Classification for the 1954 Census. A short description of the 1957 version of the Standard Industrial Classification and its relationship to earlier classifications is found in *Concentration Ratios in Manufacturing Industry 1958* (Washington, D.C.: Government Printing Office, 1962), p. 1-6.

fifteen years. If oligopoly is defined in terms of fewness, one aspect of analysis should be to establish the nature and significance of interdependence that exists among rival firms of different sizes and numbers.

There are a number of objections that may be raised against the use of the census data on concentration. They may be listed as follows: (1) Coverage of the different products is uneven, with economically important products usually being treated in greater detail. (2) The number of products and product classes is small relative to the number of products about which business decisions are made and regulatory action is taken. (3) Account is not taken of quantities exported or imported. (4) Classifications sometimes follow type of raw material used or type of producer, rather than market criteria, in defining the industry or product. (5) Shipments from one plant to another within the same firm are not excluded. (6) Competition with stocks of used equipment is ignored. (7) Potential competition is not included. These criticisms apply to 5-digit and 7-digit data as well as to the 4-digit, although it is now possible to avoid some of them.

Another that applies particularly to the most commonly used 4-digit industry data is that they assign the total value of a plant's shipment to the industry in which the firm is most active. Many plants produce products in more than one industry classification, even in more than one of the twenty 2-digit industry groups. The 5- and 7-digit, and some compilations of 4-digit data, however, cover all of the production of a commodity regardless of the 4-digit classification of the producing firms. In Bureau of the Census terminology, such data are compiled according to a "commodity" rather than an "industry" basis.

In this book we are concerned statistically only with the first two of these criticisms, although the models used in Chapters V and VII pay homage to points 3 and 7. Note might be made of Professor Weston's complaint that the influence of imports on concentration appears to be much more limited than Stigler has implied, perhaps being limited to few, if any, more than nine of the 1,807 product categories analyzed by Crowder and Thorp.[11] Criticisms listed 3, 4, and 5 can be rectified if 7-digit data relating to value-added by establishment are used appropriately, and can be reduced in some instances by approximate combinations of 5-digit and even 4-digit classes.

[11] G. J. Stigler, "Extent and Bases of Monopoly," *American Economic Review,* XXXII, No. 1 (June 1942).; and J. Fred Weston, *The Role of Mergers in the Growth of Large Firms* (Berkeley, Calif.: University of California Press, 1953), pp. 114-6.

a. Use of Census Data

If operationally defined products are desired there is, nevertheless, much to be said in favor of census definitions and data. Human judgment is not going to be eliminated because of the insurmountable obstacles that prevent the direct use of objective measures of interdependence. Products must be related to firms, and firms grouped into industries, and industries into industry groups, for the analysis of different problems at different levels of analysis. The census does these things. The definitions are carefully drawn in cooperation with industry representatives, technicians and professional advisers specifically to make the information as useful as possible to all classes of users. The definitions of each level of aggregation from the 2-digit to the 7-digit level are constantly scrutinized and revised as improvements become possible.[12] Data collection and assembly are accomplished in a highly professional manner, and alternative classifications are made.[13]

From a practical point of view the best practice is to work with these data, combining 5- and 7-digit products where they are too narrow, distinguishing market regions where possible, and working with the Bureau in revisions of definitions and procedures. Disclosure rules will continue to prevent free use of these data. But much can be done with modern data processing to combine raw data and to state results in such a way as to avoid disclosure while providing much clearer insights into industry structure.

Once a product is defined in a satisfactory way, one can attempt to determine whether the industry structure related to it falls into an oligopoly class or some other. Because the number of firms and the concentration of production, or of employment, is given for the products thus defined, this important evidence relevant to the degree of monopoly is known at once when census data are used. This provides a strong additional incentive to base operational definitions upon census definitions and data.

---

[12] A good brief treatment of the virtues and shortcomings of census industry data may be found in M. R. Conklin and H. T. Goldstein, "Census Principles and Industry and Product Classification," *Business Concentration and Price Policy, A Symposium* (Princeton, N. J.: Princeton University Press, National Bureau of Economic Research, 1955). Also, read the comments by Fabricant, Kottke, and Suits.

[13] A good example is the presentation of 4-digit data, both in terms of industry groups where shipments are classified according to the principal activity of the producers, and in terms of shipments of specific products. The first makes possible a comparison with earlier data, and the latter makes possible more accurate analysis of concentration in specific product markets.

D. An Operational Definition of Oligopoly

Because of the advantages outlined earlier, and in light of the very great logical and operational difficulties inherent in the interdependence definition and the impropriety of defining a structure by its effects, the following definition is adopted. Oligopoly is said to exist if the four leading firms produce 50 per cent or more of a narrowly defined product. A product is narrowly defined if there is good reason to believe that there is some central product produced by one firm which is a reasonably good substitute for each other product in the grouping. A product is too narrowly defined if some reasonably good substitute is excluded from the group. This definition is weak, in that considerable room is left for subjective judgment and because it seemingly excludes the effect of many poor substitutes; but this is not serious if the conclusions reached in the subsequent chapters are correct. Census data cannot be used in their present form to exactly illustrate oligopolies defined in this way. Approximations can be made, and manipulation of census data can, at considerable cost, produce reasonably close approximations in the future without involving disclosure.

The 50 per cent figure is chosen because the empirical studies made by Bain and Schwartzman reveal a dichotomy. Both report a statistically significant difference, the more concentrated industries enjoying the higher profit rates. George J. Stigler also finds evidence of a dichotomy, but suggests four-firm concentration ratio of 80 or a Herfindahl index of 0.250 as the critical values.[14] The lower value is retained for present

---

[14] J. S. Bain, "Relation of Profit Rates to Industry Concentration: American Manufacturing, 1936-1940," *Quarterly Journal of Economics*, LXV, No. 3 (August 1951), 312-4; and David Schwartzman. "The Burden of Monopoly," *Journal of Political Economy*, LXVIII, No. 6 (December 1960), 629.

Bain's data refer to the share of the value-added by the eight largest firms, where the break in profit rates is found at the 70 per cent concentration level. Schwartzman finds this to be equivalent to 50 per cent concentration in the four largest firms.

Bain's findings may be summarized as follows:

Profit Rate	Number of Industries	
	Concentration Ratio over 70 per cent	Concentration Ratio less than 70 per cent
over 10 per cent	13	3
between 5 per cent and 10 per cent	6	12
less than 5 per cent	2	6

G. J. Stigler, "A Theory of Oligopoly," *Journal of Political Economy*, LXXII, No. 1 (February 1964). See Chapter IX, p. 211-12 and related footnote for additional discussion.

purposes because it rests on a broader base and a more complete coverage of the firms in the relevant industries.

The dichotomy rather than a continuous functional relationship between profits and concentration is particularly convenient for the present purposes. Perhaps a higher rate of concentration should be used for the more narrowly defined products advocated here. The findings presented in the next section of this chapter and in Chapter IV suggest, however, that the degree of concentration in the more narrowly defined census industries is similar to the degree of concentration shown for their elements. Hence 50 per cent is retained as the critical ratio.

E. Size and Breadth of Product Classes

Studies of industrial concentration which are presently available are subject to error primarily because the product classifications have not been defined in a uniform way. The number of separate products identified in the various studies ranges from as few as twenty selected[15] to as many as 1,807.[16]

Perhaps the most careful recent analysis of industry structure which uses census data to estimate the incidence of oligopoly in the American economy is that made by Kaysen and Turner.[17] Since we rely on concentration data to define oligopoly in subsequent chapters, the validity of Kaysen and Turner's approach is analyzed in some detail. The authors make use of 1954 Bureau of Census data for product groups as defined by the Bureau's 4-digit industry code. There are 440 census product groups in the 1954 compilation. The shipments of the specific products of each manufacturing firm are separated out and assigned to each of the 440 groups in which the firm was active. Some firms are leading producers of several products.

Kaysen and Turner consolidate 332 of these 4-digit products into 83 groups, reducing the total to 191, of which 173 are termed "economically meaningful" and eighteen represent catch-all, miscellaneous industries. This consolidation of industries is defended on the ground that in some cases census definitions turn upon raw materials used (beet versus cane sugar) or upon processes (steel produced and fabricated by an integrated producer versus that fabricated by a nonintegrated pro-

[15] J. S. Bain, *Barriers to New Competition* (Cambridge, Mass.: Harvard University Press, 1956).
[16] W. L. Thorp, and W. F. Crowder, "Concentration of Production in American Manufacturing," *The Structure of Industry* (Temporary Economic Committee, Monograph No. 27, Part III (Washington, D.C.: Government Printing Office, 1941).
[17] Kaysen and Turner, *Anti-Trust Policy*.

ducer) or upon particular products between which supply shifts could occur quickly (men's suits versus separate trousers) which are meaningless from the standpoint of market power and should therefore be counted as alternative sources of supply although men's suits may not be close substitutes for separate trousers in the opinion of consumers.[18]

Finally, dissimilar industries are combined if the value of shipments is small. Of the 191 industry groups, 27 are regional and 18 are catchalls of relatively minor products. An examination of 6 of the 27 regional products suggests that the classification of 12 as oligopolistic is probably an underestimate.

The 5-digit data were available to Kaysen and Turner; but there are approximately one thousand 5-digit product classes and the larger number of consolidations required if "unimportant" products were to be left to one side complicates the calculation of concentration ratios. The economy involved in working with a short list of products is most welcome if it yields satisfactory results. But Kaysen and Turner's procedure involves classifying unlike products together in some cases, and it is interesting to see how the degree of concentration is affected by consolidation. Three examples based upon their classification are presented in Tables III-1, 2, and 3.

In the first case, sugar, little if any undesirable consequence follows from the combination of 5-digit into 4-digit product classes, or even from the combination of the 4-digit products. This is shown in Table III-1. Apparently sugar is highly concentrated whether the subgroups are combined or not. Even the 7-digit products will probably show a similar degree of concentration, because each firm tends to produce a full range of subproducts. Kaysen and Turner calculate the minimum and the maximum possible concentration ratios for each of their combined groups. The eight-firm ratios work out to 63 per cent and 85 per cent in this case.

---

[18] *Ibid.*, pp. 295-99. The consolidation of sugar and of steels rests upon high cross elasticities of demand. In contrast, the consolidations of two types of men's clothing manufacturers are examples of cross elasticity of supply.

Consolidations based upon high potential elasticities of supply raise a fundamental point. Such consolidations are appropriate to the Kaysen-Turner study because it is directed to antitrust policy, not to the definition of products or of industry structure per se. "Monopoly" power is small, as we have noted above, if a product or subproduct can be added to a product line without incurring a cost disadvantage. Kaysen and Turner assume that entry is easy in some cases, but hard in others. However, entry may be possible at negligible cost in many lines. If it were ubiquitous, *all* products would be classified together by this test. We prefer, therefore, to *define* structure in terms of the number of firms actively producing a given product, and to analyze their power position as a separate step of analysis.

Table III-1

The Effect of Fineness of Classification on Concentration.
Examples of 4-Digit, 5-Digit, and 7-Digit Classes: Sugar
(4-firm, 8-firm, and 20-firm concentration ratios)*

	Product	Concentration Ratio			Number of
		4-f	8-f	20-firm	7-D Products
2061–	raw cane sugar	40	53	78	
1	" " "	44	57	85	16
2	other cane mill prods. & by-products (six 7-d classes)	46	68	88	
2062–	cane sugar refining	67	87	100	
1	refined cane sugar	67	86	100	16
2	other refined cane sugar and by-products (7-d: types, package, syrups)	61	86	100	
2063–	beet sugar	66	96	100	
1	refined beet sugar	66	96	100	15
2	other beet prod. & by-prod. (7-d not identical to cane)	67	96	100	

Combination of 2061, 2062, 2063 (Kaysen)   (min.   63)
                                                  (max.   85)

* Source: *Concentration in American Industry,* U.S. Senate, 85th Congress, 1st Session, 1957, p. 65. Number of 7-digit products from *Numerical List of Manufactured Products,* 1958 Census of Manufacturers, MC58-300, p. 224.

The similarity of concentration ratio at 4-, 5-, and probably 7-digit levels is not found in the other two cases, shown in Tables III-2 and III-3, neither of which is an isolated case among Kaysen and Turner's nonmiscellaneous industry groupings.

Cutlery provides an example of a nonheterogeneous, nonmiscellaneous industry that Kaysen and Turner classify as unconcentrated. Nevertheless, two of the six 4-digit industries meet their test for Type I oligopoly (largest 8 firms ship 50 per cent or more, and the largest 20 firms ship 75 per cent or more) and two others exceed the threshold

Table III-2

The Effect of Fineness of Classification on Concentration.
Examples of 4-Digit, 5-Digit, and 7-Digit Classes:
Cutlery*

| Product | Concentration Ratio | | | No. of |
	4-f	8-f	20-f	7-D Products
3421– cutlery	48	57	73	
1 cutlery (scissors, shears, trimmers, snips, butchers', kitchen, table, & pocket knives)	24	26	60	9
2 razor blades, non-electric razors	97	99	100	2
3422– edge tools (farm tools, axes, cutting dies, machine knives, can openers, woodworking tools)	18	32	53	9
3423– hand tools N.E.C.	19	29	45	
1 mech. hand service tools	25	37	57	8
2 other hand tools	31	40	59	5
3424– files**	92	97	99	2
3425– hand saws and blades	44	60	84	12
3429– hardware N.E.C.	33	40	51	
1 transp. equip. hardware	71	77	87	5
2 furniture hardware	54	76	89	2
3 vacuum bottles and jugs	83	98	100	2
4 builder's hardware (padlocks, locks, hinges)	24	36	54	8
5 other hardware (casket, fireplace equip., hose fittings & couplings)	14	24	41	8

* Sources: *op. cit.,* p. 84 and MC 58-300, p. 244 and 143.
** In the 1958 revision of the Census classification files and rasps were made 7-digit products in a 5-digit product class that includes shovels, hammers, and electric soldering irons.

(largest 8 firms ship 33 per cent) for oligopoly. Moreover, three of the more well-defined 5-digit products—razor blades and nonelectric razors; transportation equipment hardware; and vacuum bottles and jugs—ex-

Table III-3

The Effect of Fineness of Classification on Concentration.
Examples of 4-Digit, 5-Digit, and 7-Digit Classes:
Soap and Glycerine, Cleaning, Polishing and
Related Products*

		Concentration Ratio			No. of
Product		4-f	8-f	20-f	7-D Products
2841– soap and glycerine		63	73	84	
1 soaps except specialty, pkgd.		76	87	95	13
2 soaps except specialty, bulk		35	44	61	6
3 specialty soaps		52	70	86	4
4 glycerine		71	87	97	3
2842– cleaning and polishing prods.		52	60	70	
1 syn. organ detrg. pkgd.		95	97	99	5
2 syn. organ detrg. bulk		33	47	74	6
3 specialty		33	44	59	11
4 polishing preps & related prod.		37	47	62	13
5 alkaline detergents		44	57	74	3
9 household insecticides & repellents		31	42	62	7
2843– sulfanated oils and assistants		30	43	60	4
2887– fatty acids		D**	69	98	8

* Source: *op. cit.* p. 78, and MC 58-300, p. 237
** Disclosure

hibit very high levels of concentration even at the four-firm level. One must doubt the severity of competition within the grouping of products shown in Table III-2 as shown by cross elasticities either of demand or of supply. The "product" is not related to allocation and consumer welfare on one hand, and it tends to conceal substantial levels of concentration which may be inimical to a maximum use of resources.

Kaysen and Turner classify the soap and glycerine group among the Class I, or highly concentrated, oligopolies where the largest eight firms ship 50 per cent or more of the total. Some product lines included in this group are much more concentrated than others. Three of the four 4-digit products exceed the criteria for Class I oligopoly, but five of the ten 5-digit products do not. This is a result of the fact that firms specialize on one or a few of the 5-digit products which are combined into a larger aggregate. Moreover, one of the 5-digit classes includes such diverse products as aerosol bombs, roach powders, mechanics' soaps, household ammonia, dry-cleaning preparations, and textile and leather assistants and finishes. These seem to be very loosely linked in the chain of substitutes either of production or of consumption. Concentration probably differs greatly among the subproducts in this group. This soap-and-glycerine grouping is not listed as one of the 18 "miscellaneous groups."

On the contrary, it is possible that categories finer than any of these may often be desirable. The Federal Trade Commission, for example, has considered a slightly thinner aluminum foil, wooden skewers which are sold to packers, and special plastic films when designed especially for use as sausage casings, to be products that may be monopolized at some cost to the community.[19] It is not feasible to reach this degree of detail in census classifications, but it may be possible to construct industries that fit the economists' preferred definition much more closely than has been done in the past. It would involve the use, and often the combination, of the seven thousand 7-digit products, according to principles deduced in Chapter II. It would avoid combining products put to dissimilar final uses even when the total values are small. It would consider alternative sources of supply as a separate step in the analysis of the significance of industry structure.

The total amount of resources devoted to the relatively unimportant cases is large. An important part of the regulatory activity of government is based on the assumption that firms consider their policies with regard to narrowly defined products, and there is little reason to suppose that the assumption is incorrect. To the extent, therefore, that economists are interested in the allocation of resources among products, and in the economic power that firms may possess in their markets, it is desirable that the products used in economic analysis be defined as narrowly as is done by the decision-making units.

When viewed thus, 191 products strike one as being clearly too few. Indeed, the seven thousand 7-digit products defined by the Bureau of the Census are conceivably too few, even if each were defined so as to

[19] For sources and other examples, see Table 7, Chapter VI, following.

require no consolidation. It is not easy to know where to stop. Nevertheless, Weston is probably in error when he follows Nutter, holding that "by narrowing product lines sufficiently fine, any desired degree of concentration might be demonstrated."[20] While this is literally true if one wishes to recognize each model and brand as a separate product, the fact that most firms are multiproduct firms in the sense of the word developed in the first section of this chapter demonstrates that there is no reason in principle why concentration ratios should consistently rise as product definitions are narrowed. Our comparison of the 4-digit and 5-digit ratios for sugar products in Table 3-1 shows that statistical concentration ratios need not rise appreciably as product definitions are narrowed. Where substantial increases in concentration do occur as product definitions are narrowed it may well be because unlike items have been inappropriately classified together in the broader categories.

F. Summary

While holding to the idea that the concept of interdependence is the most appropriate way to classify industry structures for problems relating to resource allocation, direct measurement of such relationships by means of cross elasticities and similar devices is abandoned because insurmountable difficulties of conceptualization, data acquisition, and econometric procedures seem unavoidable. Instead, the use of census data on concentration is advocated. Nevertheless, 4-digit industry classes and even 4-digit, 5-digit, and 7-digit product classes have serious shortcomings for many problems of industry structure.

The 7-digit census products may be combined so as to construct products that conform more faithfully to interdependence in the market and to provide more nearly equal coverage. Thus product-centered rather than firm-centered analysis is sought. Oligopoly is defined as existing when the largest four firms produce 50 per cent or more of a product, when the product is defined according to the guidelines chosen in Chapter II.

This definition of oligopoly in product markets is not appropriate for all purposes. Financial power, research and development activity, and political power rest to some extent on the aggregate size of the firm rather than on any monopoly in particular markets. We consider oligopoly in the broader sense in Chapters VIII and IX. In the intervening chapters, however, attention is confined to structure and performance in individual product markets.

---

[20] Weston, *The Role of Mergers*, p. 113.

Chapter IV

The Incidence of Oligopoly
in the American Economy

THIS CHAPTER summarizes three studies that offer estimates of the prevalence of oligopoly in the American economy and presents evidence from a sample of 1954 census data indicating that these are underestimates. This evidence rests upon a sample of about 4 per cent of the 1,023 5-digit product classes used in the 1954 census of manufacturers. No implications concerning trends in concentration can be inferred from this sample, but evidence is presented which suggests that no very substantial trend exists during the period since 1935.

It has been customary to use concentration ratios relating to 4-digit industry or 4-digit product classes when attempting to divide the economy into "monopolistic" and "competitive" sectors, or to measure the incidence of oligopoly in the American economy. The general validity of this procedure is supported by studies made by Bain and Schwartzman which indicate that profits are significantly larger where the four-firm concentration ratios are in excess of 50 per cent or eight-firm ratios exceed 70 per cent.[1]

A. Prevalence of Oligopoly

1. Stigler's, Kaysen and Turner's, and Nutter's Studies

Three studies making use of broad product classes are summarized.

[1] See Chapter III, section D, and related footnotes. It is quite possible that they would have found more dramatic differences if narrower product classes had been used. This would be true if profits are positively correlated with concentration in specific markets, because consolidation tends to reduce average profits of the concentrated industries when some low concentration products are included, while the profits of unconcentrated industries are raised by the inclusion of some concentrated products.

Stigler does not make direct use of concentration ratios but uses the 1939 data developed by the Temporary National Economic Committee to classify economic activity as competitive, monopolistic, compulsory cartel, or not allocable, and carries the breakdown back to 1870 with the aid of other data.[2] His procedure is to separate out the industries appropriate to the latter classifications and list the remainder as "other." It is, therefore, particularly inappropriate to count the number of industries that are monopolistic or competitive. In terms of income originating in manufacturing, however, Stigler finds 53.4 per cent coming from the competitive, 40.4 per cent from the monopolistic and 6.2 per cent from the non-allocable sectors.

Kaysen and Turner use 1954 4-digit data in the study described in Chapter III to estimate the prevalence of oligopoly and monopoly. Because they combine a large number of the industries into admittedly broad groupings, they adopt 33 per cent by the eight largest firms as the minimum concentration ratio required for oligopoly. "Type I" oligopolies are those with an eight-firm ratio of 50 per cent or more and a twenty-firm ratio of 75 per cent or more.

Using these criteria, oligopoly is found to exist in 66 per cent of the industries which account for 62 per cent of total shipments. Type I oligopoly is found for 36 per cent of the industries. They ship 22 per cent of the total.

G. Warren Nutter has also estimated the share of income originating in monopolistic industry in the United States.[3] In general, he utilizes the industry categories developed by Professor Clair Wilcox's careful study for the TNEC; but some additions such as fluid milk and manufacturing industries not included by Wilcox are made if they had four-firm concentration ratios of 50 per cent or more in 1935, or if an industry were of major value and had concentration ratios of 75 per cent or more in 1937 and were not specifically characterized as effectively competitive by Wilcox. Nutter finds that 39 per cent of income originating in manufacturing came from monopolized industry in 1937 and 39.6 per cent in 1939. This compares closely to Stigler's estimate of 40.4 per cent for the latter year, when account is taken of the crudities of the two estimation procedures, and is about halfway between Kaysen and

[2] G. J. Stigler, *Five Lectures* (New York: Macmillan, 1950), Lecture Five.
[3] G. Warren Nutter, *The Extent of Enterprise Monopoly in the United States, 1899-1939* (Chicago, Ill.: University of Chicago Press, 1951). He utilizes the industry classifications made by Clair Wilcox, *Monopoly and Competition in American Industry,* Temporary Economic Committee Monograph No. 21 (Washington, D.C.: Government Printing Office, 1940).

Turner's estimate for shipments by Type I oligopolies and their estimate for the outer limit of oligopoly in 1954.

If no important change in concentration occurred between 1939 and 1954, the 62 per cent and the 40 per cent may be taken as establishing the limits of the probable range of the incidence of oligopoly in the American economy when the problem is viewed in terms of possible demand and/or supply substitutions among 4-digit products and when minor products are grouped into relatively broad categories.

Stigler and Nutter agree that the data fail to establish any clear trend toward a larger proportion of monopoly in American industry.[4] Stigler compares 1904 with 1939, while Nutter compares 1899 with 1937 and 1939 and attempts quantitative estimates based upon alternative definitions. He finds 32 per cent of manufacturing industry to be monopolistic in 1899, and from 28 per cent to 38.3 per cent monopolized in 1937. Both authors agree that the data are not satisfactory.

Much better data are available since 1947.

2. A Trend in Oligopoly?

R. L. Nelson, utilizing data constructed by Irving Rottenberg, computes weighted average concentration ratios for the 375 4-digit industries that remained comparable between 1947 and 1954.[5] He finds an increase in the average concentration ratio from 34.6 to 35.3, utilizing current-year weights. If 1947 weights are used for both years a lesser increase, from 34.6 to 34.7 is recorded. If 1954 weights are used for both years, concentration is shown to decline from 35.9 to 35.3. Seventy-two industries showed changes of less than 1 per cent, 142 between 1 and 5 per cent, and 161 more than 5 per cent. These changes are not large, and are probably exaggerated somewhat because 1947 was a year of rapid recovery, while 1954 was a relatively bad year.

No over-all estimates of concentration in 1958 or subsequent years are presented by Nelson. A very sketchy test for change between 1954 and 1958 can be made by comparing 1954 data utilized in a sample of 5-digit 1954 census data, to be described later, to comparable product classes for 1958. Ten of the 45 5-digit product classes used in our sample are not comparable in 1958. Table IV-1 shows the average concentration ratios for the concentrated and the unconcentrated groups

---

[4] Stigler, p. 54; Nutter, p. 40.

[5] R. L. Nelson, *Concentration in Manufacturing Industries in the United States* (New Haven: Yale University Press, 1963), pp. 52-3. Nelson reports (p. 49) that there were 453 industry classes in 1947 and 446 in 1954. The industry classification assigns a firm's production to its principal product, rather than separating its products into various product classes.

Table IV-1

Five-Digit Concentration Ratios For
35 Comparable Products,
1954 and 1958

	4-firm	*8-firm*	*20-firm*
Concentrated Products			
1954	85.7	92.2	95.3
1958	83.1	91.3	98.9
Unconcentrated Products			
1954	11.2	17.6	29.5
1958	11.7	17.6	28.3

Table IV-2

Share of Total Value Added by Manufacture Accounted for by
Largest Manufacturing Companies in 1958 Compared with Share Accounted
For by Largest Companies in 1954 and 1947

Company Rankings In Respective Year	*Percentage of Value Added by Manufacture 1958*	*Percentage of Value Added by Manufacture 1954*	*Percentage of Value Added by Manufacture 1947*
Largest 50 companies	23 (23)	23 (23)	17 (17)
Largest 100 companies	30 (7)	30 (7)	23 (6)
Largest 150 companies	35 (5)	34 (4)	27 (4)
Largest 200 companies	38 (3)	37 (3)	30 (3)

Source: *Concentration Ratios in Manufacturing Industry, 1958* (Washington, D.C., Government Printing Office, 1962), p. 8.

taken separately. No trend is visible given the small size of the sample. We must conclude that no evidence of a trend toward higher concentration is discernible from these studies.

Many economists are reluctant to accept the conclusion that no trend toward oligopoly is evident. They show particular interest in the position of the largest companies regardless of the degree of concentration in particular markets. Census data on value added show a substantial increase in the shares of the two hundred largest manufacturers between 1947 and 1954, and a continued but lesser gain between 1954 and 1958.

Table IV-2 reproduces the basic table. The numbers in parentheses are the share added by the marginal group of fifty firms.

Such concentration tells one nothing about the concentration of output in particular product markets and is irrelevant to oligopoly as the word is normally defined. Big business and oligopoly are not synonymous. Nevertheless, it is interesting to analyze these data for evidence of trend.

The composition of the largest two hundred companies has changed over the years as the relative significance of the various products and firms has fluctuated, but the same general pattern remains. It is evident that the principal reason for the growth of the share of value added by the largest two hundred firms is the 6-point expansion of the fifty largest firms between 1947 and 1954 and the ability of the next largest 150 to expand slightly faster than the average of all manufacturing.

This apparent increase probably reflects cyclical shifts, not trend. Unfortunately, earlier data on concentration are for shipments, not for value added. Data for shipments by the fifty largest firms are available for the relatively good years 1937 and 1947 and the relatively bad year 1954. Crowder, Abramson, and Staudt found the leading fifty manufacturing industries to be shipping the relatively high share, 27.7 per cent of the total value of manufactures in 1937.[6] Nelson calculated shipments for the largest fifty firms for 1947 and 1954 and discovered that the share of shipments enjoyed by the fifty largest firms had increased only 2.2 percentage points, from 22.6 to 24.8. He concludes:

> The largest companies thus proved to have a lower ratio of value added to sales than for all manufacturing companies in both years, suggesting that on the average, they were less vertically integrated than all companies. The greater relative increase in their value-added share than in their shipments share reflected two developments. First, the profit margin of the largest companies rose slightly, even though the margin for all manufacturing companies fell off in the 1954 recession. Second, the vertical integration of the largest companies, though remaining lower than average, apparently increased relatively more than that for all companies.[7]

So the decline in the position of the largest firms between 1937 and 1947 may be more significant than the rise between 1947 and 1954.

The fact that reliable trends cannot be established may be significant. It lends inferential support to the conclusion that no great changes have

[6] Walter F. Crowder, Adolph J. Abramson, Ester W. Staudt, *The Structure of Industry*, T.N.E.C. Monograph No. 27, Part VI (Washington, D.C.: Government Printing Office, 1941), 583.
[7] Nelson, pp. 12-13.

taken place. The larger firms seem to have grown little if any faster than their markets and seem to specialize in mass-production industries where value added is relatively small. This may be more significant than market power as an explanation of their relatively large size.

If no trend in concentration is observable in the 4-digit manufacturing shipments, there is no reason to assert at this time that 5-digit or 7-digit data would show increasing concentration. Instead, it is reasonable to suppose that the concentration ratio among narrowly defined products as well as among broadly defined products has been rather stable.

The incidence of oligopoly may be underestimated in each of the studies reviewed thus far in this chapter. There are at least two reasons why this may be the case: (1) bias in the definition of product classes and (2) the exclusion of highly concentrated industries where power is limited by highly probable potential entry. We will consider only the first of these.

B. Data Conceal Oligopoly

It is interesting that the 36 per cent of the industries classed by Kaysen and Turner as Type I oligopolies shipped only 22 per cent of the total, while the 34 per cent of the total number of industries classed as unconcentrated shipped 38 per cent.[8] If Nelson is correct, this cannot be due to a greater degree of vertical integration in the concentrated sector which makes value added a larger proportion of value of shipments. It may be due to oligopolistic restriction of output. But it may simply reflect the practice of including relatively remote substitutes in a given industry when the value of shipments is small, as suggested by the relationships revealed in Tables III-2 and III-3. If the latter explanation is the more important, Kaysen and Turner are correct when they state that if their criteria for oligopoly are accepted their estimates of its prevalence in manufacturing are understated. Many small oligopolies have gone undetected.

The Standard Industrial Classification lists economic significance among the criteria used in classifying products, but its relative importance is unclear.[9] Kaysen and Turner explicitly include economic significance as an important criterion.[10] To the extent that heterogeneous products are grouped together simply because each is shipped in rela-

---

[8] Kaysen and Turner, p. 36-37.

[9] For a brief discussion see *Concentration Ratios in Manufacturing Industry, 1958* (Washington, D.C.: Government Printing Office, 1962), pp. 2-3. For a fuller discussion see Conklin and Goldstein.

[10] Kaysen and Turner, pp. 296-97.

tively small volume, products produced in large volume will be more homogeneously defined than those produced in small volume, with the result that concentration in small-volume products is underestimated.

If homogeneous products produced in large volume tend to have 4- and 5-digit product classes of their own, while equally distinct products arc groupcd togcthcr whcn thcir volumcs of output arc small, onc would expect (1) 4-digit products which include many 5-digit products to have lower concentration ratios than the others, and (2) some tendency for the homogeneous, high-concentration product classes to be shipped in smaller volume than the more heterogeneous lower concentration classes. While many exceptions would exist to the latter tendency, one would expect the median concentration ratios to show this bias. One would also expect (3) that if more homogeneous groups of 4- and 5-digit products are isolated from the others quite similar concentration ratios will be found regardless of the size of the value of shipments.

Ralph L. Nelson presents data compiled from the 1954 Census that support each of these hypotheses.[11] This suggests that significant numbers of monopolistic and oligopolistic markets may be overlooked in studies based upon 4-digit-and-coarser industry or product classes. As one moves toward more and more homogeneously defined products one must find higher concentration in particular markets, unless firms are multiproduct enterprises and produce for different markets in the same or offsetting proportions. One might also expect to find greater diversity of industry structure and, therefore, of concentration, although the range of the concentration ratio already extends from virtually zero to 100 at the 4-digit level. It is also possible, at least in principle, for each product to be produced by a rather small group of firms and for the apparent degree of concentration to be a function of the number of products included in a product group and the number of firms that happen to produce two or more of the included products.

Nelson's tables suggest that the latter explanation may be of some importance. Thus the 213 4-digit products which are unchanged in the 5-digit classification, and which are therefore probably rather homogeneous, show about the same concentration ratio in each class of value of shipments. Moreover, the more highly concentrated products in this group appear about as often as one would expect from the total distribution at each level of the value of shipments.[12] Finally, taken as a whole, the 5-digit data show the expected higher concentration ratios; so that far

---

[11] *Concentration in the Manufacturing Industries in the United States* (New Haven: Yale University Press, 1963), ch. iii, especially pp. 44-48.

[12] *Ibid.,* p. 46-47.

more high-concentration ratios are found for the products shipped in smaller volume.[13] It is possible, therefore, that the 5-digit data continue to conceal considerable amounts of oligopoly structure. The next section examines the relationship between 5- and 7-digit data in an effort to ascertain if this is true.

C. Concentration of 5- and 7-Digit Products

Approximately 7,000 seven-digit products are encompassed by the 1,023 5-digit product classes. As will be pointed out, 7-digit products are isolated for a variety of purposes and sometimes differ only in being produced by one class of producers (integrated) rather than another (nonintegrated). Nevertheless, most 7-digit products are themselves aggregates of several, even many, subproducts. In this section, and in chapters V and VI, it is assumed that 7-digit products are more commonly defined in a way that makes them generic products as defined in Chapter III. In some cases, 5- and 7-digit products may be identical, as were the 213 4-digit categories mentioned above. We will argue that even when the 7-digit classification is too narrow its concentration may often be a reasonably accurate indicator of concentration of the properly defined group. But if the concentration ratio is based on a too broadly defined product group, serious underestimation is almost unavoidable.

The procedure used cannot yield an accurate estimate of the incidence of oligopoly in the American economy because the sample used is taken from the extremes of the array of concentration ratios. It does suggest that Kaysen and Turner's maximum estimate of 66 per cent of the product classes is too low.[14]

Our procedure is to draw two samples from the 5-digit product classes of the 1954 Census of Manufactures.[15] One is from products with the highest concentration ratios, and the other is from the opposite extreme. Data for the 7-digit constituent products are then examined. The share of shipments by the largest firm and by the largest two firms for various groups of products is shown. To the writer's knowledge, data on the

---

[13] *Ibid.*

[14] Our estimates neglect potential supply from firms in closely related fields. That is related more to the power of an oligopoly than to its existence. This is the subject of Chapter V.

[15] It is entitled *The Proportion of the Shipments (or Employees) of Each Industry or the Shipments of Each Group of Products Accounted for by the Largest Companies as Reported in the 1954 Census of Manufactures* (Washington, D.C.: Government Printing Office, 1957). This was subsequently reprinted in expanded form by the Subcommittee of the Judiciary under the title, *Concentration in American Industry, U.S. Senate*, 85th Cong., 2d Sess., 1962.

relative size of the leading firms at the 5- and 7-digit levels have not been published heretofore.[16]

1. Products were included in this study if:

    a. The four largest firms produced 80 per cent or more of the 5-digit class and the largest twenty produced 99 per cent or more. These are divided into four subgroups designated *A, B, D* and *E,* as described below.

    b. The twenty largest firms produced approximately 40 per cent or less of the 5-digit class. This unconcentrated group is called group *C.*

2. Products were excluded even when they fell into one of these two major groups if:

    a. They were thought (on general knowledge) to have regional markets.

    b. They contained only one published 7-digit subgroup.

    c. The products were known to be involved in antimerger proceedings.

The last criterion requires explanation. The omission of products known to be involved in antimerger proceedings is based upon the expectation that the firm's share of market can be found from other sources in those cases, and that the averages obtained in this tabulation may be used to test the hypothesis that there is a difference in the rate of progression of firm size that characterizes a tendency to merge. In a number of cases, however, antimerger cases rest upon a much narrower definition of products than any shown separately in census data—for example, power switch gear sold to utilities, and liquid bleach.[17] As long as the enforcement agencies act on the monopolization of such narrowly defined products one may imagine that oligopolists must also make decisions on this level. As a result of the overlap, several 5-digit product classes are included in this list which in turn encompass 7-digit products involved in FTC proceedings in spite of limitation 2c.

The lists of products are subdivided further to separate those 5-digit product groups which enjoy an expanding market, groups *A* and *D,*

---

[16] All of the tabulations shown in this and succeeding chapters which relate to the value of shipments by the largest, next largest, third, and fourth largest firms at the 5- and 7- digit levels were made by census employees. Only the totals shown here, calculated so as to avoid disclosure, have been permitted to be taken from Census premises. The author wishes to express his great appreciation for the courtesy, concern, time, aid, and unfailing good humor of executives and staff of the Bureau of the Census.

[17] See Table VI-7, p. 118-19 following for additional products of this type.

from those where the market is either stable or declining, groups *B* and
E. The *Annual Surveys* closest to 1954 are used to make this subclassi-
fication. It happens that virtually all products falling in the unconcentrated classification, group *C*, enjoyed expanding markets at that time.
Finally, the concentrated group was divided into (1) those products all
or virtually all of which are produced by eight or fewer firms, groups *A*
and *B*; and (2) those products 99 per cent or more of which are
produced by more than eight but fewer than twenty firms, groups *D* and
E. Thus groups *A* and *B* are without much of a "competitive fringe,"
while firms in groups *D* and *E* may have a considerable fringe.[18] Table 1
of Appendix A lists the products included and Table 2 of Appendix A
summarizes the sample.

The reader will have noticed that the criteria used for the choice of
high concentration of production are very much in excess of the criteria
used by Kaysen and Turner. A four-firm concentration ratio of 80 per
cent is used in place of their eight-firm ratio of 50 per cent or, alternatively, of 33 per cent. Part of this higher critical concentration ratio
may be necessary because a sample is taken of a universe of 1,023
5-digit products rather than of the 191 groups of 4-digit industries. The
principal reasons for this high threshold, however, are a desire to limit
the size of the sample, on one hand, and the belief that if substantial
similarity exists among the components of this sample of the most highly
concentrated industries and those of the least concentrated industries it
is reasonable to infer the relationship to the remainder of the universe.
Finally, as stated before, it is hoped that this sample may stimulate a
full-dress study of the 1954 and the more recent data which have become
available.

Two theses are advanced and tested here: one, that the 7-digit data
are in general not so narrow as to be worse definitions of products than
the 5- or 4-digit classifications; and two, that concentration among
7-digit components of 5-digit products indicates more nearly comparable
and generally high degrees of concentration.

---

[18] Indeed, more than 100 firms sometimes share the last one per cent of a
highly concentrated market. However, it is possible for small firms to be in
special niches in the market and not in substantial competition with the major
producers. Bocar may not even be a competitor of Corvette nor, in another field,
Bergdorf-Goodman with Gimbels. Since firm names were not consulted in drawing
this sample, no correction for this type of error was made, and the distinction
between *A* and *B* groups on one hand and *D* and *E* groups on the other hand
may not be significant. But we do not know how much influence a "competitive
fringe" exerts in any case, and the distinction drawn here is objective. One can
see if behavior differs between the groups.

D. 7-Digit vs. 5-Digit Concentration Ratios and Oligopoly

It is possible that a narrower definition always increases the apparent concentration. If, however, firms usually produce a full line of specific products, and the product classes are approximately homogeneous, the firms classified together will typically produce much the same product lines, perhaps in similar or offsetting proportions. In that case, the 5-digit and the 7-digit concentration ratios will tend to be about the same. If a heterogeneous grouping is made at the 5-digit level, *but not at the 7-digit level,* much higher concentration ratios will be found at the 7-digit level when oligopoly is characteristic of homogeneous product groups. This difference will be found because where different markets are placed into a single classification each firm's output is compared to a large total production including much outside of its "proper" group. Thus the largest firm may have a small share of the group output, while having no close rivals for its particular product. On the other hand, when each firm produces, for example, the same percentage of each of a number of 7-digit products which are grouped into a 5-digit class, the concentration ratio is the same whether calculated for the 5- or for any of the 7-digit products.

It is, therefore, quite possible that 7-digit products are better measures of economically meaningful products than are 5-digit product classes. But it is especially significant that where they are not actually better measures they may nonetheless, *and for that very reason,* yield concentration ratios that are the same as or very similar to those of the appropriately defined product. Thus, the very fact that large changes occur in the concentration ratio as subclasses are considered separately is evidence that the subclasses are improperly classified together.

The notion that concentration ratios must approach 100 per cent for one firm as product classes are narrowed is a corollary to the standard simplifying assumption that each firm produces a single "product." There is little danger that the 7,000 7-digit products used by the Bureau of the Census will come close to providing one product for each of the 300,000-odd manufacturers in the United States.

On the other hand, there is no reason to believe that each 7-digit product is a well-defined entity. To begin with, census product groups are isolated because of similarity of processes and materials as well as similarity of uses. Thus concentration ratios at the 5-digit level are sometimes too high from the latter point of view, because nearly perfect substitutes exist made of other materials or by other processes. In these instances, 7-digit products continue to show the too-high concentration rather than to ameliorate it, because they follow the parent 5-digit class. Under these circumstances the use of 7-digit products does not reveal economic markets any better (nor perhaps any worse) than do 5-digit product classes.

The 7-digit data are sometimes more misleading than 5-digit data. The Bureau of the Census collects 7-digit data for several reasons, only one of which is to show greater detail when economically significant values of shipments are recorded for particular product classes. In some cases, part of the data may be poor, or disclosure rules would be violated if a certain grouping were made, while if several 7-digit classes are made, one or more of them may yield useful publishable data. For these reasons the number of 7-digit products for which data are collected differs somewhat from the 7-digit products which are published. Working with the work sheets, I was not aware of this distinction, with the result that some of the 292 7-digit products may be for collected—but unpublished—categories which relate to insignificant product classes. Error from this source has been minimized by elimination of all miscellaneous categories among the 7-digit data and by dropping from all of the tables all 7-digit products where the number of published categories differs more than slightly from the number collected. The principal effect is to decrease the apparent concentration for 7-digit products within the most highly concentrated 5-digit product groups.

When a 7-digit class is broken out only because its inclusion would preclude publication because of disclosure, the unpublished class is superior to the published one for the present purpose. If the 7-digit class is composed of a miscellany of poor data constructed to isolate it from useful data it is better omitted.

It should be noted that the Bureau of the Census does not claim to make any accurate count of the total number of firms producing 7-digit products, and does not publish such counts largely because special short forms are used for the smaller firms. This procedure must understate the extent of the competitive fringe, but it is not a limitation to the present use of these categories because the present study considers only the shipments of the two largest firms as compared to total shipments of each 7-digit product.

Although the 292 7-digit products included in this study have not been individually scrutinized with a view to combining substitute products made of different processes, and although some meaningless categories may remain, the considerations outlined above give reason to believe that this 4.2 per cent sample provides some useful information

Table IV-3

Concentration Ratios for 5-Digit and 7-Digit Products, 1954

Major Group	5-Digit	7-Digit	Percentage Increase	Percentage Approach to 100 Per Cent
Concentrated[a]				
4-Firm	88	—	—	—
2-Firm	70	79	13	30
Unconcentrated[b]				
Total				
4-Firm	11	—	—	—
2-Firm	6.5	43	561	39
Regional				
2-Firm	6.5	50	669	47

[a] Four largest firms at the 5-digit level ship 80 per cent or more, and the 20 largest 99 per cent or more.

[b] Twenty largest firms at the 5-digit level ship 40 per cent or less.

and, hopefully, can stimulate interest in making a full-scale study in the future.

The remainder of this chapter compares 5- and 7-digit data to see if differences in 5-digit concentration ratios may not be largely accounted for by relative diversity of product within the product classes.

Table IV-3 shows the average four-firm and two-firm concentration ratios for the most concentrated group of 5-digit products and for the least concentrated group, and the average two-firm concentration ratios for the 7-digit products included in each of them. The averages are constructed to show the typical position of the leading firms in their product class. Thus a firm's position in its 7-digit market is given weight both when ascertaining the concentration in groups of 7-digit markets and in combining 5-digit markets.[19]

[19] This was done by using the number of 7-digit products in a 5-digit product class as weights when combining 5-digit classes. The procedure is also used in Table IV and in Chapter VI, where the typical position of the leading firm, the second firm, and so on, in their particular markets is sought. This procedure is appropriate for the purpose, which is to find the typical size of the leading firm, the second firm, etc. in their markets regardless of the size of the various markets.

We do not weigh the market shares by value of shipments or some other indicator of importance, because we are not trying to judge the overall significance

Table IV-3 is designed to test the hypothesis that because firms usually produce a reasonably full line of products, narrowing the definition of products will not markedly increase concentration ratios where products are already narrowly defined, but that marked increases are encountered when the broader classes are not homogeneous. Nelson's study of the 1954 census, alluded to earlier, supports this hypothesis as a result of a comparison of 4- and 5-digit products. The present test carries this comparison to the 5- and 7-digit products. If those 5-digit products among the 1,023 which are highly concentrated at the 5-digit level are relatively homogeneous, while the unconcentrated 5-digit products are collections of noncompeting products, the subdivision of 5-digit products into 7-digit products will not increase the concentration ratio very much in the former case, but will increase it substantially in the second. Table IV-3 shows that this is the case.

One- and two-firm concentration ratios must be used for purposes of comparison at the 7-digit level because of data limitations, but the four-firm ratios at the 5-digit level are also presented. The typical position of the four leading firms in the most highly concentrated 5-digit product markets is to enjoy 88 per cent of the market. The largest two firms have 70 per cent and the next two only 18 per cent. The position of the leading firms in the unconcentrated 5-digit industries is vastly smaller, the typical "big four" having only 11 per cent of the market and the leading two, 6.5 per cent.

The relative share of shipments of the two largest firms rises by 9

---

of the different products. If each 7-digit product were to be weighted, say, by its proportion of the value shipments of its 5-digit class, the calculated concentration ratio for the class using the 7-digit products would be the same as that given for the class by the census, and nothing would be revealed about the relative size of the leading firms. Such an effort is relevant to a different problem—that of finding the importance of oligopoly once it has been adequately defined statistically.

Weighting each major group by the number of 7-digit products found in it enables one to compare the average position of the largest, next largest, etc., firm as shown by 5-digit product data with the average position of the largest, next largest, etc., firm as shown by the 7-digit data. If the statistical problems discussed above—i.e., classification by material used and process employed, devices used to avoid disclosure, collection of some products only to sharpen the definition of others, and the overriding test that the category be large enough to have economic significance—do not rob these data of usefulness, the weighting system is appropriate.

The concentration ratios given here for groups of 5-digit products, such as groups A,B,C,D and E, weight the share of the leading firms according to the number of 7-digit products in the 5-digit product class. This makes the result comparable to the average position of the leading producers of the 7-digit products which are included in the 5-digit product classes.

percentage points when the 7-digit products included in highly concentrated 5-product classes are considered. This is a 13 per cent increase. When the least concentrated product classes are examined the comparable increases are 36.5 percentage points, or 561 per cent. The largest two firms then typically enjoy 43 per cent of their market.

Although 5-digit cases thought to serve regional markets are eliminated from the sample used, the possibility exists that some of the 7-digit products associated with the 5-digit product classes may serve regional markets. Rather than rely upon the writer's judgment, the following convention is adopted: a 7-digit product is classified as "regional" if the number of establishments differs more than a small amount from the number of firms. This rule rests on the hypothesis that when there are meaningful regions, plants located within the region will possess an advantage over the plants located outside of the region. Therefore, where several firms exist, at least some of them will wish to serve more than one region, and will do so through regional establishments. When this test is applied, the 151 7-digit product groups are narrowed to 101, and the share of markets enjoyed by the largest two firms rises from 6.5 per cent to 50 per cent—a rise of 43.5 percentage points, or 669 per cent.

The large percentage increases shown for the 7-digit products may be an exaggeration, because the upper limit is 100 per cent, and both the absolute number of percentage points and especially the percentage increase possible in the concentrated industries is limited. A much harder test of the meaningfulness of this rise in the two-firm concentration ratio is percentage of the distance toward 100 per cent shares by the leading two firms accomplished by division of 5-digit product classes into 7-digit products. Such a test is biased against our hypothesis because a small change in the concentrated sector yields a very large percentage rise toward 100 per cent concentration. The result of this calculation is shown in the last column of Table IV-3. Even by this test the unconcentrated group shows a larger increase in concentration: 47 per cent for the more relevant nonregional group of unconcentrated products, 39 per cent for the total unconcentrated group, but only 30 per cent for the concentrated group. The data support our hypothesis.

E. One-Firm and Two-Firm Shares of "Unconcentrated" Products

It is possible to go one step further and show a distribution of one-firm and two-firm 7-digit concentration ratios for the products of the unconcentrated 5-digit product classes, Group C.

Table IV-4 presents a distribution of the shares of the 101 nonre-

Table IV-4

Share of Shipments of 101 7-Digit Products
Thought to Have National Markets
Selected from the Least Concentrated 5-Digit Product Classes

Percentage Share of Market of the Largest or Two Largest Firms	Number of Products			
	Largest Firm's Share		Largest Two Firms' Share	
	No.	Cum.	No.	Cum.
90-100	6	6	10	10
80-89	0	6	5	15
70-79	5	11	7	22
60-69	4	15	7	29
50-59	6	21	14	43
40-49	7	28	18	61
30-39	21	49	20	81
20-29	22	71	11	92
10-19	22	93	4	96
0-9	8	101	5	101

gional 7-digit markets held by the largest firm and the largest two firms by decile classes. One notes from Table IV-4 that almost half of the 7-digit products were produced by industries in which the largest firm shipped 30 per cent or more of the total output, and that in the typical case the two largest firms shipped in excess of 40 per cent. Moreover, the largest firm shipped 50 per cent or more of the product in about a fifth of the cases, while the largest two firms shipped more than 70 per cent in about a fifth of the cases. Concentration ratios for the largest four or eight firms are not calculated because of the high cost involved. But in only eight cases did the leading firm produce as little as 9 per cent, which compares with the average of 11 per cent for the largest *four* firms in the parent 5-digit product class.

Each of the 5-digit products included in Group C was produced by 250 to 5000 firms. Yet on the basis of the 7-digit classification, five products were produced in their entirety by one firm, three by three, two by four, four by five, and thirty-one more by six to twenty firms. This accounts for 45 of the 151 7-digit products included in this group of least-concentrated 5-digit products. A substantial majority of these qualify for investigation under the policy urged by Kaysen and Turner, who suggest for a presumptive lower boundary of oligopoly an eight-firm concentration ratio of 50 for "more precisely defined markets" and a one-firm market share of 35 per cent when the next largest firm is much smaller in very narrowly defined markets.[20]

Approximately forty of the 151 7-digit products were produced by more than 100 firms. Even among these, in one sixth of the cases, the two leading firms produced 30 per cent or more of the value of shipments while the remaining 98 or more firms divided less than 70 per cent of the market.

F. Extent of Oligopoly

The sample used in the study of concentration at the 7-digit level does not permit a satisfactory estimate of the extent of oligopoly. The sample is inadequate for this purpose because it is too small, because it is taken exclusively from the extremes of the 5-digit concentration, and because no effort is made to combine products when product classes are too narrow. Finally, some bias, probably toward understatement of concentration, exists in the sample in that it excludes products when the 5-digit and the 7-digit product definition is the same and because it excludes industries where antimerger complaints were filed.

A rough estimate of the extent of high concentration can nevertheless be made. Table IV-5 summarizes the necessary data. The top line shows the percentage distribution of the 1,023 5-digit product classes in 1954 according to their four-firm concentration ratios. A roughly equal distribution is shown, although one should bear in mind that the two extreme classes are twice as broad as the others. The median concentration ratio is 42.8.[21] Our sample was taken from the two extreme groups 0-19 and 80-100. The reader will recall that the average four-firm concentration ratio for the 5-digit products in our concentrated groups is 88 per cent and for these products in our unconcentrated group is 11 per cent.

The lower line in Table IV-5 shows the distribution of the relevant two-firm concentration ratios for only those 7-digit products which compose the least concentrated of all 5-digit products. The median two-firm concentration ratio is 46, and the average is 50. The ratios

<hr/>

[20] Kaysen and Turner, pp. 102, 104. It is possible that some of the 7-digit products are those collected to isolate other classes, which would otherwise be a disclosure, heterogeneous, or contaminated by inaccurate reporting. In the former, but not in the latter case, the 7-digit category would be useful for our purposes. In the intermediate case, the data would be more appropriate than the 5-digit figure in spite of the probability that the economic value involved is small. See *ibid.*, pp. 4-8, 9, 10.

[21] Nelson, *Concentration*, p. 41.

Table IV-5

Concentration Classes, All 5-Digit and 7-Digit
Samples Compared: 1954

Product Class			*Concentration Class*				
	0-19	20-29	30-39	40-49	50-59	60-69	70-79	80-100
Percentage of 5-digit product classes (4-firm)*	14.3	14.9	15.8	15.0	12.3	10.2	7.1	10.0
				42.8				
			median concentration ratio					
Number of 7-digit product classes; unconcentrated 5-digit parent class (2-firm)	9	11	20	18	14	7	7	15
				46 median CR	50 average CR			

*Source: Nelson, p. 41. Also *Concentration in American Industry,* Table 7, p. 14, and Table 40, pp. 133-65. Note: Detail does not add to 100.0 because of rounding in the census study.

are for the 101 products found to have national markets by the test described above. The corresponding average two-firm concentration ratio for the 141 7-digit products associated with the highly concentrated 5-digit product classes is 79.

We do not know the size of the market shares of the third and fourth largest firms. But if relative firm sizes approximate the log-normal distribution, as asserted by Simon and Bonini, and others, and as confirmed in a general way below, the four-firm concentration ratios exceed 60 per cent in 43 of the 101 7-digit products which compose the least concentrated product groups in American manufacturing industry. The top 61 of the 101 products have four-firm concentration ratios of 50 per cent or more if relative firm size follows the log-normal rule. Thus three fifths of the products in the least-concentrated sector meet our test for oligopoly.

It is reasonable to suppose (1) that virtually all 7-digit products have four-firm concentration ratios of 50 or more when the parent 5-digit classes have concentration ratios of 100 and (2) that the proportion of 7-digit products with four-firm ratios above 50 rises in a linear fashion from 61 per cent where the 5-digit concentration ratio is 6.5, to 100 per cent where it is 100. This yields an estimated average proportion of oligopolistic 7-digit products for each of the concentration classes given in Table IV-5.

Table IV-5 indicates the proportion of 5-digit products found in each concentration class. The number of 7-digit products associated with a given 5-digit class differs somewhat according to the concentration ratio of the 5-digit class. In our sample 7.8 7-digit products are found per concentrated product, while 9.2 are associated with the typical unconcentrated 5-digit product. Both of these averages are somewhat high as compared to the total universe, since a 5-digit product is included in the study only if it contains a considerable number of associated 7-digit products. Applying these two sets of weights we estimate that somewhat more than 76 per cent of the 7-digit products may have four-firm concentration ratios of 50 or more. This is more than the percentage that Kaysen and Turner advance as an outer limit to oligopoly when they apply their criterion of an eight-firm concentration ratio of 33 per cent to 191 consolidated product classes. In contrast, our estimate is based upon a sample of 242 7-digit products taken from the extremes of 7,000 much more narrowly defined products.

Little weight should be attached to this specific figure. Aside from the long interpolation, certain biases are present. The omission of one-product 5-digit product classes and products involved in antimerger proceedings biases the sample, probably toward an underestimate. The failure to combine certain 7-digit products, or the inclusion of one without certain others, probably produces some bias in the opposite direction. Nevertheless, it seems probable that manufacturing industry is highly concentrated in the United States by the usual test of fewness of important producers in well-defined markets.

G. Summary

This chapter reviews other studies of concentration in American industry and also presents some new data relevant to the more narrowly defined 7-digit products collected by the Bureau of the Census. No significant evidence of a trend toward increased concentration is found from an examination of the position of the leading firms, but a tendency toward substantial understatement of significant concentration is detected which has resulted from the use of 4-digit and coarser industry categories. Definitional categories narrow enough to produce 7,000 products of manufacturing industry are not found to be so narrow as to arbitrarily produce high concentration.

The principal exception to this rule is found in those cases where substitute products are classified in different groups because they are made of different materials, by different processes, or by integrated rather than by nonintegrated producers. All of these classification errors are found at the 4- and 5-digit level as well as at the 7, and to the extent that the latter merely follow the parent class, the error is not necessarily greater at the 7-digit level than at the others.

On the other hand, combination of unlike products has a strong tendency to arbitrarily produce low concentration. An analysis of the 7-digit products included in the least concentrated of the 5-digit product groups reveals a large number of highly concentrated products. A crude estimate of the number of 7-digit products, 50 per cent or more of which are shipped by the four largest firms, suggests that three fourths of such products are the output of oligopolies by this definition.

High concentration is often considered to be strong evidence of poor economic performance. Because concentration is more easily and less ambiguously measured than is performance itself, economists and administrators are tempted to frame policies in terms of the former. In this chapter we have confined discussion to definitional matters: hence, no implications with regard to the relationship between concentration and performance are appropriate. An attempt is made in Chapters V and VII to evaluate existing models of oligopoly and to construct alternative models which are more in accord with what is known about concentrated structure. Such models provide a basis for an evaluation of the effect of concentration upon performance which is attempted in the final chapters.

Chapter V

The Independent Maximization Hypothesis

THE PRINCIPAL purpose of this chapter is to present the independent maximization hypothesis in such a way as to make it subject to test. The hypothesis applies most appropriately to elements, but it is expected that it will also hold moderately well for generic products and can, therefore, be subjected to an indirect test with census data.

The hypothesis rests upon two major findings and a semidynamic point of view toward industry structure. The first finding is empirical. Various studies seem to show that there are negligible economies of scale over wide levels of output. The second finding is deduced in the following pages. The finding is that profit advantage is obtained by firms which concentrate on maintaining or expanding their output position rather than maintaining or increasing industry price. The point of view is that each elementary product, hereafter also referred to as "subproduct," is initially the product of a single firm, so that where more than one firm exists, entry must have occurred. The questions are: why was this permitted and what determines the relative size of each firm's share?

The independent maximization hypothesis states that under these conditions high concentration and greatly disparate firm size in particular subproduct markets follow from rational behavior by innovators and entrants whose actions are independent in the sense that they are neither designed to discourage entry nor are they collusive. Specific progressions of firm size logically follow from different curvatures of the demand curve, but such distinctions are probably too fine to be clearly observed. A simple quantity leadership rule yields the same results as independent maximization when demand curve is a straight line. It is taken as a first approximation.

The quantity leadership rule yields a log-normal distribution of firm size. This corollary of the independent maximization hypothesis is expected to hold for the first three firms. That is to say, the largest firm is expected to be twice the size of the second largest, and the second largest twice the size of the third largest. Even where firms follow independent maximization, this rate of progression can be thrown off if two or more firms enter at once, if one or more of the firms is mistaken about the size of the market, if quality changes occur in one firm's variant but not in the others', or if there is considerable curvature of the demand curve. Still the log-normal distribution is expected to be found as a strong central tendency, and departures may also be attributed to alternative policies that firms adopt.

In particular, the following alternative policies and size distributions are expected. If innovators expand to fill a market so as to inhibit entry, single-firm monopoly or very unequal sizes of firms in specific subproduct markets is expected. Alternative explanations of the relative size of firms not based upon policy decisions are considered here and in Chapter VI because of a reluctance to ascribe economic phenomena such as these to sheer policy choices; but persuasive alternatives are not found.

The independent maximization hypothesis also emerges as the more rational policy choice when sales cost, degree of profit differentiation, and investment in applied and developmental (but not basic) research are taken as variables. No corollaries subject to statistical test follow from these findings, however, so they are analyzed separately in Chapters VII and VIII.

A. Economies of Scale and Firm Size

One of the notable failures of oligopoly theory has been its failure to account for widely disparate sizes of firms.

Attempts to explain firm size rest primarily on economies and diseconomies of scale. Scale economies account for the extreme disparity —single-firm monopoly. A direct extension of this line of thinking implies that where economies of scale extend to only one half or one third of the market, two or three firms of approximately equal size will appear.

Where firms are quite different in size the popular view is that the large firms manage to hold prices up a little, providing an "umbrella" under which smaller firms can survive although their costs are rather high. Their survival is thought to depend upon their success in finding specialized niches in the market and upon the antitrust laws and the public opinion which favors them. This theory has been brought into question by more elaborate cost theories which, in essence, generalize the niche theory by attempting to relate availability of resources, including managerial talent in given locations, to sizes of productive enterprises.[1] In such cases, variable cost per unit may be quite different from firm to firm, but rents tend to equalize average costs and profits on invested capital. According to this theory relative firm size, while reflecting cost structures, has a highly skewed distribution because of the rational tendency for the best managerial talent to become associated with the best resources and to attract the most favorable financing. The result is a distribution of sizes of enterprises rather like that for the distribution of income where exceptional size is the result of the combination of a number of top qualities each of which, taken separately, may be randomly distributed.

Another effort to account for widely disparate firm sizes abandons economic analysis for the laws of chance.[2] Simon and Bonini find examples of a log-normal distribution of firm size to be "numerous and monotonously similar" in published empirical studies, whether "sales, assets, number of employees, value added, or profits are used as a size measure" and whether an "entire economy" or a "single industry" is examined.

These authors apply the theory of the random walk to the recent findings of Bain and others to the effect that few, if any, economies or diseconomies of scale are found over an indefinitely large range above some minimum size. On the assumption that any firm above this minimum has an equal chance to grow or to shrink by a given percentage, log-normal (or, more exactly, Yule) distributions of firm size are generated that fit quite closely the actual distribution of firm size reported in the *Fortune* surveys, and of producers of steel ingots in the U.S.

Hymer and Pashigian and Mansfield have investigated and have enlarged upon this approach in two studies.[3] It turns out that while the mean growth rates of firms in all size classes are closely similar, the variance is less in the larger size categories. The various authors disagree

---

[1] Thomas Saving, "Estimation of the Optimum Size of Plant," *Quarterly Journal of Economics,* LXXV, No. 4 (November 1961). I am indebted to Professor Saving for several helpful discussions on this topic.

[2] H. A. Simon and C. P. Bonini, "The Size Distribution of Business Firms," *American Economic Review,* XLVIII, No. 4 (September 1958), 6-12.

[3] Stephen Hymer and Peter Pashigian "Firm Size and the Rate of Growth," *Journal of Political Economy,* LXX, No. 6 (December 1962), 556-69; and Edwin Mansfield, "Entry, Gilbrat's Law, Innovation and the Growth of Firms," *American Economic Review,* LII, No. 5 (December 1962), 1023-51. See also Simon's comment on Hymer and Pashigian's article, *Journal of Political Economy,* LXXII, No. 1. (February 1964), 81-2; and Hymer and Pashigian's reply, *ibid.,* pp. 83-4.

about the appropriate interpretation of this finding.[4] Several conclusions are, nevertheless, warranted. The economies of scale, if any, are not pronounced enough to prevent the entry and financing of new firms, many of which are small. There exist reasonably well-defined lower limits of size necessary for survival and, by presumption, for economical operation; but no well-defined upper limit is found. Dispersion of firm size between the lower and the upper limit appears to be best described by a statistical relationship which has little, if any, basis in rational behavior of maximizing business units.

Michael Gort's study of the diversification of 111 large manufacturing enterprises also fails to find evidence of important economies of scale.[5] He finds 4-digit product additions to be concentrated in high-growth industries, in industries where the labor productivity and the proportion of technical personnel are relatively high and where the investment opportunity is high. He did not find that high capital cost impaired entry, but rather concluded that it contributed to entry by these large firms, only partly because entry was sometimes effected by merger. While large firms made some progress toward a position among the leading eight or the leading four producers, Gort concluded that, "In a substantial majority of instances, entry on the part of even large firms into industries that are new to them does not result in a leading role in the industry for the entering firm. This apparently was true even after a lapse of roughly two decades following initial entry—a conclusion that is even more significant since some entries were achieved through merger."[6]

It would be interesting to know if this is also true of 5-digit and 7-digit products.

Surprisingly, an investigation by Leonard Weiss finds a large part of total output to be produced by firms of seemingly suboptimal size, although adjustment toward a more nearly optimal size is quite rapid. Taken together, these findings suggest that the diseconomies of suboptimal plants may often, but not always, be small. They also suggest rational behavior in response to rather small differences in profit opportunities. This is not random behavior. The rationality postulate derives additional support because some suboptimal capacity is unquestionably

[4] We offer a tentative explanation in following Chapter VIII, p. 18f.

[5] Michael Gort, *Diversification and Integration in American Industry* (Princeton, N. J.: Princeton University Press, 1962), pp. 112-21. In general, the data for the 111 firms in this study are similar to those for the largest 100 firms among the largest 1,000 analyzed in the Appendix to Chapter VI, insofar as the same characteristics are reported in both studies.

[6] *Ibid.,* p. 129.

protected by geographical isolation in small markets, and because some small firms are growing in accordance with rational expectations.[7]

All of these investigations have avoided explicit definition of products and cost per unit. This practice is continued throughout this chapter. In a formal sense, it is strictly correct only where the product under consideration is homogeneous, but it is useful where broader groups of products are treated as if they were alike. Where the products in a given class are identical and the producing firms are few, "pure" oligopoly is said to exist. It is most commonly approximated in producers' goods markets where goods are bought by specification or by professional buyers. We return to differentiated products in Chapter VII.

B. Quantity vs. Price Emphasis

The self-defeating nature of price leadership is shown elsewhere.[8] The disadvantages of collusion that maintains maximum industry profits are shown in connection with the analysis of the independent maximization hypothesis that appears in the next section of this chapter, but formal analysis is found in Chapter VII because price interrelationships are not conveniently shown for an undifferentiated product where, by definition, only one price can exist under given conditions.

C. The Independent Maximization Hypothesis

We approach the independent maximization hypothesis with the aid of a formal model. The product begins as the monopoly of a single seller. Entry is assumed to occur at the rate of one new firm per "year" as long as an entrant's profit prospects are positive. The demand function is assumed to have a constant negative slope, and the long-run marginal cost function is horizontal where output is larger than some relatively small amount and is virtually identical for all firms. Once a plant size is chosen, short-run marginal costs are thought to rise and to intersect the long-run marginal cost function. We suppose further that the demand function is stable and that each firm correctly forecasts its position. Restrictions on the shape and stability of the demand function are modified shortly.

Profits of the innovating firm are maximized over time, under these circumstances, if it produces the simple monopoly output in the first

[7] Leonard W. Weiss, "The Survival Technique and the Extent of Suboptimal Capacity," *Journal of Political Economy*, LXXII, No. 3 (June 1964), 246-61. An explanation for the survival of suboptimal firms may be found in research and development costs and benefits. See Chapter VIII p. 13-5, below.

[8] D. A. Worcester, Jr., "Why Dominant Firms Decline," *Journal of Political Economy*, LXV, No. 4 (August 1957), 338-46.

period and maintains that output as entry occurs. Where a maximum
return is sought, we call this independent maximization.[9] This proposition is supported by comparison with three alternatives: (1) adopting
a larger output and a lower price to limit the opportunities of entrants,
(2) adopting a lesser output and a higher price in the initial period,
and (3) colluding with the entrants to achieve a continued monopoly
return to be split among the firms.

The analysis can make use of a revised interpretation of the traditional
duopoly diagram for the first two steps, monopoly and duopoly, which
in turn may be elucidated somewhat with the aid of an additional diagram for Firm A. When the demand curve for a product is a straight
line and long-run average and marginal costs are constant as shown in
the inserted diagram for firm A, the profit indifference system for a

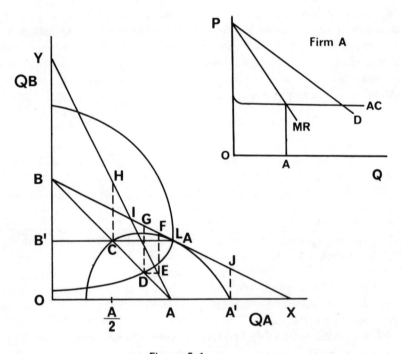

Figure 5-1

[9] It amounts to the application of a "Sylos postulate" by each firm to successive
rivals, so that each is limited to the "marginal demand curve." See Franco
Modigliani, "New Developments on the Oligopoly Front," *Journal of Political
Economy*, LXVI, No. 3 (June 1958), 217; also see footnote 13, below.

pair of duopolists is as shown in Figure 5-1.[10] In the first period, only firm A is in production, and according to the argument just given, it establishes the monopoly output (OA on both diagrams) and price. Industry output is identical to Firm A's. Firm B, of course, produces nothing in period 1; it enters in period 2. The various lines on Figure 5-1 are relevant to this two-firm situation.

Figure 5-1 represents objective, not subjective, phenomena. It can be described in the following way. The two axes represent the quantity produced by A and the quantity produced by B. Each point in the diagram denotes a particular level of output divided between the firms in a specific way. Total output determines price, so a specific level of profits for each firm is also associated with each point. All points in the

[10] The relationships are developed as follows: Let P = price; π = total profit; πA = A's profit; πB = B's profit; x = A's quantity; y = B's quantity; x + y = total quantity. P = a − b(x + y) is the industry demand curve, and π = P(x + y) = a(x + y) − b(x + y)^2 are the total industry profits.

dπ/d(x + y) = a − 2b(x + y) = 0; x + y = a/2b represents all combinations of x and y yielding maximum industry profits. A's and B's profit indifference curves are respectively: πA = Px = ax − bx^2 − bxy and πB = Py = ay −by^2 − bxy.

Their reaction functions are, therefore,

$$d\pi A/dx = a - 2bx - by = 0 \text{ or } x = \frac{a - by}{2b}$$

(Note that the output of the rival is entered as a constant on the

right side of their equations.) $$d\pi B/dy = a - 2by - bx = 0 \text{ or } y = \frac{a - bx}{2b}$$

The leadership points are found where the indifference curve of one is tangent to the reaction function of the other, or, for A,

$$\begin{cases} \pi A = ax - bx^2 - bxy \\ a - 2by - bx = 0 \\ 2b\pi A - abx + b^2x^2 = 0; \ x = \end{cases} - \frac{(-ab) + \sqrt{a^2b^2 - 8b^3\pi A}}{2b^2}$$

$$\begin{cases} \pi A = a^2/8b \\ x = a/2b; y = a/4b \end{cases} \quad \text{Outputs of A and B where A leads}$$

$$\begin{cases} \pi B = a^2/8b \\ y = a/2b; x = a/4b \end{cases} \quad \text{Outputs of A and B where B leads}$$

$$\begin{cases} - bx^2 - bxy + ax = a^2/8b \\ - by^2 - bxy + ay = a^2/8b \end{cases}$$

x = a/4b; y = a/4b; x + y = a/2b   Output of A and B where they collude on equal terms.

This analysis neglects costs, which is tantamount to the assumption that the long run marginal and average costs are constant.

quadrant below a straight line connecting points Y and X (not shown) represent positive net revenues for both firms. If all of the points yielding the same profit for one firm are connected, a profit indifference curve is formed. One is drawn for each firm. For each output of the rival, there is some output that maximizes a firm's profits. The locus of such points, which are the high points of the indifference curves, is called the reaction function of the firm. This curve is YA for firm *A*, XB for firm *B*. There is only one point on each reaction function that is tangent to one of the rival's indifference curves. Such points are called leadership points because they indicate the maximum profit for a leading firm which is consistent with the rival's reaction function. Thus if *A* holds fast to output OA, firm *B* gains its highest profit with output OB'. Either a larger or a smaller output puts it on a lower profit indifference curve.

To repeat, there is nothing subjective about the functions illustrated on this diagram if the objectivity of the demand curve and the cost curves is granted. Each pair of outputs yields a total output that determines the cost to each firm, and the industry price. That price, times *A*'s output, yields the total revenue for *A*. Likewise $P(Q_B)$ yields *B*'s total revenue. The division of production between the firms can be in any proportion, so that there is no reason to rule out some portion of the diagram.

Examination of Figure 5-1 reveals the special characteristics of this specific case. The monopoly output for *A*, OA, is the same as the leadership output for *A* when a second firm, *B*, enters. Thus, in this case, *A* will maximize in the second period by producing the same output and accepting the decline in price that is involved if *B* maximizes its profits in the portion of the market that *A* has declined to satisfy. Thus total output rises by one third in the second period, to OA + OB', and the margin of price over unit cost drops to one half of what it was in period one.

It is interesting to consider three alternative actions that might be taken by firm *A*. Knowing that *B* will enter, *A* might attempt to improve matters for both by seeking joint-profit maximization. Every point along contract curve AB represents long-run maximum industry profits in this situation where each firm has constant and equal long-run marginal costs. Any point between points C and D represents superior long-run profits for both firms as compared to point L_A. Neglect, for the moment, any accelerated rate of entry that might be stimulated by the maintenance of the larger profit margin and by the major producer's policy of making room for rivals; neglect further the higher costs suffered by firm *A* due to (1) the cost of obtaining and enforcing an agreement, and (2) under-utilization of the specific plant that it has constructed; and consider this as a two-person game.

If A succeeds in striking the most favorable honest bargain, the two firms would collude at point D, yielding B profits just equal to what it would have received had firm A stuck to its original output, while firm A achieves a much higher profit indifference curve (not drawn) much closer to its maximum profit position at A. But agreements of this sort are often broken, particularly where they are not enforceable at law. If B breaks faith, his optimal move is to point G, and any countermove by A to improve profits requires A to further reduce his output by moving (horizontally) towards his reaction function, YA. If any future bargains are struck, B is in a better position to serve his interest as compared to the point from which bargaining started, L_A. Nor is A's position improved as compared with L_A if he breaks the agreement first. If firm A breaks the agreement and makes his optimal move to point E, firm B is freed to counter with a move to point F. Firm A is again placed on a lower profit curve than the one enjoyed at point L_A and is again at a disadvantage in any future collusive negotiation.

Any other initial point on line CD is even worse for firm A. Should he accept a position as poor as C, firm B could reverse the relative sizes of the two firms, and the profits that go with them, by moving to point H. One may conclude that collusion is inferior to independent maximization on the basis of risk costs alone.

Alternatively, A could expand output to discourage B's entry. But expansion to point A' (which is equal to OA plus OB') would lower profits to the level it would get at L_A and B would still enter with quantity A'J putting A on a still lower profit curve comparable to its situation at H.

A unilateral price leadership policy is even less attractive. If firm A attempts to be a price leader who holds prices at the monopoly level as rivals' output rises, he must reduce his output by whatever amount firm B puts on the market. The ultimate conclusion is A's withdrawal, and a monopoly output by B. If the rate of entry is a positive function of the level of profits, A has a stronger incentive to hold to output OA, because reduction of his output or collusion to maintain prices can only speed the rate of entry and hasten the end of his profitable operations. In like manner, he is more likely to hold to his initial output the more sharply U-shaped his short-run costs are. Reduction of output lowers profits because of higher unit costs in the short run, although it is true that the loss is a failure to cover sunk costs.

Thus a rational manager of firm A could conclude that maintenance of its dominant quantity position would yield optimal returns as compared to its alternatives.

While this diagram pertains to a special case, it holds approximately for all instances where the reaction functions slope from one axis to the other. This covers all of the reasonable conditions of which I can conceive.[11] The modification necessary when the demand curve is not linear is discussed below.

1. Additional Entry

The appearance of additional rivals is not conveniently handled with profit indifference diagrams such as Figure 5-1. Figure 5-2 can illustrate the essential points although it is accurate even in this special case only at points of equilibrium.[12]

The industry demand function is shown as PP'. Long-run marginal and average cost for each firm is represented as CC'. Firm A maximizes in the first period by setting output where his marginal cost equals his marginal revenue MR_A. In the second period firm B enters, setting its output at the level shown by the intersection of its marginal cost and it marginal revenue, MR_B. This marginal revenue is appropriate to the portion of the market that firm A declines to serve, the segment P_AP', hereafter referred to as the "marginal demand curve." The position of MR_B rests on the hypothesis that firm A is following an independent maximization strategy. Entry of firm C continues the process.

Firm A sells quantity OA at price AP_A in the first period and the same quantity, but at price BP_B, in the second period. Since the profit margin is halved in the second year, he would have received the same profit if he had cut his output in half and shared the market equally with firm B at the monopoly price P_A. Firm B probably could have been induced to

[11] There are conceivable but unreasonable exceptions: for example, where the reaction functions slope outwards so that the leader finds himself in a better bargaining position if collusion breaks down. This situation is realized if the marginal revenue curve for the industry is upward sloping, and long-run marginal costs are also upward sloping, but more slowly, so that stable equilibria are found. In that case the second firm must expand output more before his marginal costs (which are assumed to start from the same level and rise at the same rate as firm A's) overtake the rising marginal revenue. Even in this case, however, collusion is not rational for two independent firms, for firm B is placed at a disadvantage if collusion breaks down. Moreover, diseconomies of scale suggest that in the longer run entry will continue, and output will be pushed to levels where marginal revenue does turn down, after which time only small firms will be efficient enough to survive.

[12] The more accurate, and more complicated, figure is presented in the next section.

leave more profit than this for firm *A*, but any collusive arrangement would have required some reduction of *A*'s output and would have compromised its position had the agreement failed. All this is as shown on Figure 5-1.

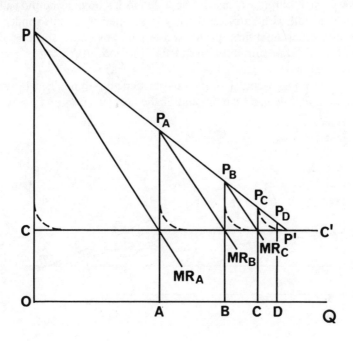

Figure 5-2

With the entry of a third firm, however, the leading firm also seems to be in a position to benefit from a collusive agreement that allocates to it only an equal share. If the third firm enters with output BC and depresses price to CP_C, firm *A*'s margin will be cut to one fourth on quantity OA, while collusion with equal shares offers one third of the original profit. The apparent net benefit from collusion continues as additional entry occurs.

But the gains of collusion involve costs. First is the cost of obtaining agreement. The second is the cost of enforcing it. A third, the risk that it will break down due to other firms' perfidy, grows with the number of sellers and the number of buyers. Finally, collusion stimulates the rate of entry, reduces the size of the firm's share, and tends to raise its average costs. The existing firms continuously lose sales and need to shrink capacity. Yet new firms must be relatively large upon entry to achieve their share. If diseconomies of small size exist, as shown by the dotted part of the cost curves, entry will, in time, cease even if collusion is unsuccessful. At that time the initial monopolist will earn normal profits on a very small output. If instead he holds to his original output, allowing prices to fall with entry until entry is stopped by profits inadequate to attract a suboptimal firm, profits somewhat above normal are enjoyed on a relatively large output for an indefinite period. At the worst normal profits are enjoyed.

The size of the eventual profit margin depends upon the elasticities of the "marginal demand curve" and of the cost function of the subopti-

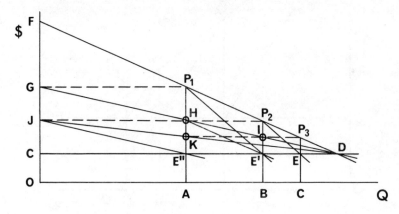

Figure 5-3

mal firm or, alternatively, of those of the potential entrants, as well as the aggregate size of output of the optimal firms. Ideally, there will be established the highest price that still excludes the marginal firm.[13] But

---

[13] This is the point established by the Sylos postulate as explained by Modigliani in his creative review of Bain's and Sylos Lambini's books. The postulate, that existing firms will not reduce output to accommodate an entrant, is substantially the same as that made in this chapter. The entrant must content himself with the segment of the demand curve to the right of the market price prior to his entry. Modigliani calls this the "marginal demand curve." The weakness of the construction employed by Bain-Sylos-Modigliani is that if the favorable price is to exist the oligopolists must contrive their outputs so as to just barely exclude the extra-marginal firm and thus to attain the largest margin over their long-run marginal cost. This assumes virtually costless and effective collusion as well as accurate knowledge of the position and slope of demand and of potential rival's costs. For if the large low-cost producers were to overexpand, or if the demand were to shift to the left, the profit margin would disappear. See also the discussion of Modigliani's article, *Journal of Political Economy*, LXVII, No. 4 (August 1959), 410-19.

no suggestion is made here that this favorable profit margin is attained. Pressure for sales, shifts of demand and lack of precise knowledge, the observed large output from apparently suboptimal firms, and frequent if not ubiquitous independence of action make supranormal profits fortuitous.

Figure 5-2 misrepresents the position of the various firms somewhat because it does not show what happens to the *ex ante* demand curves that the various firms face as entry proceeds. Figure 5-2 implies that the portion of the industry demand curve above P_A remains accessible to firm A after B has entered, and that the segment PP′ is relevant for B when C enters, and so on. This is not the case under independent maximization, as is shown for two firms in Figure 5-1. Figure 5-3 yields the same equilibrium positions as Figures 5-1 and 5-2 for this particular case, but rectifies the analysis of Figure 5-2.

If firm A were, for example, to reduce its output to zero when firm B entered, firm B would set price P_1. Therefore, under independent maximization, $P_1 = OG$ is the highest possible price for firm A after firm B has entered. Now let firm A produce any fixed amount greater than zero, such as OA or OB. B's marginal revenue beyond that point will fall twice as fast as the marginal demand curve, leading a maximizing entrant to establish price BP_2 or CP_3 depending upon the output chosen by firm A. Thus A's demand curve connects prices H and I with outputs OA and OB respectively. Firm A's *mutatis mutandis* demand curve has one half the slope of the industry demand curve, passing through points G, H, I, and D. The marginal revenue to this curve indicates the maximizing output OA at price AH $= P_2$ for firm A. This is necessarily consistent with the maximization of B's profits on the section of the demand curve not served by A. P_2 is an equilibrium price for both firm A and firm B. Since marginal revenues are the same for both firms, the elasticity of demand confronting each is the same although their slopes differ.

When firm C enters, A's demand curve becomes flatter still if firms B and C maximize. For if firm A were to produce nothing, firm B would produce OA and firm C would produce AB. Consequently, the highest price that A can charge for an infinitesimally small quantity without collusion is $P_2 = OJ$. This is likewise the highest price possible for firm B, because firm C will sell AB while firm A sells quantity OA if B reduces its output to near zero. Thus firm A's *mutatis mutandis* demand curve is JD, firm B's is HD, and firm C's is P_2D if each firm pursues independent maximization policies. The appropriate marginal revenue curves all start at the level J, H, P_2. Each firm operates where marginal revenue is equal to marginal cost—that is, where each has the same demand elasticity. As one would expect, the demand curve for each firm becomes flatter as the number of rivals increases. The original monopolist, A, sees his demand curve pivot downward from the industry curve FD to GD with one rival producing a close substitute, to JD with two rivals. Concentration is 100 per cent for three firms. Firm sizes are greatly disparate, the leading firm having 4/7 of the market, the second having 2/7, and the third, 1/7. Collusion is of questionable profitability because of the strategic reasons discussed above. Potential entry also inhibits collusion.

It is evident from the foregoing that each firm's demand curve is fixed if the other firms are rational. If either firm A or firm B produces at an irrational level of output, the maximizing outputs of their rivals shift along their *mutatis mutandis* curve in such a fashion as to make their equilibrium price equal to the disequilibrium price established by the irrational firm. But if the last firm in, firm C, produces irrational quantity, the effect is to shift the *mutatis mutandis* curves of the other firms, and their equilibrium prices cannot be read off any curve shown in Figure 5-3 except in the extreme case where C produces nothing and the next higher curves shown again become relevant.

2. Quantity Leadership Approximates Independent Maximization

Independent maximization requires accurate knowledge about the slope and position of the industry demand curve and of one's marginal cost and marginal revenue if the cost curve is not horizontal and/or the demand function is not linear, as is seen below. Many economists are unconvinced that firms either have such detailed knowledge or would apply it to make precise maximizing adjustments if they did have it. In the place of refined adjustments, an easy approximation, quantity leadership, may be employed.

Quantity leadership is not a maximizing strategy and does not require nearly as much information as does independent maximization, but it yields a maximum in the straight-line, constant-cost case. Under quantity leadership each firm tries to at least hold its absolute sales position in the face of competition of rivals. It meets price reductions by rivals when they attempt to break into its market, if price reduction is necessary to meet the output goal. A similar goal is to hold a specific percentage share of the market. This is a higher goal more appropriate to established markets, because a decline in relative share is implicit in adherence to a given physical output. Sometimes these principles are combined, the maintenance of a percentage share of market being regarded as an optimum goal and the maintenance of the level of physical sales as a minimum goal.[14]

The correspondence of the independent maximization and the "hold-one's-own" strategies in practice will be less than perfect. Quite aside from the effects of curvilinear cost and demand curves, dropping the assumption of near-perfect knowledge involves dropping the notion that either the original firm or the followers set profit-maximizing outputs and prices when they enter. If the original firm sets too small an output, firm sizes tend to be more equal. Such errors can be expected to fall on either side of the optimum, so that a central tendency will be found which closely approximates the log-normal progression if the average market shares of the first, second, and third firms are found for a reasonably large sample of products.

D. Causes of Non-Log-Normal Distributions of Firm Size

As asserted above, the disparity of firm size will depart from the log-normal distribution under the independent maximization hypothesis for various reasons. A number of these are now examined.

1. Non-Linear Industry Demand Curves

Independent maximization yields a different progression of firm sizes when the demand curve is not linear. I know of no general mathematical statement that defines the relationship. That the progression is dominated by the relative share of the largest firm can be illustrated by a simple figure for which I am indebted to Professor John C. H. Fei. It parallels Figure 5-2 and requires the same sort of adjustment made in Figure 5-3 for exact accuracy. The principal modification is that existing firms must adjust their output to obtain a maximum as additional firms enter. The shift is not large enough to materially alter the first approximation.

Suppose that two firms have access to the average cost curves XBCK as shown in Figure 5-4. Let APD be the industry demand curve, AB the industry curve for either of two firms if collusion is practiced, and AC the marginal revenue curve associated with APD. Note that the industry demand curve is concave to origin. When firm A possesses simple monopoly power it maximizes profit at output OC' and price C'P. Suppose firm A adopts the quantity leadership strategy and so

[14] Mr. Howard G. Vesper, President of Standard Oil of California, Western Operations, Inc, told the author that this is approximately the policy of Standard of California. The norm is to retain the share of market, the minimum goal is the retention of the absolute level of sales. Over the years Standard has managed to stay well above the minimum goal in the western region but has not attained its optimum goal in the rapidly expanding market.

adheres to output OC′ when firm B enters. The best that B can do is to cater to the "marginal demand curve" PP′D. It will set its maximizing price, P′, and raise the total output to OE′.[15] The former monopolist, A, must accept this price if he is to maintain his output. In this case the second firm produces less than half as much as the leading firm. This is because the marginal revenue for a monopolist lies to the right of OB, the industry share curve for two firms, so that the tendency is for the leading firm to produce more than half the competitive level.

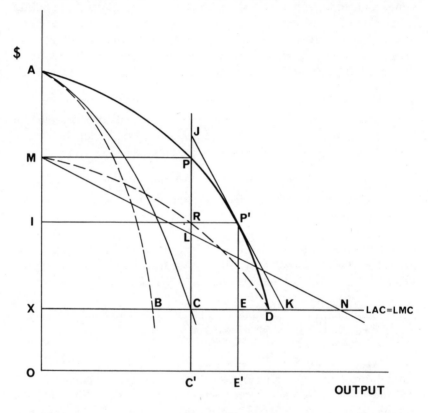

Figure 5-4

The opposite tendency is shown in Figure 5-5, where the industry demand curve is convex to origin. The analysis is parallel to that associated with Figure 5-4, and the lettering is the same to facilitate comparison.

[15] This is found, of course, by setting marginal revenue equal to long-run marginal cost. Diagrammatically, we find the point of tangency P′, such that the line segments JP′ and P′K are equal.

Unlike the linear case, this is not a maximum. Independent maximization requires some adjustment where the industry demand curves are not linear. This is shown for Figure 5-4 only. Following the same logic as for Figure 5-3, the leading firm's demand curve loses slope. The maximum price possible for A is C′P = OM because B will set this price if A withdraws. Price P′ cannot be an optimum for A at output OC′. If price P′ were to be the equilibrium price for firm A after B's appearance, A's *mutatis mutandis* demand curve, MRD, would have to be tangent to line MLN at its midpoint, L, because only then would A's marginal revenue equal its marginal cost at point C. But this is impossible,

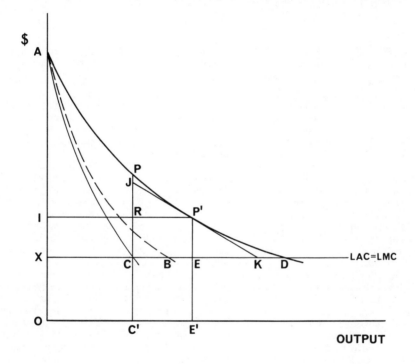

Figure 5-5

because MRD and MLN necessarily start at the same point, point L is the midpoint of MN, and segment CD is shorter than CN because of the postulated curvature of MD. Since MD intersects line MN from above it cannot be tangent to it, and its marginal must be below point C. Firm A must find its maximum profit at a lower output on its new demand curve, and firm B will sell at a somewhat higher price in the somewhat expanded market thus made available to it. The modification is not enough, however, to bring the progression of firm size back to the 2:1 ratio found in the straight-line case. The opposite adjustments are required in the longer run, when the industry demand curve is concave to the origin.[16]

Independent maximizing behavior provides one possible explanation both of highly disparate firm size in individual product markets and of variation in the size distribution. Where demand functions are straight lines, the log-normal distribution is generated. Where the demand function is concave to origin, the disparity is greater, but where it is convex to origin the disparity of firm size is less.

2. Demand Curve Shifts over Time

Rightward and leftward shifts of the demand curve over time can be expected to influence the disparity of firm size in an industry. Leftward shifts tend to eliminate small firms and produce consolidation. Right-

---

[16] These relationships have been worked out exactly by elaborating the profit indifference analysis presented in footnote 10, above. No way has been found to state a proof in terms of the sign of the second derivative of a general function, but it holds for one class of functions. This proof is not given here, however. I am indebted to Dr. Fred C. Hung for his work on it.

An interesting sidelight can be thrown on the gain to the leader from collusion. As noted above, collusion is dangerous strategy for the leader, even when he makes an optimum bargain. The straight line case used as a basis for that illustration yielded the leader no less than his profit as a leader, even if he accepted the worst bargain—point C on Figure 5-1. The bargaining range is shifted with the curvature of the demand curves, and may be illustrated somewhat inexactly with figures 5-4 and 5-5. We consider a needlessly poor bargain for the leading firm, i.e. what it would get were the two to collude so as to share the maximum industry profit equally. Each would then receive ½ CP(OC'). That this would yield the quantity leader in figure 5-4 a lower profit can be demonstrated in the following way. The alternative average net revenues for the entrant are shown by the alternative points under PP'D. The maximum profit for the entrant, in the absence of collusion, is at price P^1. The tangent to point P^1 must be composed of two equal segments, JP^1 and P^1K, because profits are maximized where the marginal revenue curve is equal to marginal cost, which is to say that the elasticity of the average *net* revenue curve is equal to unity. Because the demand curve is falling at an increasing rate, any tangent to the segment PP'D must intersect line CJ above point P. Therefore, the tangent to the demand curve at firm B's maximizing price, P^1, must intersect line CJ above point P. It follows that JR=RC and CE=EK. Equal collusive sharing of the market would have allotted one half of the maximum industry profits to firm A. As we have seen, this can be expressed as ½ CP(O'C). But the price set by the entrant allows profits per unit which are greater than ½ CP since CR = RJ and RJ > RP. Therefore, A will receive higher profits if it sticks to quantity leadership, accepting the price set by the entrant B, rather than acquiescing in collusion. Firm A gets a larger profit from collusion and equal sharing than from independent behavior when the demand curve falls at a decreasing rate, as shown by Figure 5-5. The strategic advantage, however, still lies with the entrant if collusion is accepted by the leader.

ward shifts will have different effects dependent upon whether they are anticipated or are a surprise. If they are not anticipated, entrants will find a relatively large market and firms will be more equal in size than otherwise. If expansion is anticipated, the initial firm will allow for this and will take note of the lesser risk involved in overestimation of his market. This can offset or more than offset the tendency for firms to be of more nearly equal size.

3. Business Strategy and Relative Firm Size

Independent maximization is a maximum constrained by the nature of the cost function, by free entry, and by the several costs and risks of collusion. It is argued above that other alternatives are inferior. They may nevertheless be tried. This seems especially probable because several them have played an important part in the theory of the firm. Two such alternatives are minimization of the risk of an unfavorable shift of the demand curve, and the setting of a limit price that will inhibit entry. Both are relevant to a firm with partial information in an uncertain world and are of the same genus as the independent maximization hypothesis. A third policy often ascribed to leading firms is that of price leadership. Each of these contains implications concerning the relative size of the leading firms. Empirical studies of relative firm size can be used to test the relative importance of the different strategies.

It is convenient to begin by analyzing a construction advanced by Fellner.[17] His basic hypothesis is very similar to the independent maximization hypothesis. It is assumed that the firm chooses and tends to adhere to a particular quantity and accepts price reductions as dictated by shifts of its *ex ante* demand function. It differs primarily because Fellner's oligopolist establishes output at a level below the monopoly level and price above it. It differs also because "unfavorable surprise" is not linked to entry and to the flattening of the firm's *ex ante* demand. The cost function chosen also produces minor differences for our present purpose.

a. Equal Sizes of Firms: Variable Price

Fellner analyzes "unfavorable surprise" where the entrepreneur has a concept of an *ex ante* demand curve but wishes to maximize his "safety" should the demand curve turn out to lie below (and parallel to) the *ex ante* demand curve, as in Figure 5-6. The entrepreneur somehow

[17] William Fellner, *Competition Among the Few* (New York: Knopf, 1949), pp. 146-57.

is cognizant of the shape of his average cost curve and can, therefore, determine the level of output where the worst demand shift consistent with normal profits would touch his cost curve. The "safety margin" held against "unfavorable surprise" is found at that quantity. Diagrammatically, P_1 is anticipated when output is held at Q_1. A price decline of as much as P_1P_{o1} can be absorbed without loss only at Q_1 should "unfavorable surprise" come to pass.

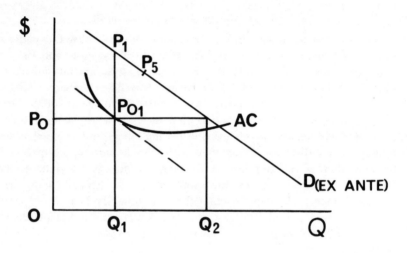

Figure 5-6

What are the implications for relative size of leading firms? Let us depart momentarily from Fellner's analysis and consider the firm to be an innovator blessed with good luck so that he realizes P_1. We can expect a rival to enter in the next period. If the original firm holds fast to output OQ_1, the second firm will face a demand curve of the same slope as P_1D with an intercept at height Q_1P_1. If the second firm maximizes its safety margin, it will also produce quantity OQ_1, doubling industry output and lowering industry price. Two firms of equal size will then exist. If the economies of scale shown are identical for all firms, no room exists for a third firm. If room does exist, additional firms of the same size will continue to enter. The important point is that those in the industry will be of the same size because the slope of the industry demand curve at height OP_o remains the same and equal to the slope of the average cost function.

It should be noted that the same result follows collusion on price, although the price will settle at a higher level.

b. Very Unequal Sizes of Firms: Variable Quantity Compared to Variable Price

An alternative way to protect oneself against "unfavorable surprise," not mentioned by Fellner, is to set price P_o and plan to produce and sell OQ_2, being prepared to sell as little as OQ_1 should the expected demand fail to materialize. This alternative is more in line with business practice, which does not make frequent price adjustments but does alter production schedules frequently as industry demand fluctuates, so that the firm does not sacrifice its position in the market. It has a further advantage because it is much more discouraging to entry by rival firms. Indeed, with these (long-run) cost functions, any price below P_5 excludes entry, yielding single-firm monopoly until cost or demand changes occur.

If there are already several firms in the market, so that P_1D represents a single oligopolist's *ex ante* (but uncertain) demand function, the firm that sets price P_1 to minimize unfavorable surprise will experience it if the others attempt to reduce unfavorable surprise by setting price P_0. In the language of game theory, strategy "P-fixed-variable Q" *dominates* strategy "Q-fixed variable P," either forcing the other firms to adopt variable quantity strategy or virtually driving from the market those who restrict output in order to maximize their prospective mark-up.[18] In this sense, at least, business practice is more rational than price-centered strategy. But all this rests upon the existence of cost curves of marked slope.

A high-output-low-price strategy is clearly preferable to the opposite when a monopolist (or a group of oligopolists) has a flat or declining long-run average cost curve in the relevant range, knows the position and slope of the industry demand function, and knows the cost functions of potential rivals. It is then rational to expand output and to lower price until the market is just filled and entry excluded, provided that there are some initial economies of scale so that some margin of profit remains. This policy requires heavier production, higher costs, and

[18] While Figure 5-6 reproduces Fellner's figure, his analysis is more plausible if the average cost curve reflects a capacity limit not much greater than Q_1. In that case a short-run, high-price strategy would be more rational. The longer-run strategy might be to expand output and exclude rivals as promptly as possible or simply to take whatever profits are possible until entry becomes complete. But typical short-run behavior reflects more output fluctuation than price adjustment, and both the testimony of businessmen and the research of economists tend to strongly support the idea that average-cost curves do not rise rapidly shortly beyond some normal output level.

lower aggregate profit in the early years in the expectation of higher profits in later years.[19] If the location of the demand function at lower prices is not known, or if the demand function fluctuates over time, the innovator's expansion may rationally stop between that sufficient to exclude entry and the short-run maximization point. The weight of these considerations is to increase the probability of firm sizes even less equal than the log-normal progression in those cases where the total number of firms is small.

The greater than log-normal disparity of firm sizes may not be extreme. Its extent depends upon the expected rate of entry, the extent to which present profits must be sacrificed, and how valuable the permanent profit stream will be if present sacrifices of profit are made as compared to its level if no sacrifices are made. At some rate of interest virtually no sacrifice of present profits will be made.[20]

c. Price Leadership

Very unequal sizes of firms may also be associated with price leadership by a dominant firm. It is argued elsewhere that this phenomenon is necessarily short-lived.[21] Depending upon the nature of costs, either the smaller rivals will grow until oligopoly or competition replaces the dominant-firm situation, or the dominant firm will expand and establish single-firm monopoly. In the former case log-normal size distributions supplant an initially extreme disparity. In the latter case, the ultimate in disparity appears.

E. Summary of Hypotheses

The analysis of this chapter leads to certain propositions that are subject to test. The propositions are: (1) Leading firms producing a given product are rarely of the same size. (2) In contrast to the usual hypothesis or assumption, the fewer the firms, the more unequal the sizes of the largest three or four will tend to be. (3) Very high disparity of firm size is more common than approximately equal size. (4) The most common pattern of firm size among the largest three or four firms

[19] An early statement of the essence of this position is found in Charles J. Bullock, "Trust Literature," W. Z. Ripley (ed.), *Trusts, Pools and Corporations* (Boston: Ginn, 1905), quoted in J. F. Weston, *The Role of Mergers in the Growth of Large Firms* (Berkeley: University of California Press, 1963), pp. 109-10.

[20] See G. J. Stigler, "Monopoly and Oligopoly by Merger," *American Economic Review*, XL, No. 2 (May 1950).

[21] Worcester, *Journal of Political Economy*, LXV, No. 4 (August 1957), 338-46.

is log-normal; that is, a 4, 2, 1 progression of relative size. (5) The leading firms will tend to be more equal in size than the log-normal distribution in industries characterized by collusion to obtain a monopoly price. (6) In young, rapidly growing industries, firm sizes are less equal than the log-normal distribution. (7) Where the shape of the industry demand curve can be ascertained, firms will be of more nearly equal size if the demand curve is convex to the origin, and less equally sized if the demand curve is concave to origin, comparison again being made to the log-normal distribution.

Some tests of some of these propositions are attempted in Chapter VI.

Chapter VI

Tests of the Hypothesis

THIS CHAPTER attempts to test the propositions derived from the models presented in Chapter V. This is done by examination of the size distributions of the leading firms in specific industries. The propositions to be tested are the following:

1. An approximation of the log-normal distribution of firm size is more common than any other among three or four largest firms.
2. Approximately equal size of leading firms is uncommon.
3. Very unequal size distribution among leading firms is less common than No. 1 but more common than No. 2.
4. Very unequal firm size is most common in industries with from two to four firms.
5. Where firms are known to have colluded, they exhibit a relative firm size more equal than the log-normal distribution.
6. Where the industry is growing, the relative firm size of the leading firms will tend to be less equal than log-normal.

If support for these propositions can be found, the independent maximization hypothesis is supported.

The first five of these propositions are adequately discussed in Chapter V. The sixth requires additional comment at this time because most industries are growing, and any bias due to growth will tend to bias the test of the other five propositions.

Proposition 6 rests upon a judgment as to which of certain contrary forces is the stronger. The predicted larger disparity is probable if the growing industry enjoys patent protection or is characterized by firms that expand beyond the simple monopoly level, because then the risks of

106

overexpansion are less and the potential gains over the longer run are larger due to the anticipated growth. On the other hand, firm size is more equal if growth is not expected or is underestimated by the innovator so that later entrants find relatively large markets. It is also probable that statistical studies of industries and products will fail to record new products separately in their first years of existence, thereby including them with other products. This will also tend to reduce the apparent disparity of firm size even if proposition 6 is correct. To summarize, proposition 6 rests on tenuous expectations, and any bias from growth is probably small.

Data to test the propositions are taken from the sample of 5- and 7-digit industries described in Chapter IV, from a Federal Trade Commission study of the 1000 largest manufacturing industries in 1950, from Nelson's analysis of the 1954 census data referred to in Chapter IV, from actions taken under Section 7 of the 1950 amendment of the Clayton Act, and from other scattered sources. The findings from each body of data are considered separately, and conclusions are drawn in the summary section.

A. Evidence From the Census Sample of 5-Digit and 7-Digit Products

1. Propositions 1 - 3

Propositions 1, 2, and 3 can be tested both with the 5-digit and with the 7-digit data collected in a special sample taken from the two extremes of the concentration range which is described in Chapter IV. Because the propositions relate to oligopoly, only the concentrated portion of the sample of the 5-digit data is relevant. Since concentration is substantial for many of the 7-digit products associated with unconcentrated 5-digit products, many of them can be used as further test of the propositions using 7-digit data.

In general, 7-digit data are considered a better test of all six propositions because they are drawn with reference to a more homogeneous product or subproduct. But both 5-digit and 7-digit data are often combinations of subproducts which belong to more than one generic product. Seven-digit products are more likely to include only members of a single generic product and tend to provide a better test of propositions 1 to 6.

The fact that 7-digit products are sometimes, perhaps usually, too narrow to be appropriate for the measurement of the intensiveness of competition is not relevant for present purposes for two reasons. High cross elasticity of supply—that is, entry by firms which suffer no cost disadvantage—is assumed, so the hypotheses to be tested relate to the

Table VI-1

Comparison of Market Shares of the Largest, Second,
Third, and Fourth Largest Firms, 5- and 7-Digit
Data, by Degree of Concentration, 1954*

Major Groups	5-Digit Percentage	7-Digit Percentage	5-Digit Percentage	7-Digit Percentage
Concentrated A & B				
Largest	55	51		
Second	20	19		
Third	8	—		
Fourth	3	—		
Concentrated D				
Largest	45	60	47	58
Second	24	22	23	21
Third	13	—	12	—
Fourth	6	—	6	—
Concentrated E				
Largest	45	62		
Second	22	21		
Third	14	—		
Fourth	8.5	—		
Unconcentrated C		(all)		
Largest	4	30	4	30
Second	2.5	13	2.5	13
Third	2.5	—	2.5	—
Fourth	2.0	—	2.0	—
	(Nonregional only)			
		35	4	35
		15	2.5	15

* Groups A and B are composed of products 80 per cent or more of which was shipped by the four largest firms and 99 per cent or more of which was shipped by 8 or fewer firms. Group D includes products 80 per cent or more of which was shipped by the four largest firms and 99 per cent or more of which was shipped by more than eight but no more than twenty firms and whose sales were rising. Group E is of the same level of concentration as D, but sales were stable or declining.

Group C is composed of products 40 per cent or less of which was produced by the twenty largest firms.

size distribution of firms which actually do produce particular products when competition is intense.

Seven-digit products are too narrowly defined for present purposes only when products that are substitutes in consumption are placed in different categories.

Seven-digit products are more likely to include only part of the sub-products associated with a particular generic product than are 5-digit products, but failure to include all subproducts is not necessarily a serious shortcoming. This is true because we expect the typical firm to produce many of the subproducts associated with a particular generic product even if it does not produce the full line. The pattern of firm size is expected to hold for subproducts no less than for generic products; indeed there is a reason to suppose that it will hold more exactly for subproducts, so that propositions relating to relative firm size are appropriately tested if the data are for categories which are "too narrow."

a. The Data

The typical positions of the leading firms within their 5-digit and 7-digit product classes are shown in Table VI-1. The first two columns show the typical shares of the market enjoyed by the leading producers of the 5-digit and the related 7-digit products included in the sample described in Chapter IV. The third and fourth columns show the relative firm size for the highly concentrated 5-digit group taken as a whole, for the unconcentrated group taken as a whole, and for the 101 unconcentrated products which are not regional according to the test described in Chapter IV.

The 5-digit data for the concentrated industries conform rather well to the log-normal distribution predicted by proposition 1. The largest four firms typically produced about 88 per cent of the total, so that the log normal distribution is 46.9; 23.4; 11.7; 5.9 which, if rounded, is exactly that shown for the 5-digit group taken as a whole. Some variation is shown among the components. Groups A plus B, which lack a fringe, show somewhat greater disparity and the fringed groups D and E somewhat less.

The averages tend to cover up differences which are basic to a test of the six propositions.

The average position of the two leading firms in the shipment of 7-digit products shows greater than log-normal disparity. The log-normal percentage shares for two firms producing 79 per cent of the industry total is 52.6 and 26.3, rather than the 58 and 21 shown for the concentrated group taken as a whole. Likewise, it is 28.6 and 14.3, rather than

30 and 13, for the 7-digit "unconcentrated" group taken as a whole; and 33.4 and 16.6 for the nonregional part of the unconcentrated group, rather than 35 and 15. Still it can be said that these averages roughly approximate the log-normal distribution Simon and Bonini find with "monotonous" regularity. But these averages also conceal the differences in disparity.

Table VI-2 presents the census data for 32 highly concentrated 5-digit product classes so as to display the diversity of relative firm size.[1] Each product class is placed into one of five "cases." In Case I, the two leading firms are approximately the same size. Case III follows the log-normal distribution, the largest firm being about twice the size of the second largest. In Case V the leading firm is eight or more times the size of the second firm. Cases II and IV are intermediate.

In these highly concentrated product groups, the four largest firms typically ship 90 per cent of the total for that product. It turns out that 15, or about 47 per cent of the 5-digit product classes fall into Case III; 9, or 28 per cent, fall in categories I and II which show less disparity; and 8, or 25 per cent, are found in categories IV and V. This table clearly shows that there is a wide variety of disparity of firm size among highly concentrated products.

It is possible for each narrowly defined component of these 5-digit product groups to have such high disparity that it should fall in Case IV or V, while firm shares in different subproduct markets differ to such an extent that 5-digit data show many patterns of relative firm size. If this is true, 7-digit data will show a stronger central tendency which will be centered on Cases IV or V.

Table VI-3 presents the distribution of relative firm sizes of the producers of 7-digit products and summarizes the 5-digit data, shown in Table VI-2, in the top row of Table VI-3. The 7-digit data where 20 or fewer firms exist show a larger number of instances at both extremes, but Case III is again the modal category. This indicates bona fide differences in relative firm size for relatively homogeneous products or subproducts. The last row of Table VI-3 reveals the incidence of the five cases where concentration is very high and is, therefore, more nearly comparable to the 5-digit data for the highly concentrated 5-digit products shown in the first row, because the share of the market produced by the largest two firms is more nearly the same. This group also shows a wider dispersion of firm disparity than the 5-digit data do.

---

[1] These 5-digit products include those listed as "additional" in Table 1, Appendix A, as well as those included in Table VI-1.

Table VI-2

Five-digit Data Classified into Five Classes to Show the
Variation of Average Relative Sizes of the Largest Four
Firms in 32 Highly Concentrated Product Classes—1954

Position of Firm	Percentage of Value of Shipments						
	Total	Middle 2/3	Case I	Case II	Case III	Case IV	Case V
1st	50	32-63	31	38	48	64	81
2nd	22	16-27	28	27	23	17	9
3rd	13	6-18	19	18	13	10	4
4th	6	2-10	7	8	6	4	2
Percentage of Industry Shipments by the Four Largest	91	—	85	91	90	95	96
Number of Cases	32	—	3	6	15	5	3
Percentage of Cases	100	—	9	19	47	16	9
Index of Disparity[a]	6.0	—	3.1	4.3	5.8	8.6	11.0
Herfindahl Index (four firms only)[a]	3189	—	2155	2561	3038	4584	6662

[a] These indexes are discussed later, on pp. 120-21 and p. 127. In general, the index of disparity measures the deviation of the market shares of the four (or eight) largest firms from their average share. A considerable variation of relative firm size can produce a given index number in most instances, and the significance of a given index is affected by the number of firms. A log-normal distribution with four firms produces an index of 6.0. The maximum index number possible with four firms is 15.0.

The Herfindahl or H-Index is the sum of the squares of the percentage market shares of the firms. It is strongly affected by the concentration ratio as well as by disparity of size and is also affected by the number of firms. The log-normal distribution where four firms produce 100 per cent is 3778, but it is 3060 when they produce only 90 per cent and the remainder is produced by many firms of negligible size.

Table VI-3[a]

Degree of Disparity of Firm Size Among the Leading Producers
of 5-Digit and 7-Digit Products, 1954

	Percentage of Cases				
	Case I	Case II	Case III	Case IV	Case V
5-Digit Data	9	19	47	16	9
7-Digit Data					
All firms	23	16	37	13	12
1-20 firms per product	14	16	36	16	17
20-2600 firms per product	37	15	38	9	2
Largest 2 firms produce 60 per cent or more	14	12	35	18	21

[a] Those 7-digit products related to 5-digit product classes classified as Group C (unconcentrated) are also included because many of them are as concentrated as the 7-digit products related to the concentrated groups A, B, D, and E. Of the 151 7-digit products shipped by firms producing the unconcentrated 5-digit product groups, 14 were shipped by fewer than 6 firms, 21 by fewer than 10, 49 by fewer than 21 and 113 by fewer than 101. About 25 per cent of these are included in the last line.

Seven-digit products are not so narrowly defined as to insure apparent monopoly, as has sometimes been implied.

The data pertaining to the more concentrated markets shown by the last line of Table VI-3 and the data presented on the third line where the total output is produced by 20 firms or fewer, provide the more relevant test for propositions 1, 2, and 3. They also provide an indication of support for proposition 4.

According to the first three propositions, Case III should be the more common one, followed by Case V and then by Case I. Ideally, the distribution is trimodal. This is the case where the two leading firms produce 60 per cent or more, although there are more instances of Case IV than of Case I. The predicted order of Cases III, V, and I, is also found when all products produced by 20 or fewer firms are considered, but the distribution is not trimodal.[2] The rather large numbers in Cases

[2] More than 60 per cent of the 292 7-digit products included in this study were produced by twenty or fewer firms. This includes about 25 per cent of the products associated with unconcentrated group C.

Table VI-4

Number and Percentage of 7-Digit and 5-Digit Products,
By Number of Shippers, by Type of Oligopoly Indicated:
Census of Manufactures, 1954

Number of Firms	Cases Supporting Hypotheses					Number of Products
	I	*II*	*III*	*IV*	*V*	
7-Digit:						
1	0	0	0	0	10	10
2	0	2	3	3	5	13
3	1	2	12	6	4	25
4	1	2	3	7	3	16
5	2	5	12	1	2	22
5 or less	4	11	30	17	24	86
(per cent)	(5)	(13)	(35)	(20)	(28)	(101)
6 - 10	12	8	19	6	4	49
11 - 20	10	11	17	6	4	48
20 or less	26	30	66	29	32	183
(per cent)	(14)	(16)	(36)	(16)	(17)	(99)
21 - 100	23	8	31	8	2	72
100 or less	49	38	97	37	34	255
(per cent)	(19)	(15)	(38)	(15)	(13)	(100)
101 - 2600	17	8	10	2	0	37
Total	66	46	107	39	34	292
(per cent)	(23)	(16)	(37)	(13)	(12)	(101)
5-Digit						
(per cent)	(9)	(19)	(47)	(16)	(9)	(100)

II and IV may reflect failures of the data to describe homogeneous
products or subproducts, the effects of nonlinear demand curves, or
non-horizontal cost conditions and demand shifts as well as failure of the
analysis underlying propositions 1 to 3.

2. Proposition 4

According to proposition 4, the disparity of size of shipments by
competing firms is inversely related to their number. This is in sharp
contrast to the usual expectation, which is based upon economies of
scale in small markets. It is often thought that if only two or three firms
exist it is because the market is so small that it can support only two or

three firms of optimal size. If so, one expects to find firms of approximately equal size. Table VI-4 shows that this is not the case. Instead, the degree of disparity is greater when there are only two, three, or four firms. The median lies between Cases IV and V for two and for four firms, and just below Case IV for three firms. This supports proposition 4. It also supports those who find virtually horizontal long-run average-cost curves, rather than economies of scale.

3. Proposition 6

Table VI-5 classifies the 7-digit products produced by 100 or fewer firms according to the disparity between the two largest firms so as to show the effect of expansion and of competitive fringe. Sales of 5-digit products in groups C, A, and D are expanding, and those in B and E are stable or contracting. No separation of the 7-digit products into these groupings is attempted. They are allocated in accordance with the position of the 5-digit parent class. This procedure probably conceals a variety of experience among the 7-digit components.

The data are inconclusive, but they tend to support proposition 6. Expanding group A-plus-D displays some tendency toward greater disparity. Found in Cases IV and V are 33 per cent of the products, as opposed to 27 per cent in Cases I and II. In addition, 37 per cent of the 7-digit products in the stable or contracting group, B-plus-E, fall in Cases I or II, while only 34 per cent are in Cases IV and V.

Table VI-5

Percentage of 7-Digit Products Falling in Cases I
Through V Related by Degree of Concentration
and Expansion or Contraction of Their
5-Digit Product Class

	Case I	Case II	Case III	Case IV	Case V	Total
A + D Expanding	15	12	40	21	12	100
B + E Stable	17	20	29	11	23	100
C[a]	26	13	41	11	10	101[b]
A + B No Fringe	15	15	40	15	15	100
D + E Fringe	15	14	37	20	15	101[b]
All Groups	19	15	38	15	13	100

[a] Excludes those products classified in group C where 101 or more firms were listed.

[b] Figures do not add up to 100 because of rounding.

Expanding group C, on the other hand, does not conform to proposition 6. Cases I and II contain 39 per cent as opposed to only 21 per cent in Cases IV and V. The relationship between growth and disparity is unclear.[3]

Nelson finds a weak negative connection between growth and concentration.[4] This implies a connection between disparity of firm size the opposite of that hypothesized above. However, one reason Nelson gives for his finding is an element of bias in the 1954 census categories. One must conclude that no relationship between growth and disparity is established.

a. Influence of a Competitive Fringe

Although no proposition under test is related to the existence of a competitive fringe, the data are of interest. Table VI-5 also presents a breakdown of the 7-digit products according to the presence or absence of a competitive fringe among the 5-digit parent products. The results may be compared to the data for the 5-digit products in Table VI-1, where greater disparity of firm size is clearly associated with absence of a fringe. Group A-plus-B is without a fringe while group C and group D-plus-E have fringes. If group C is ignored, one observes in Table VI-5 a slight tendency toward greater disparity when a competitive fringe exists. Fringed group D-plus-E has 35 per cent in Case IV and V and 29 per cent in Case I and II, while group A-plus-B has 30 per cent in each. Fringed group C is strongly represented in Cases I and II, however, and does not support the relationship. Although the data are inadequate to be more than suggestive, they tend to cast doubt on the importance of a competitive fringe as an explanation of the degree of disparity among the leading firms.

B. Proposition 5

1. Collusion and Disparity

No substantial body of evidence exists which summarizes the relative sizes of firms which follow collusive practices. The relative sizes of firms

---

[3] Group B-plus-E is remarkable in the weakness of the mode at Case III. The wider group of 7-digit products alluded to in Chapter IV, page 74, yields broadly similar results except that the highly concentrated and the expanding groups were more likely to be found in Group V; the B-plus-E group was not low in Case III; and the distribution for all groups was trimodal. Case III is always the major modal group, however, and there is little if any indication that the degree of disparity of size is explicable either by the presence of a competitive fringe or by shifting of the demand curves.

[4] Nelson, *Concentration*, p. 50-56.

Table VI-6

Relative Sizes of Producers of Heavy Electrical Equipment

| Product | Percentage of Market | | | | | No. of Firms in Market | CASE | H-index[a] | Measures of Disparity | |
| | 1st | 2nd | 3rd | 4th | 5th | | | | Index of Disparity[a] | |
									Actual	Log-N
Navy Switchgear[b]	50	30	20	—	—	3	III	3800	3.3	4.8
Marine Switchgear[b]	40	30	30	—	—	3	II	3400	1.3	4.8
Power Switchgear[c] to utilities etc.	39	35	11	8	7	5	II	2980	6.8	7.6
Power Switchgear[d] assembly to Govt. 1956	42	38	11	9	—	4	I	3410	6.0	6.0
Large Circuit Breakers[e] to Govt. 1957	45	35	10	10	—	4	II	3450	6.0	6.0
to non Govt. 1958	40.3	31.3	15.6	8.8	4.0	5	II	2939	6.2	7.6
Phase Buses and Related Structures[e]	42	34	14	10	—	4	II	3216	5.2	6.0
Power Transformers[c] (6 producers given)	30	30	15	10	8.5	6 or more	I	2197	5.7	8.6

[a] For definition see Table VI-2; p. 111, note a.

Herfindahl Index
No. of Firms   Log-Normal
3   4287
4   3778
5   3548
6   3438

Sources:

[b] Complaint before the United States District Court for the Eastern District of Pennsylvania—Civil No. 20399

[c] do Criminal No. 28090

[d] do Civil No. 27716

[e] do Civil No. 27717

[f] do Civil No. 28089

[g] do Civil No. 28105

prosecuted for collusion and those involved in merger complaints provide two sources of information. The relative sizes of electrical manufacturers in certain product markets are taken from Federal Trade Commission and Department of Justice complaints. They yield the data shown in Table VI-6.

When disparity is measured by the relative size of the two largest firms, and five "cases" distinguished, one instance is classified as Case III, five as Case II, and two as Case I. Several are borderline. These products are very narrowly defined and might be expected to show greater disparity for that reason. But the relative size of shipment tends to be somewhat more evenly distributed among the leading firms than is characteristic of 5-digit or 7-digit products overall. In general, the leading producer enjoyed less than one half of the market. However, the total number of firms is apparently smaller than usual, and this is undoubtedly an important factor in enforcing collusive agreements. The influence of foreign competition is neglected in these cases. The Index of Disparity and the Herfindahl index numbers yield approximately similar results.

These findings are consistent with proposition 5.

2. Concentration Data from FTC and Department of Justice Complaints

The Federal Trade Commission and the Department of Justice have prosecuted a number of companies under Section 7 of the Clayton Act as amended in 1950. The actions are justified under the law as necessary to prevent the monopolization of a product as a result of mergers. Product classes are defined in these complaints, and about one fifth of them estimate the market shares of the leading companies. Table VI-7 summarizes the data drawn from the more than thirty complaints including such estimates. They are divided into two groups—those selling in national markets, and those selling in regional or local markets.

Quite aside from the expectation that antimerger complaints are probably directed against the more monopolistic sectors of the economy, one might reasonably expect unusually high disparity to be found because of the narrow product definitions used in these cases. More than two thirds of them are either 7-digit products or are too narrowly defined to be found in the Standard Industrial Classification.

Nevertheless, comparison of the market shares revealed in these complaints with those presented elsewhere in this chapter for 4- and 5-digit manufactured products shows the complaints to be directed against firms whose relative size and share of the market are approximately typical of industry at the 5-digit level.

Table VI-7

Market Shares of Larger Firms:
National and Regional Markets, FTC and
Department of Justice Data*

National Markets				*Regional Markets*		
	(Percentage)				(Percentage)	
Product	*1st*	*2nd*	*3rd*	*Product*	*1st*	*2nd*
Insulated electrical				Bleach (average of		
tapes	29	29	—	6 regions)[a]	45	30
Barite[a]	44	38	—	Refined sugar	29	13
Facial tissues[a]	51	20	6	Prepared mixes[a]	45	—
Waxed paper[a]	51	14	—	Sanitary tissue[a]	68	—
Toilet paper[a]	40	12	—	Coarse papers[a]	53	18
Paper towels[a]	31	13	—	Dry salt:		
Paper napkins[a]	11	10	—	west	84	—
Polyethelene:				south	91	—
film grade resins[a]	46	20	—	Ready-mix concrete	50	—
film[a]	40	—	—	Cement	25	25
cans[a]	65	—	—	Lake sand[a]	61	31
Phenolic molding				Vending machines[a]	50	—
materials[a]	43	24	13		42	—
Aluminum truck					72	—
bodies:						
dump[a]	27	—	20			
other[a]	37	—	18			
Steel wool:						
household[a]	51	41	1	Family flour	11	10
industrial[a]	29	20	20	Cold finished		
Primary aluminum				steel bars	31	22
(FTC)	45	28	25	LP gas products	46	24
Cellophane caps and						
bands[a]	78	22	—			
Athletic goods:						
baseballs[a]	19	18	17			
basketballs[a]	24	18	16			
footballs[a]	37	14	13			
softballs[a]	18	15	12	Leading firm: Total 50 per cent		
volleyballs[a]	42	13	11	When two are given 38 22%		
soccerballs[a]	52	12	8	(Index of disparity = 2.7)		

Table VI-7—Continued

National Markets			
	(Percentage)		
Product	*1st*	*2nd*	*3rd*
Cake mixes[a]	35	31	10
Fiberboard boxes	7	5	5
Particle accelerators[a]	70	20	—
Melamine (plastic in certain dinnerware)	86	—	—
Primary aluminum (Justice)	35	30	23
New and rebuilt railway locomotives	85	—	—
Carbonated gas	29	—	—

Averages	*Percentage*			*Index of Disparity*	*Log-Normal Disparity*
Leading firms: Total	42	—	—		
Where two firms given	39	20	—	3.2	3.3
Where three firms given	35	21	13	3.5	4.8

* Some of these percentages are from complaints, and have not been subjected to counter testimony.
a 7-digit or narrower class.

The indexes of disparity, applied to the average market share where two firms' market shares are given, are 3.2 for the national markets and 2.7 for the regional ones. The log-normal index number is 3.33 when only two firms are included. Where three firms are given in the complaints, the index of disparity is 3.5, which compares to the log-normal of 4.76.

The absolute shares of the largest firms may be compared to those derived from the 1954 Census by referring to Tables VI-1 and VI-2. On the average, the leading firm producing a 7-digit product among the *least concentrated* 5-digit products in American manufacturing produces

30 per cent of the total, and the second firm produces 13 per cent. If only the 101 products most likely to enjoy national markets are included, the leading firm's share is 35 per cent and the second firm ships 15 per cent. The two-firm index of disparity is 4.0 in both cases. These data tend to support proposition 5, that collusive tendencies are associated with industries with relatively equal firm sizes.

C. Other Studies of Disparity of Firm Size

The remainder of this chapter reviews and analyzes other studies of relative firm size in order to corroborate as many of the stated propositions as possible. These investigations do not deal directly with the relative size of firms, but offer two indexes which provide rough estimates of relative size for 4-digit and/or 5-digit product classes. These studies have limitations of their own, but they do tend to cover a wider range of concentration, not being limited to the two extremes as was our sample. Index numbers calculated with their indexes appear in Tables VI-2, VI-6, and VI-7. This section analyzes them more carefully.

1. The Federal Trade Commission's Index of Disparity

In 1957 the Federal Trade Commission published a comprehensive study of the 1000 largest industrial firms as of 1950.[5] This section summarizes the findings elaborated in Appendix VI-A. The principal objective of Appendix VI-A is to show that the FTC data are more representative of total manufacturing than they may appear to be on the surface, for if this is so the findings are more relevant to the theses of this book.

Examination of the evidence shows that the smallest firms among the largest 1000 are closer in many important ways to the typical companies among the 303,000 manufacturing firms in the United States than they are to the largest firms. This statement seems to hold for relative size of shipments of particular 5-digit products, number of products shipped, number of establishments per firm, concentration of products per establishment, concentration of shipments of a given product in particular establishments, diversity of output in more narrowly defined product classes, dependence on leading product lines, and frequency of product leadership. It may not, therefore, be unreasonable to extend certain tentative conclusions, or hypotheses, based upon the pattern of behavior among the 1000 largest firms through our sample of census data to the

---

[5] *Report of the Federal Trade Commission of Industrial Concentration and Product Diversification in the 1000 Largest Manufacturing Companies: 1950.* U.S. Superintendent of Documents, Washington, D.C., 1957.

vast number of unincluded smaller firms. The FTC data reveal some surprises, such as the failure of the largest firms to be leading producers as frequently as their relative size would suggest, and the smaller scope of their influence when one considers their coverage of product classes rather than industries, and industries rather than industry groups.

The FTC study includes an analysis of the relative sizes of the largest four and the largest eight producers of each 5-digit product class. To avoid disclosure, an "index of disparity" is used which is computed by dividing the total dispersion of the value of shipments of the leading four (or, alternatively, of eight) firms from their average share by the total shipments of the four (or eight). To avoid confusion with the concentration ratio, the resulting dividend is multiplied by ten.[6]

The greater the variation in firm size the larger the index of disparity. When all firms are of the same size, the index is zero, but the maximum varies with the number of firms. It is 10 with two firms, 13.3 with three, 15.0 with four, 17.5 with eight, and so on to a maximum of 20.[7]

The index of disparity does not disclose even the relative position of any given firm because the same index number is produced by any distribution of sizes which yields the same total of dispersion. But there are limits: if the index is 5.0, the largest firm must ship from 37½ per cent to 50 per cent of the product shipped by the leading four firms. The second must ship between 25 per cent and 37½ per cent, the third from 12½ per cent to 25 per cent, while the limits for the fourth are 0 per cent and 12½ per cent. The total must, of course, add to 100 per cent. An infinite number of intermediate shares will also produce an index of 5.0 or any other number not at a "corner," such as 15.0 when there are four firms. In general, as the index of disparity rises, the possible range of sizes of the larger firms increases, and the possible range of sizes of the smaller two firms decreases.

The FTC data differ from the census data because only shipments of the 1000 largest firms are included. In some cases, a specialized firm which is too small to be among the largest 1000 will be among the first

---

[6] *Ibid.*, p. 7.

[7] For example, suppose that the four largest shippers sell 80, 40, 20, and 10 respectively for a total value of shipments of 150. The average shipment is $150/4 = 37.5$ and the dispersion is $42.5 + 2.5 + 17.5 + 27.5 = 90$. The index of disparity is $(90/150) \, 10 = 6.0$. The maximum disparity for four firms would occur if one firm shipped virtually 100 per cent, while the other three shipped negligible quantities. The total shipments would then be 100, the dispersion 150 and the index of disparity 15.0. High indexes of disparity may be associated with low concentration ratios. Thus the same index of disparity may be found whether the leading firms ship 100 per cent or 1 per cent of the products in their class if the number of firms is large.

Table VI-8

Industries and Product Classes in Which as Many as 4 and as Many as
8 Companies Among the Largest 1000 Manufacturing Companies Make
Shipments, by Size of the Index Disparity for the 4 and for the 8
Leading Companies; 1950

Index of Disparity	Industries (4-digit plus 4-digit =5-digit)		Product Classes[a] (5-digit only)		Census[b]
	4 leading companies	8 leading companies	4 leading companies	8 leading companies	
15.05 less than 15.55	—	2	—	—	
14.55 less than 15.05	—	1	1	1	
14.05 less than 14.55	—	—	2	2	
13.55 less than 14.05	—	1	—	2	
13.05 less than 13.55	2	—	1	3	
12.55 less than 13.05	3	4	2	3	
12.05 less than 12.55	3	1	1	6	
11.55 less than 12.05	3	5	—	14	
11.05 less than 11.55	1	5	3	13	
10.55 less than 11.05	2	7	4	8	3
10.05 less than 10.55	3	6	3	6	
9.55 less than 10.05	3	3	6	13	
9.05 less than 9.55	5	7	8	12	
8.55 less than 9.05	13	12	11	—	5
8.05 less than 8.55	5	11	16	22	
7.55 less than 8.05	6	10	24	13	
7.05 less than 7.55	14	17	18	17	
6.55 less than 7.05	11	9	19	16	
6.05 less than 6.55	18	14	26	15	
5.55 less than 6.05	18	17	29	21 **	15
5.05 less than 5.55	19	8	28	19	
4.55 less than 5.05	19	13	28	12	
**4.05 less than 4.55	15	17	20	19	6
3.55 less than 4.05	23	13	22	11	
3.05 less than 3.55	22	5	37	13	3
2.55 less than 3.05	19	8	26	11	
2.05 less than 2.55	13	7	26	6	
1.55 less than 2.05	16	—	19	3	
1.05 less than 1.55	7	—	18	—	
.55 less than 1.05	5	—	6	1	
less than .55	2	—	1	—	
Total	270	203	404	282	32
**Range of Common Occurrence, % within	56.7	53.2	59.9	54.6	

[a] Excluding product classes that contain all the products primary to any industry.

[b] From Table VI-2 above.

*Source: FTC Study—p. 132

four for a particular product. Thus the index of disparity may be incorrect. In such cases, the effect is probably to make the index too high. Some effort was made by the FTC to exclude products which were not sold in national markets. Table VI-8 reproduces the frequency distributions of indexes of disparity which are given in Table A-2 of the FTC Report.

These indexes of disparity indicate a great range in the relative sizes of the larger firms in a given industry. A four-firm index of 6.0 or an eight-firm index of 10.0 is produced when a log-normal size progression exists.[8] Table VI-8 shows the range of the values for the index of disparity for the 4-digit industry classification including those 5-digit products which are identical to their 4-digit class, and for the 5-digit products not included with 4-digit data. If a four-firm index of disparity of 5.05 to 7.05 is taken as approximating a log-normal progression of firm size, we find that 29 per cent of the 4-digit industries and 30 per cent of the 5-digit products fall in this rather narrow range. Greater disparity occurs in 18 per cent of the 4-digit and 20 per cent of the 5-digit categories, while 52 per cent and 50 per cent, respectively, show less. The log-normal distribution, shown in the boxes, is not atypical of the four-firm indexes, but is of the eight-firm indexes. This indicates that firms of more nearly equal relative size are found once one gets below the largest three or four.

It is argued in Chapter IV that many of the less important products tend to be combined into rather heterogeneous categories, and that homogeneous classifications tend to have four-firm concentration ratios of 50 or above. The average two-firm ratio for the 101 nonregional 7-digit components of the unconcentrated classes is 50. Using that for a guide, Table VI-9 is constructed presenting the indexes of disparity for the 103 5-digit products having concentration ratios of 50 or more. The result is approximately an equal division between the log-normal, the more disparate, and the less disparate firm sizes with 35, 36, and 32 instances respectively. As expected, a somewhat larger share is more unequal in size, but the log-normal is not the most common size although a small adjustment of its upper boundary would make it so. Propositions 1, 2, and 3 obtain modest support from these data. In particular the 3 modes are consistent with our expectation. The 5-digit data for the highly concentrated groups included in our sample of the census data are

---

[8] *Report of the Federal Trade Commission,* p. 132f. It is of interest to note in passing that pig iron had 4-firm and 8-firm indexes of 6.0 and 7.1 in 1950; refined aluminum, indexes of 6.7 and 11.5; and passenger cars, 5.4 and 9.9. These indexes are by no means exceptional in American industry.

shown in the right-hand column to facilitate comparison. It is seen that the 5-digit data from the FTC study support propositions 2 and 3 as well or better than the small sample of 5-digit data discussed above. It is therefore probable that more narrowly defined 7-digit classifications from the broader FTC sample would also give better support to all three propositions if the data were available.

The fact that the indexes of disparity shown for eight firms are too low adds support to our expectation that the log-normal disparity tends to be confined to the largest three or four firms.

Table VI-9

Indexes of Disparity
Concentrated Industry and Product Classes—1950
Number of Cases

Index	4-firm Concentration Ratio over 50		Census Sample[a] by Groups High Concentration	
	4-firm	8-firm	4-firm	5-digit
15-over	1[b]	1	—	(Index of
14-15	0	2	—	Disparity)
13-14	0	3	—	
12-13	2	3	—	
11-12	2	13 mode	3	(11.0) Case V
10-11 36	2	5	—	
9-10	9	11	—	
8-9	12 mode	10 M (7.8)	5	(8.6) Case IV
7-8	8	15 mode	—	
6-7 35	23 mode M (6.3)	4	—	
5-6	12	3	15	(5.8) Case III
4-5	9	6 mode	6	(4.3) Case II
3-4	14 mode	1	3	(3.1) Case I
2-3 32	7	0	—	
1-2	2	1	—	
0-1	0	0	—	
	103	79	32	

a From Table VI-2.
b This represents the five-digit class 37311, "Motorcycles, motorbikes, and motor-scooters, and parts." The largest manufacturers of motorscooters are omitted, as are imports. It rounds up to 15.

2. The Stability of the Index of Disparity Over Time

Inferential support accrues to our hypotheses with regard to the formation of oligopolies if the index of disparity for the four largest firms is relatively stable. Table VI-10 presents the available data for as many of our 32 selected highly concentrated 5-digit product classes as had comparable definitions for two or more years and whose indexes of disparity do not involve disclosure according to Department of Commerce criteria. Thirteen comparisons are possible between 1950 and 1954, ten between 1954 and 1958, and seven between 1950 and 1958. The seven are also comparable for all three years. It should be remembered that the FTC data for 1950 include only the largest one thousand manufacturing firms, but it seems probable that these include the largest four for each of the product classes shown in Table VI-10, although primary batteries and files may be exceptions. The Bureau of the Census very kindly prepared the 1958 indexes of disparity.

Inspection of Table VI-10 shows considerable stability. The coefficient of correlation between the indexes for 1950 and 1954 is only $+.50$, but rises to $+. 79$ if primary batteries are omitted.[9] It will be recalled that this period includes part of the readjustments to a peacetime economy following World War II and to reimposed controls of the Korean War. The correlation for 1954-1958 is $+.90$. The higher correlation is to be expected because of the greater assurance that the largest four firms are in fact those used to compute the indexes in both years. The coefficient of correlation for the seven products of the years 1950 and 1958 is $+.59$ if primary batteries are included, but is $+.89$ if they are excluded.[10]

These calculations do not preclude changes in the rank order of firms, or displacement of one or more of those in the leading group, but they do indicate considerable stability in the relative sizes of the leading firms. A better test of the propositions advanced in this chapter would be possible if this sort of information were available for 7-digit and even finer products, because differential changes in the fortunes of various 7-digit products will change the ranking of firms at the 4-digit and 5-digit level although very similar relative rankings persist for each of the 7-digit products. Firms' ranks change because some expand into

[9] It was thought that the apparent decline in disparity in primary batteries and in files was a result of the failure of some of the leading producers to be included among the 1000 largest firms in 1950. A check of industry data accounts neither for this explanation nor for any other explanation of the large change in these indexes of disparity.

[10] These coefficients are statistically significant. However, the degree of significance is overstated because the observations are not sufficiently separated in time to make them independent.

Table VI-10

Indexes of Disparity for Largest Four Companies
For Selected 5-Digit Product Classes:
1950, 1954 and 1958

1954 Code		1950	1954	1958[a]
22741	Linoleum	6.1	6.8	—
28251	Acetate yarn	5.0	3.7	5.6
28231	Cellulosic plastic materials	6.5	7.2	—
28620	Softwood distillation products	8.2	5.6	7.4
32311	Laminated glass	6.7	4.1	—
32720	Gypsum products	7.2	7.0	—
34240	Files	12.2	8.9	—
34920	Safes and vaults	—	5.0	4.7
36131	Integrating instruments, electric	—	2.8	2.6
36152	Power distribution transformers	5.5	4.2	4.6
36510	Electric lamps	—	5.7	5.2
36920	Primary batteries	11.3	4.4	6.0
37230	Aircraft propellers	7.7	4.9	6.9

Products whose 5-digit number varied slightly in 1950,
but whose description was the same.

28523	Non-cellulosic synthetic fibers	14.5	D[b]	——
28421	Synthetic organic detergents, packaged	8.4	6.3	6.2
33521	Aluminum plates and sheet	5.0	4.9	—
38615	Photographic films and plates, silver halide type	10.5	11.1	10.4

[a] Supplied by the Bureau of Census
[b] Disclosure

new regional markets or introduce new products or subproducts. Dynamic factors such as those relating to the quality of management or exhaustion of particular sources of raw materials must also play an important role.[11]

[11] N. R. Collins and L. E. Preston have studied the long-term stability of relative firm size and have concluded that over the period 1909-1958 relatively little change has taken place. Their findings do not bear directly on the matter at hand because the position of narrowly defined products is not at issue, but rather what might be termed macro-micro economics of the sort considered in Chapters VIII and IX, to follow. See "The Size Structure of Industrial Firms," *American Economic Review,* LI (December 1961), 986-1012.

3. The Herfindahl Index

Data for the 32 very highly concentrated and the 12 least concentrated 5-digit product groups and their associated 7-digit products constitute a narrow basis from which to support a general hypothesis related to industry structure. So, indeed, do the FTC data for the 1000 largest manufacturing firms. Fortunately, the Herfindahl index has been computed for many of the 5-digit products included in the censuses of 1954 and 1947.[12] The following is an analysis of the implication of the Herfindahl index, or H-index, for those 5-digit products having a four-firm concentration ratio of 60 or more. There are 101 such products recorded for 1954 and 76 for 1947. A considerable number of products are eliminated because the concentration ratio and/or the H-index involve disclosures. This produces an underrepresentation of the products whose production is undertaken by firms of greatly disparate size.

The H-index is the sum of the squares of percentages of the market enjoyed by the individual firms. The Herfindahl index measures the disparity of firm size, but it is affected by the size of the concentration ratio (CR) and the number of firms. The influence of the number of firms is reduced, since Nelson includes only the 50 largest for each product. Figure 6-1 attempts to eliminate the influence of the concentration ratio by plotting it against the H-index. The maximum value is that which would result if one firm produced virtually the total for the four largest and all other firms, of course, produced negligible amounts. The minimum value shows the effect of equal size among the four largest firms. Since the four together must produce the amount designated by the relevant concentration ratio, the minimum value for the industry is found if each of the other firms produces a negligible amount, thus spreading the share not produced by the four leading firms among so many firms that their squared shares approach zero. Note that 2500 is the maximum H-index if CR=50, but is the minimum if CR=100.

The thin section that originates with an H-index of 3778 and a concentration ratio of 100 shows the limits of a strictly construed log-normal distribution among the largest four firms.[13] It is a band, rather than a line, because the number and size-distribution of firms not among the largest four affects the value of the index for a log-normal distribution among the largest four taken separately. The lower edge of the band is found by assuming a log-normal distribution among the largest four

---

[12] Nelson, *Concentration in the United States.* Table A5, p. 197-231.
[13] It is recalled that proposition 2 involves the size distribution among the largest two or three firms only.

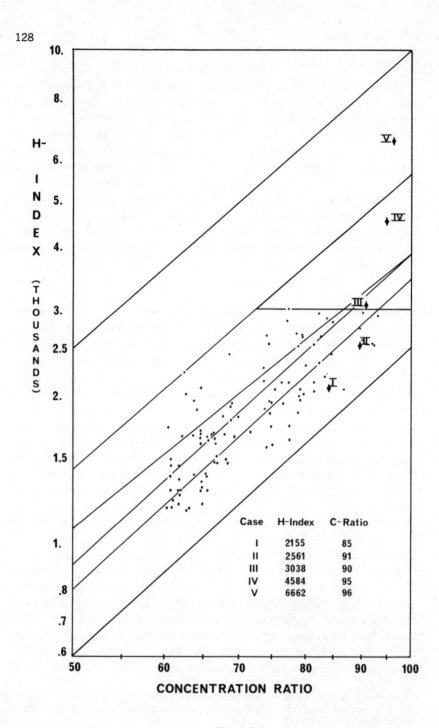

Case	H-Index	C-Ratio
I	2155	85
II	2561	91
III	3038	90
IV	4584	95
V	6662	96

CONCENTRATION RATIO

Figure 6-1

firms, and a sum of the squared shares of the (extremely numerous) other firms of virtually zero. The upper edge is found by assuming that the firms not included in the top four are equal in size to the fourth firm.

Size distributions of leading firms other than the log normal can yield H-indexes within the narrow band.[14] Industries with firms whose size is close to the log normal can lie outside of the band. There are limits to the disparity of firm size that is associated with each combination of concentration ratio and H-index, but no general statement of these limits is found. They get narrower as one gets closer to the upper right-hand corner of the Figure 6-1.

The lack of any instances of H-indexes above 3000 suggests that high disparity of firm size is underrepresented. This is particularly true where the four-firm concentration ratio is also high, because disclosure becomes a more acute problem when the industry can be cross-referenced by two such measures.

This is a serious element of bias that impairs the usefulness of this study for present purposes. It appears probable that all highly disparate instances categorized above as Case V have been eliminated as well as the instances of cases II, III, and IV that would have fallen in the triangular area marked on the figure. This is illustrated by the 32 highly concentrated products analyzed above which come from the same source used by Nelson. The average H-index for the five cases shown in Table VI-2 lies over 3000 for log-normal Case III as well as for Cases IV and V. The data for the five cases are shown in a table on Figure 6-1 where each ratio is appropriately located on the figure with a roman numeral. These calculations are based upon the largest four firms only, not the largest 50. Inclusion of the remaining firms would further increase the H-index by a small amount. The exclusion of H-indexes over 3000 is particularly unfortunate when the concentration ratio is high, because the more narrowly defined products are considered the best available test of the six propositions.

The effect of these sources of bias can be reduced for purposes of testing propositions 1 to 3 by counting only those products least subject to bias. Some of the overrepresentation of groups I and II can be avoided by including only those products with CR's of 60 or more. Exclusion of products whose H-indexes exceed 3000 seems to most affect products whose concentration ratios exceed 87. These can also

[14] For example, a CR of 80 and an H-index of 2500 can be produced with either a log-normal distribution with the largest firm producing about 42.6 per cent or by a 35 per cent, 35 per cent, 5 per cent, 5 per cent progression of firm size.

be ignored. The first limit tends to exclude the broadly defined product and the second tends to exclude those products whose high disparity produces an H-index which is a disclosure. A count of the remaining products reveals 22 in the "thin" log-normal section, 18 which are more disparate in size, and 54 less disparate. These data support proposition 2.

These findings do not support propositions 1 and 3 as they stand. But the second most common disparity class found in other data seems to have been completely eliminated by disclosure rules and a substantial number of instances of Case III are also apparently passed over. This probably accounts for the failure of propositions 1 and 3. A very restrictive statistical definition of Case III has also been employed. If the latter is defined as extending down to H-indexes of 3500 at 100 CR, and 800 at 50 CR, as illustrated, the primacy of Case III is reestablished as called for in proposition 1. Proposition 2 finds limited support, in that only 10 per cent show approximately equal firm size for the four leading firms.

A lesser body of data exists for 1947. These relate to 4-digit industries rather than 5-digit products and can be expected to show a somewhat greater bias toward Cases I and II than 5-digit data do. Examination of a scattergram like that used for Figure 6-1 confirms this expectation. The pattern of instances is very similar except that they lie at a slightly lower level.

Nelson calculates the 1947 and the 1954 H-indexes for comparable 4-digit industries. There are 42 of these with concentration ratios between 60 and 80. These 42 pairs are used to throw additional light upon the stability of the degree of disparity among leading firms. A simple correlation of the H-indexes yields a coefficient of correlation of .875. This is significant at the 1 per cent level in a formal sense, but since a given H-index denotes a different disparity if the concentration ratio changes, it is not a very clear test. As already pointed out, a given H-index can continue at a given level of concentration although disparity has changed somewhat. It is, therefore, possible for changes to be offsetting as well as distorting, and a given correlation may or may not indicate a given probability of variation in disparity. These data can be said not to reject propositions 1 through 3.

D. Summary and Conclusions

This chapter has attempted to test six of the hypotheses that follow from the analysis of Chapter V. The propositions are that:

1. A log-normal distribution of firm size among the largest three or four firms is relatively most common.

2. Leading firms of approximately equal size are relatively uncommon.

3. Distribution of firm size more disparate than log normal is found with an incidence between 1 and 2.

4. When four or fewer firms ship all of a product, the fewer the firms the greater the disparity of firm size.

5. Firms that collude will tend to be of more equal firm size.

6. Industries that are growing will display greater than average disparity of firm size.

Limited support is found for each proposition except number 6. Opposite forces are at work in growing industries, and it is possible that two or more subtypes should be recognized.

Appendix to Chapter VI

Summary of FTC Study Showing the Degree To Which the 1,000 Largest Manufacturing Firms Are Typical of All Manufacturing Firms

The main purpose of this Appendix is to show the degree to which the characteristics of the smaller firms among the largest one thousand manufacturing firms are similar to the nearly 300,000 excluded firms. The data are interesting on their own merit, but gain interest for present purposes if indexes of disparity of size among these firms in their product markets can be considered indicative of manufacturing more generally.[1]

The data presented in Chapter VI indicate that concentration and disparity among the largest firms are probably relevant to the larger group because it is found that the disparities and concentration ratios for narrowly-defined 5-digit product classes are approached by those for 7-digit products whether they are associated with the narrowly-defined or with the loosely-defined 5-digit product classes. However, the more characteristics there are in common between a major portion of the largest one thousand firms and the others, the more relevant will appear to be the data for the largest firms.

A. Relative Size

Figure 6-A offers an impression of the relative position of the firms with shipments of various sizes. The small circles denote the value of shipments given by the FTC for the smallest firm in each size group,

---

[1] Michael Gort's study, cited in Chapter IV, offers an analysis of diversification which is more sophisticated and more extensive through time than the FTC study under examination in this appendix. Its basic data are confined to 111 of the largest manufacturing firms. Although they seem to be relevant to the theses under construction, they are less representative of manufacturing as a whole than are the one thousand largest firms.

except for the circled point which is the calculated average value of shipments for all industrial firms smaller than the largest 1000. The points marked with crosses are the calculated averages for each size group.[2] A straight line projected freehand through these points appears to be a reasonably good fit, and yields a projected value of shipments of $14.6 billion for the largest firm and $70,000 for the smallest. No effort has been made to check these extreme projections, but the rather close correspondence of projected line to the average of the smallest 302,000 provides some basis for inferring typical relationships from data for the largest 1000 firms. One may note that the smallest of the 1000 largest firms is more than halfway down the diagonal line.

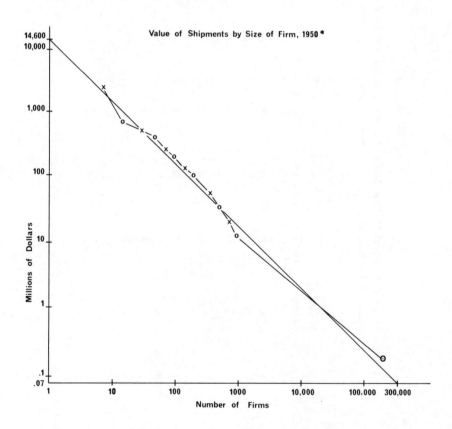

Figure 6-A

[2] *Op. cit., Report of the Federal Trade Commission.*

Table A

Dependence of the Largest 50, the Median 50, and the Smallest 50 Firms among the Largest 1000 Industrial Firms upon Their Leading Product Classes: 1950

Percentage of Total Value of Shipments Of a Firm	Number of Companies Depending Upon:								
	One Product Class			Two or Fewer Product Classes			Five or Fewer Product Classes		
	Largest 50	Median 50	Smallest 50	Largest 50	Median 50	Smallest 50	Largest 50	Median 50	Smallest 50
10 and under	2	0	0	0	0	0	0	0	0
10 to 20	5	0	0	2	0	0	0	0	0
20 to 30	8	2	0	2	0	0	1	0	0
30 to 40	6	11	7	7	0	0	1	0	0
40 to 50	11	7	8	5	2	0	1	0	0
50 to 60	11	9	10	9	8	5	3	0	0
60 to 70	4	2	0	9	7	6	5	1	0
70 to 80	1	8	4	5	8	5	9	1	0
80 to 90	2	6	6	3	8	6	17	6	4
90 to 100	0	5	15	8	17	28	13	42	46
50 to 100	18	30	35	34	48	50	47	50	50

* FTC Report, p. 148.

B. Size, Number of Products, and Dependence on Leading Products

The larger the company, in general, the larger the number of the approximately 1000 5-digit product classes produced. The largest company produced 129 5-digit product classes, twelve companies shipped 21 to 75 product classes, but 118 of the 1000 largest companies shipped only one.[3]

Individual firms differ greatly in their dependence upon their leading product but not as much as one might have expected. Table A presents the findings of the FTC study. Fifteen of the fifty, or 30 per cent of the smallest firms among the largest 1000, derive 90 per cent or more of their sales from a single product class, 56 per cent from two product classes, and 92 per cent from five. The Federal Trade Commission argues that because in a few cases as many as five product classes may be virtually joint products it may be wisest to direct primary attention to the third group of figures, for five or fewer product classes. Whether we look to the influence of a single product, two products or five, however, it is evident that the position of a substantial minority of the largest firms is similar to that of smaller firms in dependence upon one or a few product groups. There is a curious bimodality, and even trimodality, that may be of interest; but it is overshadowed by the tendency toward concentration of value of shipments among relatively few product classes

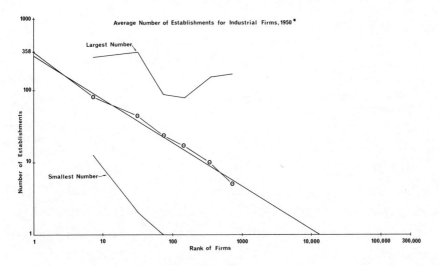

Figure 6-B

[3] *Ibid.*, pp. 26-28.

by all except a half dozen or so firms. The smaller firms among the largest 1,000 are similar to the many excluded firms.

C. Number of Establishments

Large firms tend to be large by virtue of control of many establishments. Table B reproduces one given on page 37 of the FTC study, and relates the average number of establishments to size of firms.

These data are plotted in Figure 6-B along with the largest and the smallest specific number of establishments for each size class. A straight line on log-log paper fits the average quite well, ranging from 358 establishments for the largest firm to one establishment per firm at approximately the largest 10,000 level. This would suggest that the smaller 293,000 firms tend to have a single establishment. Although the smaller of the 1000 largest tend to have few establishments, the range is wide and the broad range surely extends to relatively small firms.

Among the largest 15 companies, 10 had more than 50 establishments, 4 had between 21 and 50, and one had between 11 and 15. Only 29 firms among the largest 500 operated only one establishment. But of the companies ranked 501-1000 only one had more than 45 establishments (but it had 175) while 262 had five or less, and 103 had only one.

Table B

Number of Establishments by Size Class of Firm
(No. jointly and equally owned by firms of different size classes are shown in parentheses.)

Size Class	Average Number of Establishments Per Company	Total No. of Establishments Per Size Class
1- 15	87	1308 (3)
16- 50	45	1569 (6)
51- 100	24	1190 (32)
101- 200	17	1684 (30)
201- 500	10	3132 (5)
501-1000	5	2606 (2)

[a] FTC Report, Table 20, pp. 33; 37.

Table C

Number and Percentage of the Establishments of Manufacturing Companies in
Each of Six Size Classes Shipping Specified Number of Product Classes: 1950

No. of Product Classes Shipped	Size Classes (Rank of Firms)											
	1st to 15th		16 to 50		51 to 100		101 to 200		201 to 500		501 to 1000	
	No.	Percentage	No.	Percentage	No.	Percentage	No.	Percentage	No.	Percentage	No.	Percentage
1	501(3)	38.3	647(5)	41.2	599(10)	50.4	833(9)	49.5	1831(5)	58.4	1443(2)	55.4
2	304	23.2	405(1)	25.8	290(10)	24.3	312(9)	18.5	627	20.0	515	19.8
3	194	14.8	191	12.2	126(6)	10.6	234(6)	13.9	303	9.7	253	9.7
4	95	7.4	125	8.0	65(4)	5.5	106(4)	6.3	168	5.4	162	6.2
5	83	6.3	74	4.7	43(1)	3.6	76(1)	4.5	88	2.8	88	3.3
over 5	131	10.0	127	8.1	67(1)	5.6	123(1)	7.3	115	3.7	145	5.6

Source: FTC Report, p. 33.

a Number of establishments jointly and equally owned by two in different size classes are shown in parentheses.

Table D

Frequency With Which the 1000 Largest Companies Shipped a
Given Class of Product from a Specified Number of Establishments: 1950

Item	Total	Product Classes of Which Shipments by the Surveyed Companies (in Millions of Dollars) Were:					
		200 and Over	100 but Under 200	50 but Under 100	10 but Under 50	5 but Under 10	Under 5
Number of instances	9,001	2,684	1,911	1,578	2,063	304	461
Percentage of instances in which a company made shipments from:							
1 establishment	58.2	49.1	56.8	59.6	64.8	71.1	74.2
2 establishments	16.9	16.7	18.4	16.1	17.3	16.4	13.4
3- 5 establishments	15.4	19.3	15.2	16.2	12.2	10.2	8.7
6-10 establishments	5.9	8.8	6.2	5.2	3.4	2.0	3.5
11-20 establishments	2.3	4.2	2.1	1.6	1.6	0.3	—
21-50 establishments	0.9	1.5	0.9	1.0	0.5	—	0.2
Over 50 establishments	0.3	0.4	0.4	0.3	0.2	—	—

Source: FTC Report, p. 39.

D. Concentration of Products per Establishment

A given establishment tends to produce a limited number of products whether it belongs to a large firm or a smaller one. Table C presents the data by size of company and number of products. At every size level of firm the leading two product classes accounted for more than 60 per cent of the value of shipments of a given establishment. There is some tendency for the larger companies to own establishments producing a larger number of product classes, but the tendency is not strong. This finding lends emphasis to the FTC's conclusion that the larger firm's size rests primarily upon control of a larger number of establishments and, perhaps, a larger average size of establishment. It also is another point of similarity between firms in the largest 1000 and smaller firms.

E. Size of Shipment per Number of Establishments

Even when the size of shipment by a single firm is very large ($200,000,000 and over) they are shipped from a single plant nearly half of the time, and from either one or two plants 65 per cent of the time. Where the value of shipments is smaller, there is a greater likelihood that they will originate in a single plant, as one would expect if there are any economies of scale to be set against transportation costs, but the tendency is not dramatic. Table D presents the relevant data.

There were 9,000 instances in which a particular product class was shipped from some establishment of one of the largest 1000 industrial companies in 1950. Companies with annual shipments of a product class amounting to $200 million and over shipped a given product from a single establishment 49.1 per cent of the time. Firms shipping less than $5 million shipped from a single establishment 74.2 per cent of the time.

The FTC study presents data which reveal a substantial range in the size of establishments producing nearly all of the products included in the food-processing, electrical machinery, and transportation equipment industries.[4] In general, the average size establishment ranked 13th to 16th in size is always less than one half the size of the average ranked 1 to 4, and for some 5-digit product classes is as small as one twenty-fifth the size of the largest establishment. However, there is nothing to connect the largest establishments with the largest companies, and no conclusions can be drawn about the size of establishments of the smaller companies from the given data.

[4] *Ibid.,* p. 10.

F. Diversity of Firm Output by Breadth of Product Class

The larger firms are found in a larger percentage of the product markets the more broadly they are defined. For example, the seven most diversified companies shipped products classified in 10 to 15 of the 21 major (2-digit) industry groups.[5] Thus, the most diversified company contended in 71 per cent of the major industrial groupings. The five most diversified companies produced products that are classified in 25 to 48 of the 150 industry subgroups, the most diversified company being active in 32 per cent of them. The twenty most diversified of the companies at the 4-digit industry level produced in 25 or more industries, and the largest most diversified single company operated in 75 to 80 of the 453 industry classifications, or in no more than 17.8 per cent of them. Eight companies shipped more than 55 5-digit product classes, and one of these shipped 129 different classes or 13.9 per cent of the 926 product classes.

The declining percentage of classes covered by the largest firms as the number of classes is increased suggests that it may be at least as appropriate to look at these distributions from the other end, noting the proportion of firms engaged in only a few products, industries, industry subgroups, and industry groups. Thus 43.2 per cent of the 1000 largest companies produced only 1 to 5 of the 926 product classes; 59.8 per cent operated in but 1 to 5 of the 453 industries, 58.9 per cent operated in 1 to 5 of the 150 industry subgroups; and 76.6 per cent operated in no more than 1 to 3 of the 21 industry groups—90 per cent shipping in 1 to 5 of these groups.[6]

G. Product Leadership and Size

The leading producers of 5-digit products are more widely dispersed than one might expect from the concentration of shipments. As noted previously, all product classes are classified among 926 categories, of which the leading 1000 firms produced 853. This leaves only 73 5-digit product classes of which the leading firm cannot be among the largest 1000 firms. To reduce the chance that leadership will be incorrectly assigned to one of the 1000 largest firms, only those firms shipping at least $13,000,000 of a particular product class are included. This is equal to the total shipments of the smallest firm included among the largest 1000 companies and eliminates any possibility that a smaller company may be the leader in a good assigned to one of the 1000. It

[5] *Ibid.*, p. 30, 32.
[6] *Ibid.*, Figure 4, p. 32, and supporting data.

also eliminates nearly one hundred product classes where the class total is less than $13 million, and an undetermined number of additional product classes where the leading firm produces less than $13 million. A $13 million cutoff finds 753 of the largest 1000 firms with no leading product. Under these restrictions one or another of the remaining 247 of the largest 1000 firms leads in 441 (48 per cent) of the 5-digit product classes. This is a minimum number of product classes led by one

Table E

Leading Producers of 5-Digit Products
By Size Group, 1950

	Total Company Shipments Exceed:			
	$13 Million		$1 Million	
Size Group	Leading Company	Among Top Four	Leading Company	Among Top Four
	(Number of Products)			
1 to 15	105	215	140	387
16 to 50	78	162	95	279
51 to 100	48	135	81	267
101 to 200	64	165	116	346
201 to 500	88	255	172	614
501 to 1000	58	167	166	566
Total	441	1,099	770	2,489
Percentage of Leadership Positions	48	30	83	67
	(Average Number per Firm)			
1 to 15	7.0	14.3	9.3	25.8
16 to 50	2.2	4.6	2.7	8.0
51 to 100	1.0	2.7	1.6	5.3
101 to 200	0.6	1.7	1.2	3.4
201 to 500	0.3	0.9	0.6	2.0
501 to 1000	0.1	0.3	0.3	1.1

Source: Computed from data in FTC Report, pp. 22, 145-50.

of the 1000 largest firms and may be compared to the 55 per cent of total shipments made by the same firms.

A $1,000,000 cutoff is also used, and something may be inferred from the difference in the incidence of leadership when that cutoff figure is used rather than $13 million. Lowering the cutoff makes one or another of 399 of the largest 1000 firms appear to be the leader in 770 of the 853 products produced by them, or 83 per cent of all products. This surely exaggerates the incidence of leadership of the 1000, because firms too small to be included in the study must sometimes be the leading producer with shipments of $1 million or more. Table E summarizes the FTC data pertaining to product class leadership.

The data in the lower part of Table E can be compared to the relative sizes of the various groups of companies to ascertain whether or not each size group got "its share" of leadership positions. The relative sizes can be found from the percentage of total value of shipments by each of the six size groups. This is done in Table F.

From Table F it can be seen that the largest firms do not ship "their share" of the leading products if one were to suppose that the number of leading products would be in proportion to firm size. The average size of the leading 15 firms is 94 times the average size of the smallest 500 among the 1000 largest firms; but they produce, on the average, only 70 times as many leading products if the $13 million cutoff point

Table F

Relative Size and Relative Frequency of Product
Class Leadership in USA Manufacturing
Industry: 1950

| | | Shipments per Company (Relative) | | | |
| | Relative | Exceed $13 million | | Exceed $1 million | |
Size Class	Size Class	1st	1st four	1st	1st four
1 - 15	94	70	48	31	23
16 - 50	21	22	15	9	7
51 - 100	12	10	9	5	5
101 - 200	6	6	6	4	3
201 - 500	2.5	3	3	2	1.8
501 - 1000	1	1	1	1	1

Source: Computed from data in FTC Report, pp. 22, 145-50.

is used and 31 times as many if the $1 million cutoff is used. Since the leading producer must sometimes be found among the firms excluded from the sample, these data must overestimate the incidence of product leadership among the largest firms. This conclusion is more strikingly shown by the data for four firms and for the $1 million cutoff. The more room there is for smaller firms in the statistical sample, the less dominating the largest firms appear.

Some of the largest firms are, nevertheless, as the FTC emphasizes, often leaders in the production of some product which is of minor import to them. This is an inevitable consequence of large size accomplished by multiple establishments and multiple products. But larger firms sometimes specialize in the mass production of some commodity. For that reason the largest firms do not lead in the number of products that would be proportionate to their size. One suspects that another survey based upon 7-digit data would reveal more cases of big-firm dominance of some meaningful products which are unimportant to it. But a more striking result would probably be the relatively few products where the largest firms lead.

This summary and comment on the 1957 report leads to these tentative conclusions:

1. The 1000 largest firms are more representative of the 303,000 manufacturing establishments than one might suppose. In particular, the smaller firms among them tend to rely upon one or a very few products, one or a few establishments, and are rarely the leading producer of a 5-digit product class.

2. The larger firms typically seem to ship several products, but only rarely does a single establishment turn out more than a very few product classes.

3. The evidence from the FTC study and the special study of 1954 Census data suggests that the size of the shipments of the leading producers of individual 5- and 7-digit product classes is typically very unequal.

4. The more narrowly defined the industry or product, the less dominant the largest firms appear to be. In particular, the leading firms do not appear to hold a share of leadership positions for 5-digit product classes proportionate to their total sales.

Chapter VII

Independent Maximization Applied
to Product Competition and Sales Expense

If independent maximization is an appropriate explanatory principle when applied to measurable variables such as price and output it is likely to be appropriate to other less objectively measurable dimensions of firms' activities as well, because measurement is needed to regulate collusive and semicollusive agreements. Independent maximization may, however, provide less profitable alternatives than collusion, leadership, or some other coordinating device. This chapter investigates choice among these three where product competition and sales expense are the key variables. It also investigates price competition where differentiated products exist. In general, independent maximization strategy is found to be the superior strategy. This conclusion is not dependent upon the difficulty of measuring sales efforts and product differences, but is reinforced thereby.

To simplify analysis, rival firms are assumed to produce the same range of subproducts and to undertake similar ranges of sales expenses. This is less of a departure from the findings of chapters V and VI than appears on the surface. Analysis centers upon diversity of subproducts associated with a particular generic product, and with sales expense related to such a product. These, especially the former, can be quite similar among rival firms although aggregate sales of all generic products differ greatly, because large companies often owe their great size to the production of several generic products and are on relatively equal footing in particular markets.[1]

---

[1] Our analysis of census data shows that the larger firms owe their relative size primarily to a larger number of establishments and only in a secondary way to larger size of establishment.

A. Product Competition

It is convenient to analyze product competition with the aid of a profit-indifference diagram for duopolists similar to that employed in Chapter V. The ideal situation for any firm is to have no rivals. In that case a group of subproducts can be marketed to obtain a monopolist's income. The number of subproducts is ascertained according to the principles discussed in Chapter II. In some cases this might be a single type, but more commonly a line of subproducts is more profitable. Figure 7-1 treats generic products as if they were made up of a continuously variable number of subproducts, and designates Oa and Ob as the monopolistic number of subproducts for Firm A and Firm B respectively. Each of these positions, of course, assumes that the other firm does not exist.

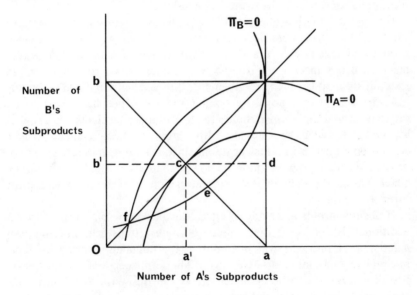

Figure 7-1

Assume for the moment that firm A's initial monopoly position is broken by entry of firm B, but that further entry is blocked. Assume initially that the presence of a rival does not affect the optimum number of subproducts as seen by the firm. In that case Firm A will produce Oa number of subproducts whether or not Firm B exists; and Firm B will produce the same number, Ob, if it enters. This is shown by the vertical reaction functions aI and bI, which show the most profitable number of subproducts for each given number offered by the rival.

There is some number of firms which will make the profits of each firm equal to zero when it produces Oa number of subproducts. This number is assumed to be two for the moment, so the normal profit indifference curve for each firm passes through point I. The costs of full lines, and the higher cross elasticities associated with the enlarged source of supply, make any point within the lens-shaped area more profitable than maintenance of the full lines. For example, collusion to reduce the number of product lines to the lesser number shown by the set [Oa', Ob'] yields higher profits for both firms, and if Firm A were to win maximum bargaining advantage it could reach a still higher profit indifference curve that passes through point e without pushing Firm B's profits below the normal level. With entry blocked, collusion to reduce the number of subproducts seems to be indicated.

Unlike the situation illustrated in Chapter V where quantities are the variable, both firms here have an incentive to enter the agreement since it offers immediate profits and either will benefit if it breaks the agreement. But this incentive is double edged, because the rival firm suffers losses if its rival breaks the agreement. For example, if Firm A breaks a 50-50 agreement (shown by point C) and expands his output to its original level while Firm B holds to the collusive level Ob', point d is attained. This yields substantial positive profits to the agreement-breaker A, and puts Firm B in a loss position, since B's profit indifference curve passing through point d must be lower than its normal profit curve, which passes through point I. Similar action by Firm B would push Firm A into the red.

If positive profits are likely to attract further entry, both firms face an additional risk of loss if they collude because a third firm entering with a full line of products will put both of the colluding firms, with their incomplete lines, at a disadvantage. Thus, independent maximization behavior turns out to be minimax strategy in the sense that a firm that sticks to Oa subproducts will never suffer a relative disadvantage.[2]

It is probable that Figure 7-1 refers to a special case, in that the most profitable number of subproducts for any firm is often a function of the number of subproducts marketed by its rivals. It is probably a positive function, so that for any given number of subproducts produced by one firm, the rival will find a larger number desirable. Thus Firm B would tend to enter with Ob' number of subproducts if Firm A is pro-

---

[2] One may note that the "leadership" positions for both firms also fall at point I.

ducing the monopolistic number, *Oa*, as shown on Figure 7-2 by the coordinates to point S.

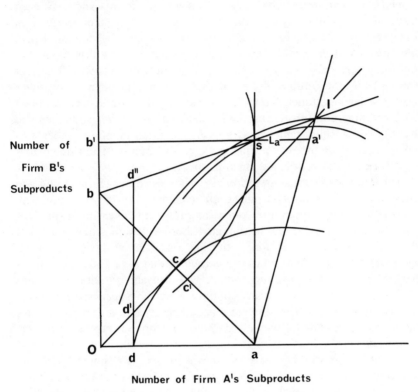

Figure 7-2

What is Firm *A*'s optimal response? The following choices exist: (1) collusion, hopefully at point *C*; (2) independent maximization, by an initial move to *A*'s reaction function at point *a'* and eventually as *B* reacts to point *I*; and (3) leadership equilibrium, by movement to point L_A if firm *A* assumes leadership.

Collusion between points *C* and *C'* offers larger profits to both firms in the case illustrated. Very similar cases can exist where the iso-profit curves upon which *C* and *C'* rest fail to intersect and, therefore, provide no basis for collusion. In the present case mutually beneficial collusion can exist. Yet both firms may not think it wise to run the risks involved in collusive policies.

There are two sources of risk: agreement failure and entry by other firms. Each is placed at a great disadvantage if the rival breaks the agreement. The agreement-breaker increases his profits and may even push his rival into negative profits. This would be the outcome in Figures 7-1 and 2. Entry by a third firm offering a full line at such a time could seal the bankruptcy of the agreement-keeping firm. Whether or not agreements are kept, greater than normal profits will attract entry. Entry by full-line firms will have an advantage not only over potential later entrants, but over the existing firms that have colluded by shortening and integrating their lines. The new firm would tend to match the full line, and would approach the status of the other two taken together should they persist in a collusive product line agreement. Collusion is, therefore, a dangerous strategy.

If the independent maximization alternative is chosen, Firm A will add substantially to its product line when B enters. It will go to point a'. Firm B would be expected to restore its profits by increasing its product line also, and point I would be obtained shortly. If we again assume that this is a normal profit position, both firms are secure at this point. If, on the other hand, positive profits are earned at that point, additional firms will enter, and additional subproducts will also appear until profits are eliminated.[3] The leading firms continue to make super-normal profits as they move toward I, and never place themselves in an inferior strategic position. At point I they continue to earn normal profits on a large volume of sales.

A third possibility is that Firm A will increase its subproducts only slightly so that Firm B will attain its maximum profits at point L_A. Firm A will take super-normal profits indefinitely but they will be lower than B's. In time, some safe way to divide the profit, or to increase it for both, by collusive agreement may be found if entry can be forestalled. But if supranormal profits attract entry, as is probable, Firm A remains in the more vulnerable position. For that reason, it is reasonable to expect

---

[3] The controversy between the production department and the sales department of the calculating machine company can be considered with the aid of Figure 7-2 if the arbitrary assumption is made that a single product line for firm A is denoted by point d. The profit at point d is considerably short of the maximum monopoly profit designated by point a, but it is higher than that associated with any non-collusive outcome when a rival is present. The production department assumes that it will drive the rival from the field and obtain point d. But the rival has the easy alternative of matching the tactic, moving both firms to the lower profit positions at point d'. And if it can continue its full line, it will obtain point d'' which yields substantial gains to the rival and absolute losses to the single subproduct firm. Of course, the revolutionary policy advocated by the production department may work so that point d is obtained. But the risk that it will not is substantial.

the original firm to choose independent maximization, the minimax alternative, rather than taking the "leadership" position, L_a. Thus the number of subproducts may be larger than optimal, according to the principles described in Chapter II.

B. Monopoly via Product Differentiation

It is possible, but not probable, that negative profits are associated with point I when only two firms exist. In that case, economies of scale in the differentiation of products exist which are sufficient to produce natural monopoly. Some initial economies of scale are required to produce this result. If this is the situation, it is possible that no production at all may be possible without differentiation of the product. In other cases, the existence of more than one firm may be dependent upon differentiation of product. This is a well-known proposition in transportation and public utility economics, and can be illustrated briefly as follows. See Figure 7-3. Let BQ be the demand curve for a product, GC its long-run average cost curve by any firm and $MFDC$ the related long-run marginal cost. The simple monopoly price is OP_a and is associ-

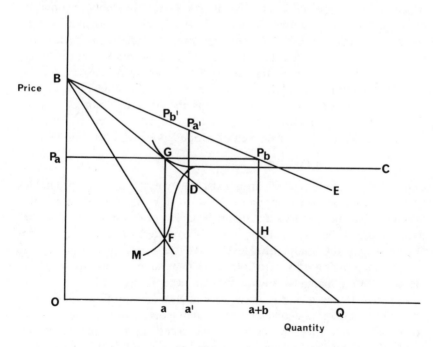

Figure 7-3

ated with quantity Oa. If the firm can achieve first-degree price discrimination which, as described in Chapter II, is equivalent to achieving complete differentiation of its product, the demand curve becomes a marginal revenue curve, because sale of an additional item does not depress the price received for the others. The firm then maximizes with a range of products selling for each price from OB to $d'D$. The average price is $d'P_a'$ which is considerably over average cost. Had the demand curve lain slightly to the left, production at a single price would have been unprofitable, but production would have been profitable with discrimination (that is, with multiple products which are joint in production.) Thus differentiation and initial economies of scale can provide a shelter from entry that allows long-term monopoly profits to exist.

In the situation illustrated, single-product monopoly yields normal profits. With multiple products, two firms can secure normal profits if they can differentiate completely without cost, so entry may occur. But it may not improve economic performance much. Each firm then produces quantity Oa for a total of $Oa+b$, prices range from B to H, for an average price of $OP_a=aG$.

The results of entry are anomalous in this case. Profits are eliminated by entry and some units are sold at low prices, but none as low as marginal cost, aF. Output is doubled, which, since marginal cost is below each price, is desirable although output remains insufficient by the usual welfare criterion that marginal cost equal price. On the other hand, consumer surplus in this industry falls, and resources are transferred from other production that yields such a surplus unless first-degree discrimination exists there also. Perhaps the most that can be said is that product differentiation that permits a larger number of firms to exist is not clearly superior on welfare grounds to simple monopoly.

1. Summary

In markets where several firms exist and where the more profitable firms produce as many subproducts as their rivals do, or more, we conclude that independent maximum behavior probably exists. On the basis of the preceding analysis, entry is expected to reduce profits to approximately the competitive level under these circumstances. There are also continuing efforts to introduce new subproducts, to supplant old ones, and to match or straddle those of other firms.

The welfare results of this activity are unclear, but profit maximization and entry produce phenomena closely analogous to those described in competitive industries by standard microeconomics. The variety of products expands and profits are reduced even when firms remain few.

While leadership and contract-curve situations are possible, the risks of collusion and entry tend to destroy them. In the absence of entry, industry profit rests upon a self-restraint of the leading firm, which is not commonly regarded as typical of American business.[4]

C. Rivalry in Selling Cost

Selling cost involves expenditures made to increase the relative desire of consumers for products. It is not strictly distinguishable from production cost, since the design, capacity, size, color, durability, and other characteristics of the product are vital "selling points." Nevertheless, the distinction is useful and important. Selling costs inform and persuade the buyer. They do not change the physical aspects of the product, its location, or its availability at a given time.

Where firms produce a full product line, there is a strong tendency for selling cost to be concentrated upon the more expensive subproducts which generally yield the largest margins. The less praise accorded to the low-price lines, the easier it is to ascribe high virtue to the higher price lines.

Although selling cost is concentrated on relatively few subproducts, all are affected. For present purposes, we take the lines of products as given and consider the effect of selling costs on the assumption that each firm makes optimum adjustments to each of its subproducts and to the selling costs of the rival firms.

The general nature of the interrelationships of selling costs is the same as of those between subproducts on Figure 7-2. A monopolist will profit from a positive expenditure for selling costs. Likewise, if a rival exists, the more a rival puts into selling costs, the more a firm will need to do to regain an optimum position. If the zero-profit point for all firms lies beyond the intersection point of their reaction functions, independent maximization will yield profits and will tend to attract additional rivals until the profits are eliminated. But if the zero-profit curves lie below the intersection point, vigorous rivalry and continuing instability are found until, perhaps, the number of firms is reduced and intersection equilibrium is established. Collusion or custom that inhibits competitive

[4] The analysis just presented may strike the reader as appropriate for game theory. The contention of this analysis is that the payoffs cannot be known with sufficient precision, particularly in the face of potential entry and a continually shifting pattern of subproducts and variants. Moreover, the lag between the introduction of a subproduct by one firm and the response of the rival which must develop a variant or reorganize his product line is necessarily too long to permit close association of decisions with payoffs. So strategic plans geared to forecasts of markets may heavily outweigh tactical plans to outmaneuver rivals. This also favors the independent maximization hypothesis.

selling expense is even less probable than is collusion to limit product lines, but it is conceivable. But in that case, custom or collusion policed by one of the stronger firms at some cost to itself must be legally possible, economically feasible in spite of the notoriously inexact nature of the relationship between selling costs and particular profit results, and desired by the stronger firm. Even then it will be abortive unless further entry can be forestalled. To list these conditions is enough to cast doubt upon the likelihood of collusive agreement in the area of selling costs. The formal analysis of selling cost is essentially identical to that of product differentiation and is not repeated here.

Selling cost rivalry may differ from subproduct rivalry in one interesting respect. In some cases, at least, it is probable that certain types of selling cost, such as advertising, are to some extent helpful to rivals because they tend to shift the demand curve for the generic product to the right as well as to provide a special advantage for the advertiser's variants. Attention is attracted to a particular class of good or service, but a rival may make the sale.

As in the case of subproducts, the tendency is similar to that of pure competition in that the activity is carried beyond the one appropriate to maximum industry profits up to the point of normal profits (point I on Figure 7-2). Again the welfare implications are ambiguous for, although the expenditures increase the total sales of the firm and the industry (in the sense of total revenue), they may also introduce or support first- or second-degree price discrimination or its equivalent.

1. A Digression on Price Relationships

The dominance of quantity leadership over price leadership is discussed in Chapter V. There attention is centered on competition between undifferentiated products. Where products are undifferentiated, only one price can exist for a given subproduct at a given time. If the products are differentiated, however, rival subproducts can sell at different prices, and indeed, if two firms produce a whole line of subproducts, small differences of prices may exist between virtual variants of each subproduct. Figure 7-4 illustrates interrelationships among prices of differentiated products, or product lines.[5]

Analysis of this figure reinforces the choice made in favor of quantity competition rather than price competition where few firms confront each

[5] This is essentially the same diagram first presented by Heinrich V. Stackelberg, *Marktform und Gleichgewicht* (Wein and Berlin: J. Springer, 1934), as summarized in William Fellner, *Competition Among the Few* (New York: Knopf, 1949), ch. iii. For a more refined treatment see Martin Shubik, *Strategy and Market Structure* (New York: John Wiley and Sons, 1959).

other in oligopolistic markets. As pointed out in Chapter V and formally demonstrated in Shubik's book, there is a specific relationship between price and quantity. If a firm chooses quantity leadership it renounces price leadership and vice versa. This figure demonstrates the relative unprofitableness of price leadership.

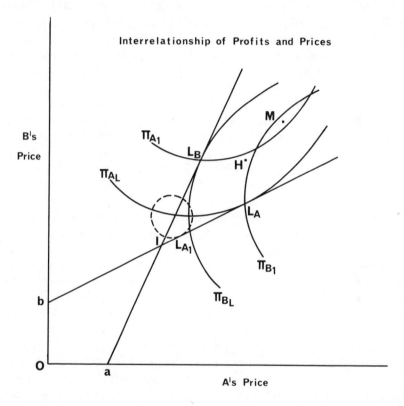

Figure 7-4

On Figure 7-4, M indicates the collusive monopoly price for a single product and may be thought of as an approximation of the simple monopoly price. Let us suppose that the zero-profit iso-profit curve for each firm passes through point I. The reaction functions denote the universally recognized condition that the higher one's rival sets his price, the higher one may profitably set his own price. Conversely, the lower the rival sets his price, the lower one is constrained to set his own. This relationship is of the same order as that for subproducts or selling costs, but in this case the tendency is for firms to lower their price in order to make inroads on rivals' markets, rather than to *raise* the number of subproducts or the amount spent on selling costs. Thus, in distinction to other situations, the higher profit positions lie above, rather than below, point I. But the paradox of leadership is the same. Firm A enjoys high profits (close to the monopoly level M) as shown by profit indifference curve πA_1 if firm B is a price leader, but considerably less than that, as shown by curve πA_L, if A assumes the burden of price leadership itself. Firm B benefits in the same way if Firm A can be made to be the price leader, as shown by the two profit indifference curves for Firm B. Both benefit from price leadership, even their own leadership (if entry is forestalled), in the sense that it is better than equilibrium at point I. But the price follower gains the most.

It is possible for each firm to be better off at its own leadership point when the products are not identical and the profit indifference curves are not symmetrical. For example, let Firm A's indifference pattern center on an iso-profit curve such as the dashed one that yields price leadership for A at L_{A1}. Firm B is better off at L_B and Firm A at L_{A1}. One would expect the lower price to dominate so L_{A1} denotes the effective price combination. But there is no reason to suppose that substantial asymmetry in price indifference curves should be typical.

As pointed out in Chapter V, price leadership is sacrificed to attain quantity leadership in situations where entry cannot be forestalled. In time, prices will approach intersection equilibrium, not because of a foolish contest to pursue one's leadership on the false assumption that the rival will not respond, but because of the entry of new firms which offer a lower price in order to make room for themselves in a market where the existing firms do not reduce output to support the market price. In terms of Figure 7-4 this causes price to fall progressively from the monopoly level to something like L_B, the price leadership point of the first entrant, Firm B, and to still lower levels as additional firms enter.[6]

D. Conclusions

Competition by means of price, by means of number of subproducts, and by means of sales expense involves the same type of interrelationships in each case. Independent maximization tends to produce lower

---

[6] It should be pointed out that if both firms were to attempt to establish their leadership positions they would establish point H which is better for both than their single leadership. But it would be unstable in the absence of agreement and some way to inhibit entry; and it would not last in the short run unless both firms reduced their outputs appropriately.

prices, higher levels of sales expense, and higher numbers of subproducts than a monopolist would find profitable. In each case, leadership tends to benefit the rival more than the leader, since it allows the rivals to hold on to a larger proportion of the market. Where rivalry takes the form of introducing subproducts or undertaking sales costs, inability to establish reasonably clear quantitative relationships between the variables and the profits of the rival firms complicates any tendency that firms might have toward collusive behavior to their mutual advantage. But this tendency is not very strong in any case because of the threat of entry and the need of the leading firms in the event of collusion to restrict their output and thereby to weaken their strategic positions.

The hypothesis of quantity leadership developed in Chapter V suggests that new entrants will tend to lead the price down, while the existing firms tend to hold to or expand their output positions. If so, there is a tendency toward intersection equilibrium for each of the three variables under consideration here. The welfare consequences of this result are mixed. Lower prices, a larger number of subproducts, and informative selling costs expand the consumers' utility frontier. To the extent that there are elements of first- and second-degree price discrimination fostered by subproduct and selling-cost competition, the utility frontier is shrunk.

Chapter VIII

Big Business and Research

This chapter examines two questions: How does market structure affect the amount of research that is conducted, and how does market structure affect the relative amounts of the various types of research that are conducted?

A. Firm-Centered Analysis Required

Research activities cannot be related to particular products in the same way that price, output, and sales policies can. The effect of research is to alter product lines, provide opportunities to enter new lines, or sell research results themselves to other firms better able to exploit new opportunities. Moreover, conglomerate firms engage extensively in research, and may have a research advantage because of their conglomerate nature. Consequently, the product-centered approach followed thus far is abandoned in favor of the traditional firm-centered approach for purposes of analyzing research.

Such a definition, however, raises serious questions about the relationship of research to monopoly or oligopoly. A conglomerate firm may be monopolistic in some markets and competitive in others. A very large firm can, in principle, even be competitive in each of its markets, and a very small firm can nonetheless be monopolistic in each of its markets.

Research is viewed as a long-standing and normal aspect of firm activity about which commercially motivated decisions are made continuously. An examination is made of the data and analyses of economists who have sought to associate the quantity of research essayed or accom-

156

plished with the size of firm. No ground is discovered that unambiguously relates research to size of firm, nor do we find that monopolistic profit provides an exceptional supply of funds nor monopolistic security an exceptional incentive to conduct research. Findings with regard to conglomerate firms are sparse but they may possess some research advantage. Interdependence is found to produce pressures that distort the kind of research conducted away from that which is socially desirable, if commercial standards are used to determine social desirability. The tendency is to put too much into development and too little into basic research. Collusion tends to increase the amount of basic research done, although not enough to reach optimal levels; but collusion will tend to reduce the amount of developmental research into suboptimal levels.

Definitional problems are involved with regard to the delineation of "research" and its major divisions, and with regard to the specific meaning which is properly attached to market structure. These problems are faced following a general statement of the economics of research.

B. Research, Profitability, and Size

Research and development are by no means new business phenomena. Product and process innovations have characterized Western business enterprise (especially in industry, transportation, and communication) for two centuries. During that time firms differing greatly in size have competed in virtually every product line, and in most cases firms of strikingly different size remain active today. Although one would scarcely expect to find full equilibrium existing at any given moment, it is reasonable to suppose that something like an optimal adjustment to research opportunities is achieved.

There is no reason to doubt that the profit motive operates in the research and development aspect in business. Studies of profit expectations related to research expenditures support this view.[1] The combina-

---

[1] Zvi Griliches finds very high rates of return to agricultural research in his "Research Costs and Social Returns: Hybrid Corn and Related Innovations," *Journal of Political Economy*, LXVI (October 1958), 419-32. Dexter Keezer, reviewing data gathered in a 1958 McGraw-Hill survey, finds that 39 per cent of the surveyed companies expect research and development expenditures to pay off in five years or less; and only 9 per cent expect the payoff to take six years or more. (See: National Science Foundation, *Proceedings of a Conference on Research and Development: Impact on the Economy*, NSF 58-36, Washington Superintendent of Documents, 1958). C. F. Carter and B. R. Williams, in a study of eighteen English firms, found ten to expect payoff in five years or less, but five companies expected ten years or more to be necessary. *Investment*

tion of long-time experience in research and in development activity for commercial purposes in the American economy would lead one to expect that optimal adjustments are approximated by the firms operating in the various industries and markets. Mansfield's study tends to confirm this expectation, for he finds that a specific model fits the entire period 1945-1959 rather well in spite of the major changes that occurred in the industries studied during that period.[2]

It is sometimes asserted that suboptimal amounts are expended on research. This view is supported by findings which show very large rates of return to research expenditures.

R. H. Elwell offers some data for the years prior to 1953.[3] He finds a close scatter between expenditures on research and development and gross national product and a somewhat less reliable relationship between research and development costs and growth rates of individual industries over the 25-year period, 1928-1953. He concludes that the return to investment in research lies between 100 per cent and 200 per cent and cites individual cases labeled "large chemical" and "major oil" which enjoyed rates of return of 200 per cent and 160 per cent.

Rates of return of this magnitude far exceed the normal returns expected from investment of funds for capital goods and, if substantiated, argue strongly in favor of the position that too little is allocated for research and development. Elwell does not distinguish between basic research and applied research and development expenditures in his statistical compilations, but he asserts that the largest returns probably come from basic research.

Zvi Griliches has also assessed the rate of return to research effort with special reference to certain agricultural products.[4] He finds the return to research in hybrid corn to be at least 700 per cent and additional agricultural research data compiled by Professor Schultz yield rates of return of 35 per cent to 171 per cent for other crops. These returns were not necessarily captured by the firms undertaking the

and Innovation (London: Oxford University Press, 1958), p. 59. Edwin Mansfield has recently published results of his econometric investigation of 35 firms in the steel, petroleum, chemical, and glass industries. He finds that expected profits, plus a time lag and an allowance for the size of the firm, yield a satisfactory explanation of the money expenditure for research and development. ("Industrial R and D Expenditures: Determinants, Prospects, and Relation to Size of Firm and Inventive Output," *Journal of Political Economy*, LXXII [August 1964], 337).

[2] *Ibid.*, p. 334.

[3] "Role of Research in Economic Growth," *Chemical and Engineering News*, XXXIII (July 18, 1955), 2980-85.

[4] *Journal of Political Economy*, LXVI, No. 5 (October, 1958), 419-32.

research and do not imply that the firms failed to push their research expenditures to the optimum level.

Edwin Mansfield's calculations for ten petroleum firms for the years 1946-1962 also indicated very high returns, averaging 40 per cent.[5]

Dexter Keezer's report cited in footnote 1 above is related more specifically to rational behavior by firms.[6] These rates of return are higher than those expected by businessmen in 1955 for investment in new plant and equipment. Keezer points out that at that time only 17 per cent expected such investment to pay off in three years or less; 69 per cent in three to five years; and fully 19 per cent expected the payout period to be six years or more. Keezer believes that the payout periods for new plant and equipment were longer in 1958 than in 1955, so that research and development is a better bargain than these figures indicate.

Although Keezer's data support those of Griliches and Elwell in a general way, one is struck by the far more modest implied rate of return.

Skepticism about the productivity of additional research is sometimes expressed. Machlup puts this case cogently.[7] He presents a priori reasons which indicate that both the supply of research talent and the supply of talent required to take advantage of an increasing flow of knowledge are likely to be quite inelastic. Carter and Williams are quoted to indicate the diminishing proportions of "firsts" won as enrollment at British universities has risen.[8] This line of reasoning cautions us not to place great reliance upon the promise of additional expenditures for research, but concedes that the allocation of funds may be somewhat short for the present.

We conclude that although rates of return to research may be higher than to investment generally, there is no compelling reason to assume that firms fail to apply commercial tests to their research activities nor that they fail to carry research to the limits justified by commercial considerations if uncertainty is taken into account. This provides a lever which enables one to analyze the questions thrown up by hypotheses

[5] Edwin Mansfield, "Rates of Return from Industrial Research and Development," *American Economic Review*, LV, No. 2 (May 1965). Mansfield does not claim a high degree of accuracy, pointing out that a one-year time lag markedly reduces the rate of return.

[6] See also, "The Outlook for Expenditures on Research and Development During the Next Decade," *American Economic Review*, L, No. 2 (May 1960), 355-69.

[7] Fritz Machlup, "The Supply of Inventors and Inventions," *The Rate and Direction of Inventive Activity* (Princeton: Princeton University Press, 1962), p. 143f.

[8] C. F. Carter and B. R. Williams, *Industry and Technical Progress* (London: Oxford University Press, 1957), pp. 90-1.

which connect size of firm, oligopoly, and monopoly with the incentive to conduct research and with efficiency in research and innovation.

C. Size and Research

J. A. Schumpeter, [9] J. S .Bain,[10] J. K. Galbraith,[11] David Lilienthal,[12] A. D. H. Kaplan,[13] J. D. Glover,[14] H. H. Villard,[15] William Baumol,[16] William Fellner,[17] D. Hamberg,[18] Ira Horowitz[19] and others have found reasons that lead them to expect the larger firms to devote the larger proportion of resources to research and innovation because of their size. Some of these writers believe that oligopoly and even monopoly power stimulates research activity by protecting its fruits and by providing larger research funds; while others stress the stimulus of competition but assert that larger firms are better able to finance research and to maintain operations of sufficient size to be efficient in research. All support the thesis that a free society tends to produce too little research and innovation because of benefits external to the firm and the limited time horizons of firms. Richard R. Nelson has given the most explicit statement of this point of view in regard only to basic research where, under strictly defined conditions, the performance of any basic research by profit-oriented enterprise can be taken as an indication of insufficient total investment in basic research.[20]

[9] J. A. Schumpeter, *Capitalism, Socialism, and Democracy* (New York: Harper, 1942).

[10] J. S. Bain, *Pricing, Distribution and Employment* (New York: Wiley, 1953).

[11] J. K. Galbraith, *American Capitalism: The Concept of Countervailing Power* (Boston: Houghton-Mifflin, 1952).

[12] David Lilienthal, *Big Business: A New Era* (New York: Harper, 1952).

[13] A. D. H. Kaplan, *Big Enterprise in a Competitive System* (Washington, D.C.: Brookings Institution, 1954).

[14] J. D. Glover, *The Attack on Big Business* (Boston: Harvard University Press, 1954).

[15] H. H. Villard, "Competition, Oligopoly and Research," *Journal of Political Economy*, LXVI (December 1958), 483-97; and *Economic Performance* (New York: Rinehart, 1959), ch. iv.

[16] William Baumol, *Business Behavior, Value and Growth* (New York: Macmillan, 1959).

[17] William Fellner, "The Influence of Market Structure on Technological Research," *Quarterly Journal of Economics*, LXV, No. 4 (reprinted in George Stocking and Richard Heflebower A.E.A. Readings, *Readings in Industrial Organization and Public Policy*, Vol. VIII [Homewood, Ill.: Irwin, 1958]).

[18] Donald Hamberg, "Size of Firm, Oligopoly, and Research," *The Canadian Journal of Economics and Political Science*, XXX, No. 1 (February 1964).

[19] Ira Horowitz, "Firm Size and Research Activity," *The Southern Economic Journal*, XXVIII, No. 3 (January 1962).

[20] R. R. Nelson, "The Simple Economics of Basic Research," *Journal of Political Economy*, LXVII, No. 3 (June 1959), 304-5.

Ten reasons have been advanced which associate size of firm positively with inventive activity, research and development.

1. Economies of scale in research and development exist.
2. Research is an outlet for monopoly profits that may yield a good
   financial return and will tend to enhance the status and accept-
   ability of the firm in the eyes of possible critics.
3. Monopolistically or oligopolistically insulated markets for final
   products of a firm provide additional security for profits of innovation, thereby stimulating research leading to innovation.
4. Diversity of output (conglomerateness) enhances the alertness to,
   and possible range of, the usefulness of accidental inventions.
5. Quality of management that is itself progressive can encompass
   disparate organizational forms and attitudes of personnel without
   blighting them.
6. The uncertainty of invention is converted to virtually predictable
   risks.
7. The technology already in use approaches the limits of scientific
   knowledge, raising the probable returns to research for some firms.
8. The firm needs to appear progressive in order to win business.
9. Public support is lacking for aid to big businesses when they suffer
   from declining markets.
10. The motivations of firms differ with size and market power.

Each of these implies some relationship between research activity and
costs and/or revenues.

The principal evidence offered is a positive relationship between size
of firm and actual expenditures for research. This relationship is a
prominent feature of the findings of the National Science Foundation
where firms are grouped into broad size catagories.

But the mere fact that larger firms devote a larger proportion of their
expenditures or manpower to research does not establish any meaningful
relationship between size of firm and research. Certain lines of activity
can be expected to yield greater returns to research effort than others.
Some of these lines may have production costs suitable to large-scale
production while others do not. More importantly, specialization within
fields can be expected to include some firms which are active in the
areas where research is relatively important, while others are active in
branches of the industry where it is not. Private firms have participated in
research activity for a long time. If there have been advantages attain-
able by research, then the laggard researchers will have shrunk in relative
size. On the other hand, if money has been more profitably invested

elsewhere, those which invested in research will have shrunk. Over time, market forces tend to produce an optimum level of research as well as an optimum size of firm in every part of the productive process.

The key question to be answered is this: Do the ten points just listed provide evidence that too much or too little research is conducted (1) *because* of the size distribution of firms, or (2) *because* of the existence of monopolistic, oligopolistic, or competitive structures of markets? We consider the effect of size distribution first.

The size of the total enterprise, not its position in specific markets, is regarded as relevant here because research is not necessarily or even typically devoted to a particular product line and because the total financial strength of the company is thought to be relevant. The firm is thought of as a multiproduct enterprise as in previous chapters, but attention is focused on the aggregate position of the firm rather than on its activities in particular markets.

1. Economies of Scale to Research

Research activity is one of the productive activities of firms. There is no more reason to assume that firms must be vertically integrated so as to produce their own research than there is to assume that they must produce the other inputs of their productive process.

It is often asserted that economies of scale exist in the conduct of research. This is undoubtedly correct for some types of research, notably those which require very expensive equipment, although it may not be true as a general statement. Contrary to the common opinion, economy of scale in the conduct of research need have no influence on the size of operating companies if a good market exists for research results. If there are continuing economies of scale in research, firms specializing in research are able to produce research results more economically than are operating companies. One must expect the research industry to be monopolistic under this circumstance, but the size distribution of the research users is then unaffected by economies of research.

The fact that so many operating companies engage in research is evidence that the economies of scale in research, if any, are modest or are offset by other factors that affect profit. Suppose that economies of scale in research do exist. What can account for the fact that many firms of all sizes do engage in research?

Even small firms will elect to conduct their own research, in spite of economies of scale that would otherwise make it more economical to have their research conducted in large enterprises specialized in a research business, if research is a joint cost or if it is a joint product. In the former case, the conduct of research lowers other costs of production, and in the latter case it expands the demand function. Both of these sources of jointness exist.

The most important reason for the vertical integration of the research input with the output of the firm is the high cost of information and other marketing costs associated with the transfer of research results from an independent firm conducting research to the research user. The cost is high because the product (research) is highly heterogeneous and its value inferential in nature. Looked at in this way, there are no economies of scale in the production of research because the unavoidable marketing costs *are* costs, and because they are sufficient to offset, or more than offset, the economies of scale in the conduct of research per se. But they amount to market imperfections that can be circumvented by integration of research into the relevant operating companies. A firm conducting its own research will have lower costs than a similar firm that buys the research results that it needs.

If economies of scale in research exist, and if jointness exists, then the larger firm doing its own research should have an advantage over a smaller firm doing its own research.

It is, therefore, reasonable to expect that economies of scale in the conduct of research will result in the decline in importance of smaller firms, a rising importance of the largest firms, and a highly skewed distribution of research expenditures among firms of different sizes. These trends and distributions should go back as far as business records go, because of the rising importance of research. The trends in the survival and growth of firms by size must be regarded as more significant than the relative expenditures for research because a presumption must be made that the market tends to direct firms of all sizes in each market to undertake the appropriate amount of research activity. Surviving firms, by hypothesis, have taken better advantage of their opportunities, including research opportunities.

Many factors other than research efficiency affect trends in the survival of firms of different sizes. Nevertheless, studies cited in previous chapters indicate a wide range of optimal sizes and no trend in the relative size of firms strong enough to be unambiguously detected. This provides implicit evidence that either economies of scale in the conduct of research are not found in all industries or that such economies are often offset by diseconomies of scale in other parts of the joint production effort. The possibility remains that economies of scale associated with joint costs remain in particular research-oriented industries. If so, large firms enjoy substantial advantages in those industries. If that is the case, industries which are research oriented will be populated over-whelmingly by large firms. A corollary of this proposition is that small firms will be found where research is not important. The validity of this thesis can be tested by ascertaining whether or not those firms which conduct research at all tend to be large. Any general presumption favoring economies of scale to research must fall if smaller firms which conduct research are as research intensive as the larger firms, and if in each size class we find some research-intensive firms and some which conduct little or no research. National Science Foundation data show this to be the case.

The National Science Foundation publishes data by size class of firm in each major industrial class which show the percentage of employees (1) who are scientists and engineers and (2) are devoted primarily to research and development, and (3) the percentage of firms which engage in some research and development activity. There are five size classes of firms ranging from "under 100" to "5,000 and more," and data are given for sixteen industry classes. Thus when data are given for each size class and each industry class, sixty-four comparisons of relative research effort by size of firm are possible.[21]

These data show that the next larger size class is not always more research intensive. In fourteen of the sixty-four comparisons, scientists and engineers were a smaller percentage of total employees in the next larger size class of firm. In the more relevant instance where attention is focused on the percentage of scientists and engineers engaged primar-ily in research and development, the percentage fell in twenty-seven of the fifty-eight cases where comparison is possible.

These facts are obscured in most summary tables by the rising per-centage of large firms that conduct some research, for in sixty-three of sixty-four cases a larger proportion of the firms in the next larger size class engaged in some research or development activity.

These data can be used to test the hypothesis under consideration, namely that economies of scale to research are probably small. If one multiplies the percentage of scientists and engineers employed by the

[21] National Science Foundation, *Scientific and Technical Personnel in Ameri-can Industry*, NSF 60-62, (Washington: U.S. Superintendent of Documents, 1962). Data showing the number of scientists and engineers as a percentage of total employment are shown on p. 29; those showing the percentage of scientists and engineers primarily engaged in research and development on p. 37; and data showing the percentage of companies of a given size class that engage in research and development activity on p. 27. The weakest link for present purposes is in the second step, where data for six categories are omitted because less than 50 cases are found. Ten additional cases are said to have standard errors of 50 per cent or more.

percentage of these employed in research and development work, the percentage of personnel employed in research and development is ascertained. It is found that larger firms devote relatively more employees to this function in 29 of 54 cases, the same percentage in 9 cases, and fewer in 16. If the numbers so employed are divided among the firms in each size class according to the number of firms actually engaged in some research and development activity it turns out that larger firms employed a larger proportion of their employees in research and development work in only 22 of the 54 cases. About the same proportion was employed in 5 cases, and fewer in 27 cases. If one omits the instances where one or both members of the size classes are subject to an error of estimate of 50 per cent or more, there are 21 instances where the larger firms directed a larger proportion of their employees to research and development activity, 21 instances where they devoted a smaller proportion, and 5 where the proportion is the same. Table VIII-1 summarizes these results.

A striking finding is the high percentage of research and development personnel in the smallest size group. Although the average for all firms employing scientists and engineers in research and development work is 1.0 per cent, the average for such firms with fewer than 100 employees is 3.1 per cent, the highest of any size group. This is true of each of the twelve industry groups for which data are given. One interpretation that may be placed on this finding is that *small* research-oriented firms have a competitive advantage. Such a finding is consistent with the rapid development of small research companies near major academic centers in recent years and the existence of relatively small research institutes attached to associations of producers.

A second striking finding is that more than 10 per cent of the firms with 5,000 employees or more conducted no research. Such firms operate in the food and kindred products; stone, clay, and glass; other manufacturing; transportation and other public utility; and other non-manufacturing industries. Again this is consistent with the hypothesis that the appropriate intensity of research work differs from industry to industry and that economies of scale of research are not substantial. Disaggregation of the sixteen industry classes is necessary if economies of scale, or lack of them, are to be definitively established, but these data tend to confirm the hypothesis that they do not exist. Jacob Schmookler comes to much the same conclusion from his analysis of six industry classes using 1953 data.[22]

[22] Jacob Schmookler, "Bigness, Fewness and Research," *Journal of Political Economy*, LXVII, No. 6 (December 1959).

Table VIII-1

Scientists and Engineers Primarily Engaged in Research and Development as a
Percentage of Total Employment in Companies Doing Some Research,
By Size of Company and Industry, January, 1959*

Industry	All Companies	Companies with Total Employment of					Range—Largest Firms[a]
		Under 100	100-499	500-999	1000-4999	5000 and more	
All Industries	1.0	3.1	.9	1.1	1.0	2.0	—
Food and kindred products	.3	[b]	.45	.34	.38	.62	.04-4.35
Textile mill products and apparel	.1	[b]	.54	[b]	.2	.2	—
Paper and allied products	.4	[b]	.25	.2 [c]	.6	.2	—
Chemicals and allied products	3.7	6.4	3.5	3.8	3.8	3.6	.9-10.94
Petroleum products and extraction	1.4	3.8[c]	.4	1.2	2.4	1.8	.47-5.85
Stone, clay, and glass products	.3	1.7[c]	.5[c]	.4	.5	.5	.27-3.96
Primary metal industries	.5	1.9[c]	.4	.4	.8	.5	.12-2.36
Fabricated metal products and ordnance	1.6	4.5[c]	.9	.3	1.7	3.0	—
Machinery (except electrical)	1.7	7.3	1.2	1.1	1.2	2.4	.3-9.5
Electrical equipment	4.3	7.8	2.4	4.8	2.5	5.7	.33-20.11
Aircraft and parts	6.8	7.8	2.2	7.3	4.9	7.4	—
Professional and scientific instruments	3.6	13.7	4.7	1.9	3.2	4.8	—
Other manufacturing industries	.6	1.6	.4	.2	.6	1.4	—
Construction	1.5	6.2[c]	[b]	[b]	.4	1.2	—
Transportation and other public utilities	.1	[b]	[b]	.8	.1	.1	.14-9.18
Other nonmanufacturing industries	.2	1.3	.5	1.0	.9	.3	—

* Computed from Table A-4 and A-13 of NSF 60-62 cited in footnote VIII-19.
[a] Worley, *JPE* (April 1961), p. 185. (Number of firms ranges from 16 to 29)
[b] Less than 50 cases.
[c] Subject to error of 50 per cent or more in one series (in addition to the error involved in multiplying rounded series).

Firms with 5,000 employees are not small, but the larger firms are giants compared to this lower limit. These data do not exclude the possibility that some advantages of scale accrue to the truly giant firms and that the advantage is largely concealed in an average which includes all firms with 5,000 or more employees. J. S. Worley studied the relationship between size and research and development expenditures by 198 very large firms.[23] He found that the percentage of research personnel among total employees varied over an extremely broad range in each of the eight industry classes examined. Moreover, he found the middle-sized firms among the largest 25 or so to be the most research intensive. The ranges found by Worley are shown in the last column of Table VIII-1. The relationship between size of firm and percentage of research and development personnel was positive and significant at the 5 per cent level for petroleum and at the 10 per cent level for electrical machinery. In the other six cases, the relationship was more uncertain, but in every case some of the largest firms devoted a much smaller share of their personnel to research and development than did the *average* firm with fewer than 100 or from 100 to 499 employees in the same industry class. Again the evidence is against any general relationship between size of firm and efficiency of research and development expenditures.

F. M. Scherer correlates the number of patents awarded and, alternatively, the employment of research and development personnel with firm size as measured by sales.[24] The relationship is found to be sensitive to the exclusion of instances of a zero level of activity by some firms, and to atypical behavior by single large firms in particular major industry groups. Scherer concludes that gigantic scale is not an essential condition for vigorous industrial research and development activity, and may even reduce its level. With the exception of chemicals, which show increasing research activity with size, all of the regressions presented have inflection points, and four of the seven show a negative relationship at high levels of sales. The positive relationships usually shown for sales levels between zero and $200 to $600 million are, with one exception, small and of questionable statistical significance.

Mansfield finds no consistent relationship between size of firm and

[23] J. S. Worley, "Industrial Research and the New Competition," *Journal of Political Economy*, LXIX, No. 2 (April 1961).

[24] F. M. Scherer, "Size of Firm, Oligopoly, and Research: A Comment," *The Canadian Journal of Economics and Political Science*, XXXI, No. 2 (May 1965). While ostensibly a review of Hamberg's article (*op. cit.* note 18) this is essentially an article on its own merit, which makes important methodological and substantive points.

expenditures for research and development as a percentage of sales. A positive relationship is found in chemical industries; a significant negative relationship is found for petroleum, drug, and glass-producing firms; and a statistically insignificant negative one for steel. He also finds that by the test of production of significant innovations, economies of scale to research and development inputs do exist among the industries tested only in the case of chemicals.[25] Worley's findings thus acquire added support, and it seems unlikely that strong economies of scale to research and development among the largest firms exist at all as a general phenomenon. That it may be strong enough to offset the findings for the whole spectrum of firm size, given above, is most improbable.

a. Economies of Scale: Summary

To summarize, economy of scale to research and development does not of itself constitute a reason why large operating firms should conduct research. The National Science Foundation has not found large companies which specialize in the production of research results for sale to operating companies. This fact implies that any economies of scale that may exist must be less than the gains which accrue to firms that combine smaller research efforts with the production of other goods and services. It is probable that imperfections in the market for research results convert research into an input which is joint with other productive inputs. If this is the case, and if economies of scale to research and development do exist, the larger firms should exhibit a competitive advantage in the production of their final products. Moreover, one would expect the larger firms to devote relatively more of their resources to research. Neither of these results is found. Data presented in earlier chapters suggest the continuing coexistence of firms of grossly different size in most industries, indicating small or nonexistent competitive advantage of size. Data summarized in this chapter show very wide differences in the expenditure for research in every size category. Economies of scale to research greater than the gain associated with research as a joint input even in small firms is not consistent with the evidence. An alternative hypothesis that research payoffs differ within and among particular industries—so that commercially-oriented firms acting efficiently will conduct much, little, or no research depending upon their positions and circumstances—is consistent with the evidence.

[25] Edwin Mansfield, *Journal of Political Economy,* LXXII, No. 4 (August, 1964), 336-37. Jora Minasian, however, finds no statistically significant relationship between size of firm and research expenditures in the chemical industry. See his "The Economics of Research and Development," *The Rate and Direction of Inventive Activity,* pp. 125-30.

2. Suboptimum Size of Firm and Research

If firm size is unrelated to efficiency in research, a paradoxical relationship between survival rates and optimal sizes of firm revealed by empirical studies can be explained.[26] Smaller firms are shown to have higher costs on the average, but nevertheless to survive. Collectively, they account for a substantial share of output in their industry classes. The relative ability of firms of different sizes to apply the insurance principle to research may account for this. The commercial value of any specific research project is dubious. But the commercial value of a large number of projects is reasonably certain within a moderate range of error. Small firms, therefore, experience both exceptionally high and exceptionally low returns. Were there no bias in recording, one would expect that the average returns would be the same for firms of all sizes unless scale economies or diseconomies exist. Sources of bias do exist which have contrary pulls. The costs incurred by small firms may be understated because individual research effort tends not be counted. Moreover, losses are cut by failures, while gains continue. On the other hand, successes often result in expansion so that the successful firm is no longer categorized as small. Finally, firms often undertake operations at a loss when breaking into a field or embarking on expansion. When firms are small, such losses tend to dominate the firms' balance sheets. Failure rates of small firms will be high, so that a survival test of optimum size applied to existing firms in given size categories would show them to be suboptimal. But although the identity of the firms changes, each size class continues to exist.

If there are economies of scale in research, larger firms tend to have an advantage. In addition, investors may prefer to invest in firms large enough to apply the insurance principle to research rather than spreading their investments among a sufficient number of smaller firms so as to achieve the same end. If they do, economies of scale are introduced although actual money costs may be the same.

The fact that firms in each size class conduct research and that firms in each size class continue to exist suggests that such economies of scale are small or nonexistent and not continuous as size of firm increases.

D. Size and Research: Reasons Other Than Economies of Scale

The remaining reasons offered to associate the size of a firm's research effort to its size may be grouped as resting upon jointness of research with conglomerate final products, jointness of research with sales oppor-

[26] See Chapter V, p. 86.

tunities, and incorrect arguments. When cogent, these apply with different force to different industries and industry groups and may help explain the variety of experience found in modern industry.

1. Research as a Joint Input and Size of Firm

Three of the ten arguments relating size of firm positively to the proportion of expenditures devoted to research and development rest upon the jointness of research with other inputs. Perhaps the most important of these is related to conglomerateness of output. It has two aspects which encompass two of the arguments. They are jointness with conglomerate output and jointness with the type of managerial skill necessary to the efficient management of a conglomerate firm.

Size may be related to the ability of firms to profit from research in spite of the absence of economies of scale in research if the larger firms produce a conglomeration of unrelated products. The survey of 5-digit data analyzed in previous chapters is consistent with such a result, because the larger firms were found to have the greater diversity of products. This relationship may also have gone undetected in Table VIII-1 because firms whose output is concentrated in one product are not treated separately from large firms whose principal product is in an industry but which have many products.

Three explanations have been advanced to account for the advantage that large conglomerate firms are said to have. They are: (1) jointness with (temporary) monopoly or oligopoly power in particular markets which ensures and enlarges the return to research, (2) jointness of research with diversity of product lines due to the special kind of managerial skill required for the conduct of conglomerate enterprise, and (3) the greater likelihood that commercial possibilities will be recognized in laboratory findings when the firm is conglomerate, thus providing more tinder upon which the creative spark of new knowledge may fall. We discuss these in the reverse order.

If the commercial potential of research findings is enhanced when research is conducted by the same firm that may produce the commercial product it must be because information flows more readily within a firm than it does between firms, or because the management encounters less resistance to innovations which originate within the firm as compared to those which originate from without. No research advantage would be enjoyed by a conglomerate firm in the absence of economies of scale in research if a perfect market for research results existed. But perfect markets are uncommon. The research market may be imperfect because a possible use must be envisioned for a research result before one can expect to merchandise it.

The degree of abstract imagination available, notoriously imperfect in any case, must be even less adequate where the selling firm has experience only in a single line of products. Moreover, the normal resistance of production departments to innovation may well be more effective when pitted against the purchase of a disturbing innovation than it can be in combatting company-produced information to which considerable company funds have already been committed. The lack of uniformity of the definitions of 5- and 7-digit products prevents an adequate test of this hypothesis, but it may be that a reasonably close relationship exists between diversity of product line and at least some types of research and development activity. This hypothesis has not, to the author's knowledge, been tested statistically.

Research and development can, as shown earlier, be a form of production in its own right. The kind of managerial skill required for the successful operation of a conglomerate enterprise, such as the selection of high grade personnel and the substantial decentralization of control, is similar to that required to encompass a research department. Carter and Williams list twenty-four characteristics that distinguish progressive from unprogressive firms.[27] Many items are related to alertness to new information, selection and motivation of staff, willingness to take new knowledge on license and to enter into joint ventures, high status for science and technology, and other characteristics which suggest a sensitive, rational approach to business and organizational problems.

One would expect firms characterized by such managements to grow and thus become larger than others. Quality of management is difficult to quantify directly, but fourteen of Carter and Williams' twenty-four points can be objectively observed, and each is widely useful in multi-product industry. Thus quality of management and conglomerateness tend to reinforce each other in providing hospitable conditions for research.

2. Monopoly, Oligopoly, and Research

A third argument that rests on jointness with inputs is the Schumpeterian one, echoed by many others, which asserts that monopolistic or oligopolistic markets for final products offer short-term protection of profits, thereby stimulating research. This is thought to be desirable

[27] Carter and Williams, *Industry and Technical Progress,* ch. xvi.

because social benefits from added research exceed private benefits as rivals come to utilize the research results. The argument when applied to the size of firms involves two questionable logical steps: (1) that absolutely large firms are required if monopoly or oligopoly is to exist in the relevant markets, and (2) that research is a joint output.

This argument is without force unless jointness exists, because without it, the market relevant to this claim would be research itself rather than some ultimate product embodying the research findings. No need for monopoly or oligopoly in the product markets would be then germane.

Monopolistic or oligopolistic protection of markets which has the effect of prolonging the period of exceptional profit on innovations may be associated sufficiently with size to produce the general but imprecise relationship between research and size that has been observed. This view of temporary monopoly is vigorously espoused by Schumpeter, and underlies the philosophy of the patent system. However, there is no direct connection between size of firm and control over specific products. The data reviewed in chapters I and II reveal striking degrees of market concentration and disparity of firm size in particular markets usually characterized as competitive in structure and performance. Since markets vary so much in size, Schumpetrian monopoly can exist for firms of small size concentrated in a particular market more readily than for a larger firm participating in many markets. Data do not exist which would enable one to make a broad study of monopoly of particular products and their effect on a firm's propensity to invest in research and development. However, Harberger's and Schwartzman's articles cited previously, and the theory favoring quantity (as opposed to price) competition developed in Chapter V, suggest that neither size nor monopoly produces large distortions. M. J. Peck's study of the aluminum industry suggests that the threat involved in the postwar development of oligopoly out of the formerly monopolistic industry structure had the effect of stimulating rather than retarding invention and innovation.[28] His Table 1 indicates that the largest single number of innovations is attributable to the equipment manufacturers—firms which are small, relative to their customers, and comparatively numerous.[29] Their innovations may well have been stimulated by the availability of patent protection. But Schumpeter's argument favoring large size and monopolistic power is not helped much by patent monopoly, since patents are available to firms of all sizes.

Jointness with monopoly, at least as it is related to size, may plausibly

[28] M. J. Peck, *Rate and Direction*, pp. 294-6.
[29] *Ibid.*, p. 285.

be related to public relations. Monopoly profits, when available, may be directed to research beyond the level indicated by profits attributable to products and processes because it is believed that high research and development expenditures are socially acceptable and will protect the company against the ill-will of consumers, lawmakers, administrators, and opinion-makers. If this is the case, rising profits will tend to precede rising expenditures for research. The only data relating directly to this hypothesis of which I am aware are presented by Minasian, who finds a strong relationship in the chemical industry which runs from research to productivity to profitability, and not in the opposite direction.[30] His data, taken from a single industry, cannot be conclusive, but strong evidence from an industry so closely connected to research carries weight.

The final type of jointness makes research and development something of a sales expense. In certain important industries, especially those selling to the Defense Department, active research may be valuable in attracting orders although it bears tangentially, if at all, on the commercial or military work done by the enterprise. Especially where a choice must be made between competent rivals, the respectability of the firm's research organization may be considered favorably. Indeed, the fact that the effort includes interesting projects of basic (noncommercial) interest may confer a crucial margin of prestige.

If this speculation is well founded, the buyer apparently regards the purchase as a joint purchase of a product plus a research effort which may have an undeterminable value. I am aware of no test that has been made of this hypothesis.

3. Other Arguments

Carter and Williams find that the amount and nature of a firm's basic research effort is related to the closeness of the industry to the frontiers of research relevant to its operation.[31] This is rational if the market for research results is imperfect, because basic research is less likely to produce results immediately useful to the firm. As long as a substantial pool of potentially useful knowledge is at hand to refresh applied and developmental research, virtually no commercial motive can be served by engaging in basic research. The better the market for research results, the wider the possible range for their internal application, and the

---

[30] "Economics of Research," p. 95. He states, "We can conclude from this study that, beyond reasonable doubt, causality runs from research and development to productivity, and finally to profitability."

[31] Carter and Williams, *Industry and Technical Progress*, ch. v.

greater the paucity of pure knowledge available, the greater are the potential returns from basic research.

There is less reason, however, to suppose that the intensity of the total research effort need be increased because of the paucity of unexploited knowledge. Applied and developmental research is by far the larger part of the research budget. And there is less reason still to relate closeness to the boundaries of knowledge with the size of firm. Small firms, even individuals, conduct basic research. The very nature of large-scale production implies operations some distance from the frontiers of knowledge. Carter and Williams' point is relevant to the division of the research budget between types of research, the central issue in the second section of this chapter.

It has been argued that the profitability of research is affected by the size of firms because the incentives and pressures under which managements operate differ according to the structure of their industries. Specifically, Villard argues that "competitive oligopolies" are most likely to maximize research and development in a free economy. "Competitive oligopoly" involves both bigness in some absolute sense, and fewness in a market. One of the social advantages of this market structure is said to be a lack of public sympathy and official protective action when one or another of the firms gets into trouble. Thus pressures are retained which stimulate efficient performance at times when combination or collusion would be publicly acceptable and quite possibly governmentally sponsored and enforced if many small businesses were involved.

Villard's argument rests on the assumption that competitive oligopolies enjoy higher profits than do smaller firms. If this is not so, harassment of the larger firms must make them less profitable and they would tend to disappear from the scene. On the basis of our findings, no superior efficiency of larger firms can be associated with firms simply because of their size, and a disproportionate research effort by competitive oligopolies can only reduce their profits.

Nevertheless, Villard is on strong ground when he argues that efficiency is well served by letting adjustments occur, and that big business may enjoy a smaller store of good will upon which it may draw to protect itself from the consequences of inefficiency. But the latter consideration provides no basis for pushing research and development beyond the point where its net marginal return is equal to the net marginal return to other expenditures. Therefore, there is no reason based on profit maximization for a competitive oligopoly to spend more on research than is spent by firms in different market situations.

Finally, one may doubt that the giant firm is actually at a disadvantage if it calls to Government for aid in a moment of peril. The Reconstruction Finance Corporation inaugurated under President Hoover and expanded by President Roosevelt is a case in point. Recently there has been much talk of the responsibility that "ought" to be assumed by the Federal Government for firms that have grown up around major defense contractors. Much of this arose from broadly based groups not associated with the managements of the large firms involved.

Pressures to aid business, great or small, are much less when the firms and employees have alternatives. Thus among large firms, less concern is expressed for those suffering poor markets for one or another of its products if the firm is conglomerate. Contrast the lack of concern about the great decline in Buick sales in the 1950's as compared to the attention given the fortunes of Studebaker or some of the American watch companies at about the same time. Conglomerateness when added to size may carry the virtue of public pressure that enforces independence, efficiency, and active research.

J. Jewkes, D. Sawers, and R. Stillerman also examine the effect of size and structure upon pressures and incentives to innovate which arise within business itself.[32] They conclude that research is stimulated: (1) more as a firm fears being surpassed by another; (2) less as it fears that its research results will be lost to a rival (dispossession); and (3) more if it believes that it can expand, presumably at the expense of rivals. The effect of market structure is determined by considering the position of an individual firm placed alternatively in a monopoly, an oligopoly, and a competitive industry. Jewkes, Sawers, and Stillerman conclude that, relatively speaking, monopolists are stimulated by the second motive, lack of fear of dispossession; that oligopolists are stimulated by fear of being supplanted, but that competitors are stimulated both by fear of being supplanted and by hope of expansion. These authors conclude, therefore, that competition is the more desirable form of organization if one wishes to stimulate technological development.

An examination of the three stimuli suggests an alternative conclusion. Consider the fear of being surpassed. Firms in any of the three market structures may be surpassed by a new product or process, but the monopolist is undoubtedly the most secure of the three and can afford to take the most complacent attitude toward innovation by others. But the competitive firm and the oligopolist are not equally insecure if we may assume industries which are of equal dynamism. The competitive

[32] J. Jewkes, *et al., The Sources of Invention* (New York: St. Martin's Press, 1958), pp. 167f and 178f.

firm is more narrowly specialized and is less able, for example, to undertake the expense of researching "second best alternatives" and patenting
them—as, for example, Du Pont did to protect its position in moisture-
proof cellophane. The smaller firm is, for lack of financial resources,
also less able to expand rapidly to take advantage of a new product or
process. The larger firm is also more likely to produce a variety of
product lines, and thereby be less vulnerable to the loss of any particular
one of them should a rival succeed in some market. Consequently, it
seems reasonable to assign rank weight of 1, 2, and 3 to the urgency to
innovate felt by monopolists, oligopolists, and competitors, respectively,
as a result of their fears of being surpassed.

The same considerations suggest that monopolists will fear (uncom-
pensated) loss of information to rivals the least, oligopolists rather
more, and competitors the most, suggesting weights of 3, 2, and 1 respectively for the second desideratum. This order of stimulus is also in
accord with the commonly observed ability of larger firms to avail themselves of legal protection and to harass rivals in patent cases.

Finally, it is clear that monopolies have the more limited ability to
expand in their existing product lines. But what may be said of competitors versus oligopolists? Competitors surely have the most room for
expansion. Nevertheless, it seems incongruous to hold with Jewkes,
Sawers, and Stillerman that oligopolists must fear being surpassed but
lack an opportunity to expand. When one oligopolist surpasses another,
one expects it to take over part of the rival's market and thus to expand.
It is true that the oligopolist may be in a better position to defend his
market than would a competitor, for his reputation imparts a certain
inertia to the market, and as Jewkes, Sawers, and Stillerman say, new
products may be met in part by price cuts and sales efforts. On the
other hand, the ability of an oligopolist to expand (in an absolute sense)
when profitable opportunity arises surely exceeds that of the competitor.
Size and competence of management, credit, and the ability to expand
by merger weigh heavily in the ability to expand. Because many product
and process opportunities require expansion well beyond the ability of a
small firm, while even minor ideas can be adopted by larger firms, the
larger firm enjoys a relative advantage. Thus the oligopolist rather than
the competitor is the more likely to be able to take advantage of the
ideas that may call for expansion. The weights for the third stimulus,
therefore, are monopoly, 1; competition, 2; and oligopoly, 3. The
summed weights are 6, 7, and 5 for competition, oligopoly, and monopoly
respectively. By this test, assuming each of these influences to carry
equal weight, some tendency for oligopolies to conduct a disproportion-

ate amount of research exists quite apart from consideration of economies of scale, jointness of research with inputs or outputs, or pressures from public opinion or government.

E. Conclusions

The implicit conclusion from all this is that no substantial advantages of size are present. Instead, there is reason to suppose that the size distribution of firms in the various industries reflects total efficiency, including efficiency in the conduct of research and the utilization of research results. Research seems to be a joint input or a joint output.

Nor does the degree of monopoly play an important role. The finding of the NBER Conference on Inventive Activity as stated by Zvi Griliches is, in general, supported and extended to research and development generally. While somewhat differing views were expressed by other participants, he states, "Whatever evidence we have . . . points to no particular relationship between monopoly, oligopoly, or competition and inventive activity. Neither the empirical evidence nor the theoretical discussion has established the presumption of a correlation between the degree of market control and the rate of inventive activity.[33] This statement relates to aggregate expenditures. It does not rule out distortions in the type of research. The probability that the market structure upsets the appropriate balance among the various types of research is discussed subsequently in this chapter.

F. Type of Research Affected by Interdependence

Research covers a wide range of human activity. It is quite possible that monopolistic or oligopolistic pressures shift resources from one type of research to another. In recent years the definitions of types used by the National Science Foundation have come into general use. Research activity is classified as "basic," "applied," and "development" and is contrasted on the one hand to engineering, and on the other to business innovational activity such as market research that involves neither processes nor products.[34]

[33] Zvi Griliches, *Rate and Direction,* p. 353. Two contributors to the conference might disagree with this statement. Kenneth J. Arrow (especially pp. 619-22) comes to the conclusion that social benefit of research exceeds private under competitive conditions and even more so under monopolistic ones. His conclusions, however, rest on purely abstract grounds. Jora Minasian offers some evidence that may indicate that the degree of monopoly has increased in the chemical industry as a result of a growing percentage of new products in the product mix which tend to yield temporary monopoly prices.

[34] The National Science Foundation definitions read as follows:

"Basic Research—Research projects which represent original investigation for

We contend that it is more fruitful to classify research into two categories rather than the three employed by the National Science Foundation. Part of the reason is that the distinctions between the various types of research are, nevertheless, difficult to draw. This is particularly true of the distinction between basic and applied research where the motivation of the research organization is decisive. Both types of research are directed to the discovery of new knowledge, the former without a commercial object and the latter with one. But even development which creates a new product or process out of accumulated knowledge also requires skills and qualities of mind that make probable the discovery of ideas and application that may be as fruitful for processes and products not included in the research objective as for those included. Thus Du Pont's investigation of nitro-cellulose for photographic film accidentally led to the development of Duco lacquers, and systematic research with tetrafluorethylene as a refrigerant produced an accidental discovery of the plastic Teflon.[35] These investigations may be classified as a development according to the accepted definitions, although the fortuitous outcomes suggest applied research. Business executives have commented upon the necessity of abandoning ordinary commercial tests when attempting to evaluate basic research. The following comments are typical of one view of research. Elisha Gray, II, president of Whirlpool-Seeger Corporation writes:

> First, research and development as practiced by aggressive companies is our most profitable frontier for the investment of money. . . . Any producing company which lacks research and development has virtually no chance for survival in the competitive struggle for the consumer market.
>
> By its very nature, pure research lacks the element upon which the ordinary management decision can be exercised. . . . Maybe we ought to be allocating a percentage of our research dollars in the pursuit of funda-

---

the advancement of scientific knowledge and which do not have specific commercial objectives, although they may be in fields of present or potential interest to the reporting company.

"Applied Research—Research projects which represent investigation directed to discovery of new scientific knowledge and which have specific commercial objectives with respect to either products or processes.

"Development Research—Technical activity concerned with non-routine problems which are encountered in translating research findings or other general scientific knowledge into products or processes." (Instructions for Survey of Industrial Research and Development During 1959, U.S. Department of Commerce, Bureau of the Census), Form RD-1, (April 26, 1960).

[35] Willard F. Mueller, "The Origins of the Basic Inventions Underlying Du Pont's Major Product and Process Innovations," *Rate and Direction of Inventive Activity*, pp. 326-27, 338.

mental scientific knowledge, uncontaminated by any commercial taint. In an ideal universe perhaps we would.[36]

Not all companies take this position. W. Wallace McDowell, vice-president in charge of engineering and research for IBM, states that in advanced planning (where products are five, ten, fifteen or more years in the future) "good people . . . enthusiastic about their work, plus a sense of urgency, and a definite sense of obligation to produce regularly things that can be moved into sales projects [are required]." He states further that "in any research and development activity, there should always be a certain amount of what might be called 'unprogrammed research.'"[37]

A study of basic research in the Shell laboratories indicates that after thirty years of experience the scientists are allowed to do "pretty much what we want" because it has been found to pay off in the past.[38] The Bell Telephone Laboratories has a similar research philosophy. James B. Fisk, president of the laboratories stated:

> Our fundamental belief is that there is no difference between good science and good science relevant to our business. Among a thousand scientific problems, a hundred or so will be interesting, but only one or two will be truly rewarding—both to the world of science and to us. What we try to provide is the atmosphere that will make selecting the one or two in a thousand a matter of individual responsibility and essentially automatic.[39]

It is probable that the research-oriented philosophy expressed here is based upon experience in laboratories that have enjoyed the presence of men who had something of the attitude of William Shockley, the head of the research team that invented the transistor. Shockley declared in his Nobel lecture:

> Frequently, I have been asked if an experiment I have planned is pure or applied science; to me it is more important to know if the experiment

[36] "The Commercialization of Research Results," (New York: American Management Association, Special Report No. 20, 1957), p. 11, 15.

[37] "Getting the Most for Product Research and Development" (New York: American Management Association, Special Report No. 6, 1955).

[38] H. Gershinowitz, "Industrial Research Programs and Academic Research," *American Scientist*, XLVI, No. 1 (March 1958), 28-29, quoted in Albert E. Hickey, Jr. "Basic Research, Should Industry Do More of It?" *Harvard Business Review*, XXXVI, No. 4 (July 1958). Hickey answers this question in the affirmative, but holds that most managements focus too much on short-run objectives and inhibit basic research by attempting to apply profit criteria to it.

[39] Quoted by Richard R. Nelson, "The Link between Science and Invention: The Case of the Transistor," *Rate of Direction of Inventive Activities,* p. 570.

will yield new and probably enduring knowledge about nature. If it is likely to yield such knowledge, it is, in my opinion, good fundamental research; and this is more important than whether the motivation is purely esthetic satisfaction on the part of the experimenter on the one hand or the improvement of the stability of a high-power transistor on the other.[40]

Aside from Shockley's statement, each man quoted above regards research as a profitable investment for his company, but they apparently differ about the profitability of basic research. The scientist no less than the businessman, however, considers the motivation to be noncritical, although awareness of applications is prized. Thus a dichotomy seems to be present.

Some research has rather definite objectives, is organized, and seems to be undertaken with rather clear profit expectations. Development and a part of applied research fall in this category. On the other hand, some research takes the form of hiring men to organize and conduct research of their own choosing with not much more than a gentlemen's understanding that they will be alert to useful applications that may follow from their work. The companies expect profits in the long run, and the scientists are interested in devices and processes as well as in the fundamental advance of knowledge. But the connection between the research done and its commercial return is obscure and rests importantly on faith. Part of applied and all of basic research done by commercial firms belongs in this category.

This dichotomy is maintained throughout these pages. The former category is denoted "developmental research," and the latter, for want of a better term to distinguish it from basic and applied research, as "pure research."

1. The Competitive Effects of Developmental Research

Developmental research is the nonroutine application of research techniques to solve well-formulated problems. It is directed to the superior solution of old problems; to the adaptation of new materials, processes, fuels, etc., to old uses; and to exploration of the practicality of new ideas. This kind of research has been dubbed "contract research," since it is the kind to which more less standard techniques can be applied to find rather concrete "answers." Developmental research is by far the most common type of research undertaken by oligopolistic companies.

[40] Quoted by Nelson, *ibid.*, p. 582.

Only a small percentage of specific research studies is crowned with commercial success. While it would seem that only a large firm can "afford" to take such risks, the data presented above show that it does not follow that only large firms actually do undertake such research. Small firms, even individual persons, are involved, and their successes count as "exceptions." But the numerous small ventures which fail may not be counted at all, since they may involve loss only to the "inventor," who may succeed on the second or the twenty-second try, financing his efforts however he can. What the individual faces as uncertainty, a large firm converts to virtually insurable risk. But the social return on resources committed may be no better in one case than in the other. Nevertheless, continued viability of each firm is in doubt until it is large enough to survive with only a normal incidence of research successes.

The fact that some firms of all sizes conduct some research, and that nine out of ten of the largest firms do so, provides concrete evidence that research is profitable. It follows that a monopoly would find it profitable to conduct some research. The question to which attention is now turned is whether or not oligopolistic or competitive pressures would lead firms to undertake more or less developmental research than would be undertaken by a monopoly. We are also interested in ascertaining how closely research expenditures may approximate the optimal level. The first question may, perhaps, be answered statistically, the latter requires analysis. An analytic approach is made to both questions here.

Profit indifference curves can be used to ascertain the general nature of the relationships. They show that interdependence tends to expand expenditures for developmental research. Let us suppose that two rivals exist, both large enough to apply the insurance principle to their research programs. Let us suppose, further, that the level of developmental research conducted by one firm has no effect upon the most profitable level of research effort by the rival. In that case, each firm would conduct the same amount of research that it would undertake if it were a monopoly.

Figure 8-1 illustrates this situation. Either firm, if a monopoly, would conduct developmental research, OM_B or OM_A for firms B and A respectively. This quantity maximizes their return from research. Any developmental research done by a rival reduces the profits obtained from such research but does not change the optimal level for each firm (in the absence of collusion). This is shown by the reaction functions, $M_B I$ and $M_A I$, which are perpendicular to their firm's axis.

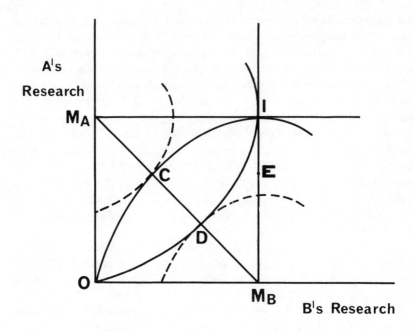

Figure 8-1

For convenience of exposition let each firm earn the normal rate of profit when both firms conduct no developmental research. Thus the zero-profit indifference curves are *ODI* for firm *A* and *OCI* for firm *B*. Again for convenience of exposition let these profit indifference curves cross at point *I*, where the reaction functions cross. It is clear that in this special case independent decisions with regard to research double the amount of research done and reduce profits to the competitive level in much the same manner that competition in product markets increases output and lowers industry profits.[41] It is likewise clear that both firms

---

[41] It is possible that the whole scale of operation of firm *A* or *B* would be larger in the absence of a rival. Thus with a rival present, but doing no research, OM_B is the optimum amount, while a larger amount is optimal in the absence of a rival in being or in prospect. Still, in the absence of economies of scale, a single firm would not get returns higher than those shown for point *I* if it doubled all inputs including research, because the profit indifference curves which intersect at point *I* are relevant to twice the research expenditures associated with two firms of equal size, and there is no obvious reason why the optimal proportion between research expense and other expenses should be modified. But profits can be expected to attract another efficient firm.

can gain by restricting their research effort to some level within the area *ODIC*; ideally, from a profit point of view, to some point on the contract curve shown by line *CD*. Such restrictions are not probable, however, because: (1) It is hard for a firm to determine and, therefore, to enforce the level of expenditures for research made by its rival. (2) Either rival by breaking the agreement tends to greatly improve his position while forcing losses on the other. (3) Because of the time lag between effort and result, the rival risks much in any misplaced trust. Consider Figure 8-1, for example. If firm *A* gains the primary benefit from an initial agreement by establishing point *C*, firm *B* can increase its research effort from *C* to *E*, greatly increasing its profits and inflicting losses on firm *A*. Firm *B* could do even better if it started from the more favorable position *D*. The best countermove that firm *A* can make is to return to the *OMA* level of research, reestablishing point *I* as soon as its expanded research effort matures. Point *I* is likely to dominate points on *CD* for a third reason: potential entry. Should unusually high profits be maintained in a field for lack of sufficient research activity, additional rivals are likely to appear.

Figure 8-1 is unrealistic on two counts: (1) the level of research undertaken by rivals probably influences the optimal research effort by a firm, and (2) there is no reason to suppose that normal profits are earned in the short run where the firms' reaction functions intersect. Consider the second point first. If the normal profit indifference curves cross to the "northeast" of point *I*, independent behavior, which results in equilibrium at point *I*, leaves firms with supranormal profits. If natural or contrived barriers to entry exist, such profits may continue indefinitely. If they do not, entry will tend to reduce the profits of each firm in the industry until normal profits are realized. This has the effect of shifting the normal profit indifference curves toward the origin until they pass through point *I* or its equivalent in a multifirm space.

Likewise, indifference curves indicating losses may pass through point *I* in the short run. Exit may then tend to reverse the shift described in the preceding paragraph. If only two firms exist, however, collusion or its equivalent is necessary for the survival of both firms. Without collusion, monopoly will be established gradually or by a cutthroat research war.

Since very few actual monopolies embracing even 7-digit products exist, it is probable that oligopolies tend to carry developmental research to the point where marginal returns, in the eyes of the managers, are approximately equal to returns available from expenditure of funds in other directions. This in turn suggests that the returns approximate the competitive level since entry, for reasons given in Chapter V, tends to drive marginal returns to that level. There is no reason to expect that a monopolistic firm will carry research to that high a level.

The second assumption to be reconsidered is that the level of research carried on by one firm does not affect the most profitable level of the research effort of rivals. This is not essential to the argument, since noncollusive policies yield larger research expenditures by oligopolists than by monopolists regardless of the direction of the inclination of the firms' reaction functions, and over a wide range of angles of inclination. But developmental research is without doubt competitive. It seems clear that within the relevant ranges, the more developmental research done by one firm, the more its rival finds to be optimal. Stated in terms of a profit indifference diagram for two firms, the reaction functions slope outward. Such an instance is illustrated in Figure 8-2.

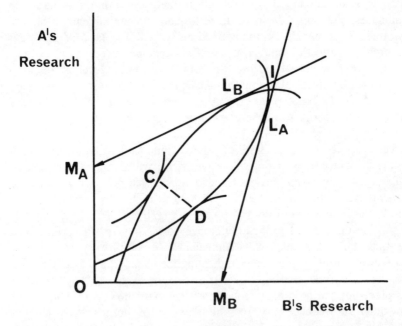

Figure 8-2

The reaction functions $M_A I$ and $M_B I$ show the most profitable level of research for firms A and B, respectively, for each fixed level of research by the other. This involves each firm in larger expenditures for research

than it would undertake if it were a monopolist. Both firms would benefit from collusion to restrict research to a point on line *CD*. But because
of difficulties of prediction and control, discussed above, independent
decisions about research effort are probable.

Independent research policies tend to produce equilibrium at point *I*,
provided that normal profits are associated with that result. If they are
not, entry of additional firms, or vigorous competition that leads to exit,
is to be expected for reasons given earlier. We may assume that there
is a tendency for normal profits to be received by both parties at point *I*.
It is evident that restraint by one firm, say *B*, could improve profits for
both firms, provided that the functions shown in Figure 8-2 can be objectively known and forecast into the future. Firm *B*, by reducing its
research effort, can make it profitable for firm *A* to reduce its effort by a
lesser amount, even in the absence of collusion. Such activity is called
"leadership." The point designated L_B is firm *B*'s optimal leadership
position. At that point firm *B* is somewhat better off that it would be at
point *I*, but firm *A* is much better off. Thus research leadership designed
to achieve supranormal profits benefits the follower more than the leader.
in the same way that price leadership, discussed in Chapter V, does.
If the follower's profits tend to exceed the normal level, additional
followers tend to appear, reducing followers' profits to the normal level
and reducing the leader's profits to a subnormal level. This provides an
additional reason for supposing that research efforts tend to be carried
to, or close to, the competitive level even when relatively few firms exist
in particular markets characterized by significant levels of developmental
research.[42]

2. Pure Research vs. Developmental Research

Large firms engage in some pure research, as defined above, as well
as in developmental research. Pure research includes investigation of
the nature of the universe without relation to any specific commercial
goal or with such goals remote from existing knowledge. Investigations

---

[42] If the reaction functions slope towards the rival's axis rather than sloping
"outward," as in Figure 8-2, or being vertical, as in Figure 8-1, a leader could
benefit at the expense of his rival. The analysis (and the geometry) are essentially
the same as that in connection with Figure 5-1. A firm that sticks rigidly to
his leadership level of research would, if his financial strength were sufficient,
bring the rival to accept this position and maximize accordingly. But Figures 8-1
and 8-2 seem to be the relevant ones for developmental research, and it is
probable that information is too poor to permit either leadership or collusive
policies. The lack of information is particularly serious because of the tendency
of research results to be relevant to markets and firms outside of the usual
industry groupings.

of this type have produced leads that, after developmental research, resulted in major business gains. Nevertheless, it is not clear that rational calculation can be employed to allocate resources to pure research, even with the application of the insurance principle, because of the substantial but vague lead time required and the unreliable connection between research and salable products or research findings.

In recent years the gap between publication of the findings of pure research and the mounting of developmental research that produces useful products seems to have been reduced. Salk vaccine, linear programming, the transistor, polymers, and electrical tapes are but a few of the examples that come readily to mind. Moreover, the larger companies have become interested in expansion into new fields and the market for research results may have improved. If so, pure research may have become a proper activity for "hardheaded" business, not merely for "public-relations-conscious" business. But one is entitled to doubt.

The international character of pure research is well known. This implies that it will not thrive when the researchers are closeted in some company laboratory surrounded by secrecy but will rather flourish where there is a maximum of interchange. This fact is recognized by many companies which encourage the publication of research papers, attendance at professional meetings, and similar activities. But this means that the investment that one company makes in research is even less likely to redound to its advantage. Moreover, each company has the alternative of employing scientists to search the literature with a view to capitalizing on pure research done by others in commercial and noncommercial laboratories. So although we assume that there are constant returns to pure research from society's viewpoint, an individual firm may profit more by concentrating its research efforts in development.[43] Were one to assume that diminishing returns to investment in pure research prevail, this will only strengthen the advantage of the firm that concentrates on development.

One may reach these conclusions with the aid of the following construction (Figure 8-3) where it is assumed that expected profits from both developmental and pure research exist. If duopoly exists, the more pure research done by firm A the more firm B may profit from developmental research because A's activities will have provided B with a

---

[43] Villard, *Economic Performance* (n. 14), pp. 367-70, has pointed to specific cases which suggest that it is in any firm's interest to let its rivals carry out the pure research, including some of the developmental research, particularly in view of the antitrust laws and consent decrees which require licensing of patents.

greater store of knowledge. Thus B's reaction function goes in a north-easterly direction showing larger optimal levels of B's developmental research associated with larger levels of A's pure research. And the more pure research done by A the higher B's profits are. But the more research talent devoted to pure research by A, the less it can devote to developmental research which creates commercial products. And the greater B's developmental effort, the lower will be A's return on its total research program. Thus A's optimum level of pure research is greater the less the amount of developmental research conducted by firm B. As illustrated in Figure 8-3, A's curves are drawn as solid lines, and B's curves as dashed lines.

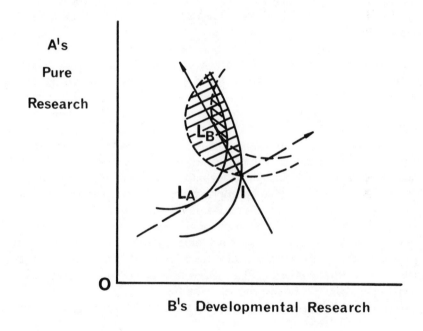

Figure 8-3

The most probable outcome in this situation is, once again, intersection equilibrium. The connection between the two firms' activities is not well known, is subect to variable time lags, and is capable of concealment. Thus point I is probable, and the long-run tendency is toward normal profits at that point.

It is interesting to notice that collusion that enhances profits for both firms involves a shift from developmental to pure research. It is even more interesting that if the firm conducting developmental research, firm B, can establish its leadership position, both firms benefit substantially. This requires the leader, firm B, to *reduce* its developmental research effort in order to induce a larger pure research effort by firm A. Note on Figure 8-3 that any point in the shaded area is preferable for both firms to independent (intersection) equilibrium. Any point in the cross-hatched area is better than own-leadership equilibrium for both. Firm B's leadership position, shown by L_B, is on the boundary of this area. Thus B's leadership would increase profits by increasing the ratio of pure to developmental research which results from a decrease of developmental research and an (induced) increase in fundamental research.

Entry would tend to destroy both leadership and possible collusion. Thus competitive pressures tend to result in relatively less pure research than is justified by the strict commercial standards underlying this analysis.

3. Collusion and Pure Research

The basic reason for underemphasis on pure research, aside from the vagueness of the connection between new knowledge and commercially valuable products, is the high probability that firms other than those paying for the research may appropriate the benefits. American patent laws may contribute to the failure of firms to profit from their additions to basic knowledge when it is developed by others. This is because the results of basic research are not patentable while the new products and processes created by developmental research are.[44] Consequently, the leakage of information is a net loss which discourages pure research and encourages secrecy at the expense of social benefits.

The unpatentability of "fundamental" additions to knowledge may be overstated. Research chemists at the University of Washington and a highly successful patent attorney have told the writer that a substance or a process may be fruitfully patented although the specific usefulness of the substance or the outcome of the process may turn out to be quite different from that envisaged. But it is true that a general statement of a scientific law, such as the law of conservation of energy, is not patentable although myriad applications are.

[44] *Ibid.*, pp. 261-62; and Richard R. Nelson, *The Simple Economics of Basic Research, op. cit.*, p. 302.

It is probable, therefore, that commercial motivation to engage in pure research is less than that for developmental research. The substantial period of time between basic discoveries and the development of useful products makes more likely the lapse of whatever patent protection may be available. Commercial motivation is further reduced if research successes are regularly licensed to rivals under pressure by governmental agencies.

Collusion can make a considerable amount of pure research commercially desirable when none would otherwise be performed. This is illustrated in Figure 8-4.

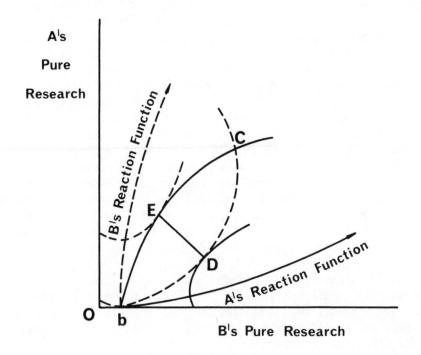

Figure 8-4

If two firms are active in a research-oriented industry, both are under similar pressures but only one may conduct pure research. Figure 8-4 illustrates a situation where firm *A* would conduct no pure research in the absence of collusion, but firm *B* would then conduct *Ob* of pure research. All curves relevant to firm *B* are shown as dashed lines. The main peculiarity of pure research is that a rival firm stands to gain from the other's work. Thus there is the tendency for one firm's reaction function to lie virtually along the rival's axis. In Figure 8-4 we show the reaction function somewhat inside the rival's axis, indicating that a large amount of pure research by one firm will induce a much smaller additional amount of that type of research by a rival following commercial motivation. The exact position of the reaction function is not important for our analysis. In either case, independent action is to be expected because of the inexact relationships between expenditure for research and profitable results, and independent action produces a very small amount of pure research. In Figure 8-4 intersection equilibrium yields no pure research by firm A and Ob by firm B.

What is important is the shape of the profit indifference curves. The indifference curves that cross at point C yield the same profits to each firm as that which they realize at intersection equilibrium. Any point inside the area $bDCE$ requires a larger level of pure research by both firms and yields larger profits to both firms. The substantially larger amount of pure research conducted by both firms is socially desirable when valued only by commercial values. Firms would maximize their profits on the contract curve, ED. If every enterprise were included, and if their joint objective were to attain a maximum joint revenue, this level is also the monopoly level of pure research. Point C represents the extension of pure research to the level that yields only competitive returns and is therefore socially optimal as calculated by cost-benefit techniques. But, unlike the situation for developmental research, the failure to establish collusion, or its breakdown if once established, leads to a minimal rather than an optimal research effort. It is competitive in its profit level but not in its allocative result.

Collusion is the only apparent device for increasing pure research towards C which is open to private motivation. It should be remembered that some desirable shift from developmental research to pure would also follow from collusion.

To the extent that collusion or monopoly is eschewed, movement toward point C may be encouraged by creating a climate favoring a variety of social conventions. Thus firms of all sizes may assume certain "social obligations," such as support to private colleges and universities, particularly graduate instruction and research, or they may allocate a certain percentage of total research funds to fundamental research carried on by special research institutes and made available to all. Subsidies, tax advantages, and other devices such as prizes may also help to expand private pure research.

If firms find it profitable to engage in collusion or to establish conventions to insure expenditures for fundamental research by special
institutes or at universities, it might seem possible for a firm to become
so large that it could avoid leakages of its findings to its rivals. Pure
research would then become a normal and substantial part of the firm's
activity. But the international character of science suggests that the firm
would have to be very great indeed, and possessed of a long time
horizon. Diseconomies of production and administration may be expected long before this size is attained. Moreover, it would aspire only to
the monopoly level of research, or *ED* in Figure 8-4, not the optimal
level.

All signs seem, therefore, to point toward an inadequate expenditure
for pure research by business, even when the test of the desirability of
research is its ability to produce profits for business. This is surely a
minimum level of research, because man's curiosity about the universe
extends to many things which have a most tenuous connection with
increasing the output and variety of goods and services. Much is of
interest for its own sake, and more must lie beyond the horizon of
merely sensible people. Therefore, public support of pure research of
all types is indicated, along with encouragement of those firms which
conduct pure research even to the extent of allowing collusion in this area.

G. Pure Research for Profit, A Contrary View

Nelson has offered a rule which may (under stringent conditions) be
used to determine the appropriate minimum level of government activity
in basic research. He declares: "However, if basic research can be
considered as a homogeneous commodity, like potato chips, and hence
the public can be assumed to be indifferent between the research results
produced in government or in industry laboratories; if the marginal cost
of research output is assumed to be no greater in non-profit laboratories
than in profit-oriented laboratories, and if industry laboratories are
assumed to operate where marginal revenue equals marginal cost, then
the fact that industry laboratories do basic research *at all* is itself evidence that we should increase our expenditure on basic research.[45]

As it is difficult to separate basic from applied research, as Nelson
himself concluded in a subsequent paper,[46] it may be appropriate to
broaden the coverage of this quotation to what we have called pure
research. The plain implication of Nelson's conclusion is that if the

[45] *Ibid.*, p. 304.
[46] *The Rate and Direction of Inventive Activities*, p. 582.

socially desirable level of pure research is to be performed it must be done by government-financed enterprises or in government laboratories, because the leakages make additions to that high level of research activity unprofitable for firms. Developmental research, however, may properly be left to profit-oriented business.

The validity of this argument rests heavily on the hypothesized homogeneity of pure research, for only under such a condition can diminishing returns to research effort cover all pure research and thereby make private research unprofitable to all firms that can profit from new knowledge.

There are three reasons to suppose that Nelson's criteria would mislead government to overexpend on pure research. (1) Basic research is not homogeneous. New dimensions and new facets are found rather frequently. Especially if patents can be had for much of what is considered to be the outcome of basic research, no level of basic research can be expected to extirpate all private research effort. Indeed one may doubt that diminishing returns characterize pure research, in which case no level of public research will eliminate pure research by all firms. (2) More important, there seems to be a complementary relationship between pure and developmental research. Just as universities find it easier to recruit and stimulate academic staff if top level personnel are present, so industrial companies have found that the quality of their developmental programs is improved by contact between the basic, applied, and development personnel.[47] Hence, the separation of pure from developmental research may reduce the effectiveness of both. (3) Finally, one may question the efficiency of the administration of any very large program of government support of research. The more empirical work of Carter and Williams, of Jewkes, Sawers and Stillerman, of Mueller, and of others cited above suggests that much useful work is done by individuals on a small scale for a variety of motives, but not least in hope of gain. Many such persons would not qualify for positions in government laboratories or even for small research grants administered according to any reasonable standards. Any total research effort that was considered to be inadequate until such time as it displaced all pure research embarked upon in hope of gain seems destined to devote an uneconomically large amount of resources to research.

Encouragement of industry-financed laboratories of the type that are becoming more common here and abroad is definitely in order, to

---

[47] This point was brought out by representatives of the Boeing Aircraft Company and of Standard Oil of California in personal interviews.

increase the quantity of pure research. Tax exemption of money so spent is probably advisable. Otherwise, such ventures can, at best, bring the research expenditures of an industry to the E-D line in Figure 8-4. Substantial expenditures of public funds through universities, research institutes, government laboratories are undoubtedly desirable, and should perhaps be increased. But incentives to private research by increasing the gains from research can also help.

Professor Kenneth Arrow has raised a different objection to research by private enterprises. Acknowledging the necessity for a return if invention is to be encouraged, he nevertheless applies the sunk cost principle to the optimal allocation of knowledge. Thus the monopoly return for research limits its application, reducing level of income and, presumably, of welfare.[48] This is precisely the kind of reasoning against which Professor Schumpeter directed his sharpest strictures about confusing static and dynamic analysis. *If* efficiency and the rate of innovation are otherwise unchanged by the return to research, Arrow's point holds—two conditions which are by no means obviously met. We agree, however, that pure research should be pushed to the "competitive" level. Independent action probably approximates this result for developmental research. But the probabilities are strongly against achieving this level of pure research in the absence of government support and what amounts to private collusion.

H. Summary

In the course of this chapter certain conclusions have been hazarded. The appropriate decision-making unit is at least as broad as the activities of the firm when research decisions are made, so the product-centered "industry" is abandoned in favor of a "firm-centered" analysis. Basic and applied research are sufficiently alike, differing primarily in the motivation of the firm, so as to make a division between pure and developmental research more useful than the usual basic, applied, and development categories. The asserted positive relationship between size-*cum*-monopoly and research activity is investigated and found to be not proven, although some advantages may accrue to large firms, particularly those producing a conglomerate product line. Evidence bearing on the proportion of national income devoted to research and development of all types is not conclusive. Research and development is not a new activity for private enterprise, so it is reasonable to suppose that the firms in the various industries have made rational allocations between

---

[48] *Rate and Direction of Inventive Activities,* pp. 609-25.

research, investment, and other expenditures. Nevertheless there is probably a deficiency in research expenditures from a social point of view, since many things of small commercial value are interesting. It is found possible for monopoly to arise because of monopolistic advantages in developmental research, but the rare occurrence of monopoly in fact suggests that the model that produced this result is not as common as the alternative model that suggests pressures toward a competitive level of developmental research. Monopoly would considerably reduce this type of research. Collusive oligopoly, on the other hand, tends to produce a larger amount of pure research than would competitive industry. Collusive arrangements would tend to reduce the amount of developmental research below optimal levels and raise basic research closer to optimal levels. However, the patentability of some pure research, the improving market for its fruits, the complementarity of the various types of research within some research organizations, the growing number of broadly-financed research institutes, and the existence of conventional support of research in universities and elsewhere by business concerns and foundations contribute to a considerable growth of pure research. While government is a proper sponsor of research and should continue to make up the apparent deficiency of pure research revealed by rather abstract analysis, Nelson's carefully hedged suggestion that it be expanded until none is profitable to private enterprise is considered extreme and inefficient.

Chapter IX

Welfare Aspects of Big Business

THIS CHAPTER attempts to assess the effect of oligopoly upon growth, income distribution, and the misallocation of resources. These effects taken together may be thought of as covering the welfare aspects of oligopoly in an operational sense of the word. It does not, however, exhaust the aspects of oligopoly about which people have strong preferences, especially those of political or sociological nature. Although that type of consideration lies outside of the scope of this book, an attempt is made to draw the issues clearly.

A. Technical Welfare Criteria

The technical welfare criteria applicable to an economic event are stringent. The eye of the needle that leads to a welfare conclusion is indeed so narrow as to discourage its use. Each consumer must so dispose of his income as to permit no higher level of satisfaction by any shift of expenditure and as a producer he must pursue the most rewarding of the available types of gainful activity to just the degree where the fruits of marginal labor balance its irksomeness. The prices to which individuals adjust must be the same to all persons similarly located and must in each case be equal to marginal cost. Any person who would prefer a different occupation and who can perform its duties must be able to make the move without discrimination. External economies and diseconomies must be absent. That is to say, for example, that all gains from investment in research will accrue to the investing firm, and that none of the costs of production will fail to be included in the costs of the firm and in the prices paid by purchasers. Finally, because no particular income distribution can be called optimal from all points of view relevant to welfare, an event that changes the distribution of income so as to better the position of one or even of many individuals at the detriment of another cannot be said to improve welfare unless those injured are adequately compensated (although some have maintained that it is enough if those injured *could* have been sufficiently compensated) so as to restore their former position.

This final criterion is at once the most crucial and the most paradoxical. It is crucial, because it is essential that some way be found to decide if the group can benefit when both gains and losses are experienced by its members, for in all important changes insufficiently compensated losses must occur to some. It is paradoxical because the impulse toward change is so strong in contemporary society that often any change is deemed preferable to none. It is galling to think that *welfare* criteria offer no guide to action in a world seemingly crying for economic development. The Communist phrase that one must break some eggs if one is to make an omelette, and the attention paid by Western nations to such matters as agriculturists' incomes, social insurance, job placement services, and bankruptcy laws, attest to the expectation that injury accompanies change which is nevertheless widely considered to be social progress. It is also paradoxical because the richer the nation and the less the resistance to change, the more likely it is that this welfare test will be violated. For the more specialized the economy the more likely it is that change will adversely affect the interest of some individuals.

It is paradoxical, too, that those nations which are regarded as having made the most rapid economic progress and have presumably best served the welfare of their inhabitants in some broad sense are precisely those which were so organized as to keep the veto power of adversely-affected economic groups at a minimum. In the Western world the limited power of government and the decentralized nature of private economic power make change appear to be a part of the natural order against which resistance is futile. In the Communist East, "reactionaries," "deviationists," "obstructionists," and others who stand in the path of change are countered with forthrightness and effectiveness at least equal to that of the West. This paradoxical aspect of the welfare test as applied to growth discourages its use.

The standard welfare test, moreover, rests upon static assumptions and does not sufficiently take into account the advantages of changes which result from a shift to new production functions or the introduction of higher levels of production attributable to a larger capital stock or to innovations that convert reserves of raw materials, land, or labor into economic resources.

The welfare test properly applies to individuals as such and not to categories of producers such as "farmers," "steelworkers," nor to geographical regions such as West Virginia, or Boston, or the like. It is difficult, therefore, to measure the gains or losses to individuals by examination of the position of such groups as these. Individuals can in some instances move at small cost and large benefit from occupations or regions damaged by growth, while others cannot. A proper microeconomic assessment of losses and gains due to change involves problems of identification and measurement that are beyond the capability of operational analysis.

For all of these reasons we regretfully retreat to some measured increase of output per head plus a measure of aggregative distribution of income plus a measurement of misallocation of resources in order to ascertain overall welfare. This amounts to the adoption of the test that the gains be large enough so that compensation *could* be made if one could discover (at zero cost) who should compensate whom—with the additional proviso that each income class benefit. It does not guard against individuals' falling from higher to lower income classes, nor does it include losses or gains that fail to be registered on the market. This crude measure is more objective and may be considered relevant as a proximate welfare test in assessing economic performance in a changing world.

B. Oligopoly and Growth

Oligopoly may affect growth in several ways. It may affect the division between consumption and investment; it may be more or less effective in the discovery and adoption of superior management techniques, broadening internal and external markets, and it may take better advantage of the opportunities that exist for research, development, and innovation.

The efficacy of the division between consumption and investment is part of the problem of allocation of resources and is discussed further on in connection with the works of Harberger and Schwartzman. Although we find reasons to be critical of both studies, the criticisms are not sufficient to overthrow their conclusions. If one accepts the usual criteria, the oligopolistic firms do seem to have invested enough to reduce their returns to approximately the normal level. Any restriction of investment which would have restrained growth, is, therefore, minor by this test. If there has been an overall failure of our economy to stress investment, the oligopolistic sector does not appear to be any more reprehensible than the other sectors.

There is nothing relating to the general efficiency of management techniques nor to management's aggressive attitude toward expansion in internal and external markets that suggests that oligopolistic managements are less progressive than those in competitive industries. The general tenor of comment suggests that the oligopolist industries are better managed and more interested in expansion, internal and foreign specialization, than competitive firms are. We do not investigate the merits of this argument but note that, if it is correct, oligopolistic structure is superior on this count as a promoter of growth.

Efficient management sometime secures special legislation and support that results in an inefficient use of resources. It is not evident that oligopolistic industries have been more successful than more competitive industries in this endeavor. The special treatment of the oil industry is matched by that of agriculture; and all sorts of special treatment is accorded small business and licensed semiprofessions. No attempt is made to establish the comparative seriousness of the distortion due to activities of managements to secure favored treatment.

We have already assessed the influence of oligopoly in the third activity relating to growth. Oligopolistic structure does undervalue fundamental research, but no more seriously than competitive structures do. Elsewhere, pressures exist which tend to produce firms of a size appropriate to the internalization of whatever economies of scale may exist for developmental research activity and innovation. Therefore, no ground is found for any dogmatic assertion as to the superiority of any particular size or structure for all classes of products. To the extent that the appropriate structure turns out to be oligopolistic, there is some tendency to carry the level of innovation beyond the level most profitable to the group, but only to the level appropriate to competition—that is, to the zero pure-profit level. Only monopoly is certain to produce distortion of developmental research.

With all market structures, public authority and private curiosity must fill a considerable gap if the optimal level of pure research is to be achieved, because of the inability of any firm or industry to encompass its potential external economies. Indeed, such economies may be beyond the compass of any nation, if welfare is considered on a global basis, as perhaps it should be.

If oligopolistic structure performs as well as or better than possible alternative structures at the growing points of the economy, it can be thought of as making its full contribution to welfare if it is not offset in some other direction.

C. Oligopoly and Income Distribution

A second dimension of welfare may be measured in an approximate way by the distribution of income. Data on the personal distribution of income show roughly proportionate gains to each income group when they are grouped by deciles. Nevertheless, a number of economists of the first rank have found the distribution of income between owners and employees to be adversely affected by oligopoly. This presumably increases the share of the income received by the top ½ to 1 per cent of the income receivers, at the expense of the remaining 99 per cent or so.

The arguments are stated more in terms of monopoly than oligopoly partly because this procedure simplifies the argument, and partly because the literature frequently uses the term monopoly in contexts that imply oligopoly. That practice is followed here. Our findings are at variance with theirs. To the extent that monopoly affects economic activity we find income distribution to be little affected. The "degree of monopoly" is found to be irrelevant to functional income distribution. And so is the degree of concentration as it relates to the functional income distribution in particular industries.

1. Alleged Relationship Between Inequality and Demand Elasticity[1]

Let us begin with the extreme case. Mrs. Joan Robinson first referred to it as a "world of monopolies."[2] Although Mrs. Robinson's analysis is thirty years old, it casts up the main points in a forthright way, and subsequent modifications are more easily understood if we use her analysis as a starting point.

The essentials of her argument are not complex. Assuming one firm to an industry, an elasticity of demand for all goods of unity, demand curves of some identical elasticity between one and infinity for each product, fixed total amounts of each factor, perfect mobility of each factor, a closed system, monopolists who perform no service whatsoever except to control output, and monetary and fiscal policies which maintain full employment, she compares the results of monopoly with perfect compe-

---

[1] I summarized and commented upon the considerable literature on this subject in "Monopoly and Income Distribution," *Proceedings of the Western Economic Association* (Salt Lake City: Western Economic Association, August 1956), pp. 36-41.

[2] Joan Robinson, *Economics of Imperfect Competition* (New York: Macmillan Company, 1934), p. 307 ff.

tition so far as the distribution of income is concerned. She concludes: "It follows . . . that the national dividend will be the same as before, . . . [and] that the proportions in which the factors are employed is the same as before, so that their relative rewards are unaltered. But the distribution of the national dividend will have been altered, and the factors of production will be exploited."[3] "The extent to which the factors are exploited will depend upon the elasticity of demand for the commodities. . . . Even with an elasticity of demand as great as two, the factors receive only half the perfectly competitive real wage."[4] This last sentence is the summary sentence in a section whose purpose is to "draw a moral for the real world." In general, we may say that by assuming short-run profit maximization, so that the marginal revenue will equal marginal cost, she finds all factors payable according to their marginal products exploited by the ratio between marginal revenue and price, or $\frac{E-1}{E}$ (If demand curves displayed an elasticity of unity or less, the factors would get zero or negative returns.)

This conclusion depends fully upon the complete elimination of the threat of entry, although when Mrs. Robinson compares a "world of monopolies" with a "world of imperfect competition" she continues to apply this reasoning and finds a virtual improvement of income distribution only through the increasing demand elasticity, offset in part by other considerations which make imperfect competition less efficient.

The effect of entry is recognized by present writers who follow Mrs. Robinson's mode of analysis. Bain and Scitovsky may be taken as examples. When they discuss the no-entry or restricted-entry case, they find a rather close relationship between elasticity and income distribution. Scitovsky uses a variant of Mrs. Robinson's formula to isolate the effect upon the shares received by the hired factors.[5] While there are important differences between non-hired factors and Mrs. Robinson's "pure owners" of businesses, inequality of income distribution is closely associated with the earning of higher than normal, or excess, profits. When the postulate of fully blockaded entry is abandoned, the size of excess profits is found to be related primarily to the ease of entry rather than to the slopes of the demand curves facing the firms. As Scitovsky says, "For restraints on the entry of newcomers may enable an established firm to make a monopoly profit even if competition between him

[3] *Ibid.*, p. 310.
[4] *Ibid.*, pp. 312-3.
[5] J. S. Bain, *Pricing, Distribution and Employment* (rev. ed.; New York; Holt, 1953), p. 243, 340, 372, 448, 514; and T. Scitovsky, *Welfare and Competition* (Homewood, Ill.: Irwin, 1951), p. 287ff, 367f.

and his established competitors is unrestrained; whereas the entry of newcomers would eliminate monopoly profit, however restrained may be the competitive behavior of the established firms among themselves."[6]

Machlup, among others, has analyzed situations where long-run monopoly gains are made without resort to sloped demand curves facing the individual firm.[7] His example of physicians' services is unfortunate, but does serve to point out the fact that doctors' incomes probably would contain a monopoly element because of the general and perhaps arbitrary scarcity of physicians even if each *were* powerless to affect his fee schedule. Perhaps a better example can be found in the fisheries, where the catch of some species, notably halibut, is limited by conservation activities. The market price for the restricted catch may be so high that large excess profits are taken so long as the number of boats and other facilities is held to a level that minimizes industry cost. As long as entry can be forestalled, large profits will accrue to those having the equipment in spite of the fact that there are so many operators that each is virtually powerless over selling price.

We must conclude, then, that maldistribution of income rests on restriction of entry, not on the presence or absence of slope of the individual firm's demand curves.

Unfortunately, Scitovsky and Bain fail to maintain the separation of the effects of slope and entry throughout their works. The disposition to associate monopoly primarily with the distribution of income remains. Scitovsky escapes the fascination with elasticity while dealing explicitly with "free competition." But when discussing the principles of price-making by the firm, both for free and for restricted competition, the profit margin is calculated as a simple relationship between marginal cost and elasticity of demand on the assumption that marginal cost will equal marginal revenue. And elasticity, as used here, makes no room for entry, being related directly to the determinants of consumer demand. He speaks of "the simple relation between the market's price elasticity and the price maker's optimum profit margin" in a way that suggests that each firm receives a certain share of the market via price matching, or some such device, which leaves little room for entry.[8]

Bain consistently refers to marginal revenue product as the demand curve for factors when discussing the effect of monopoly on the distribu-

[6] *Ibid.*, p. 23.

[7] Fritz Machlup, *The Political Economy of Monopoly* (Baltimore: The Johns Hopkins Press, 1952), p. 508f. Scitovsky also considers a similar case, *Welfare and Competition*, p. 23.

[8] Scitovsky, *Welfare,* p. 298.

tion of income when, in fact, it is irrelevant to his conclusion. For it is clear from the preceding discussion that a discrepancy between marginal revenue and price is not even a necessary, let alone a sufficient, condition for the emergence of monopolistic profits. Restriction of entry is a necessary condition, the only other condition being that there is some manner of operation that will yield excess profits, if monopoly is to affect the distribution of income between hired factors on one side and pure owners on the other.

Historians of doctrine may some day be interested in the continued significance given the discrepancy between the value of the marginal product and the marginal revenue product in distribution theory. Perhaps one of the reasons for its continued survival is the clever use of the closely related concept, "degree of monopoly" by Kalecki. Abba Lerner fathered the formulation in 1934.[9] It is very similar to Mrs. Robinson's formula expressing the degree of exploitation, but does not rest upon the concept of profit maximization. The degree of monopoly, to which we will hereafter refer as *d,* is defined as $\dfrac{\text{price-marginal cost}}{\text{price.}}$

If profit is maximized, marginal cost will be equal to marginal revenue and the degree of monopoly will be the reciprocal of the elasticity of demand. This concept makes the degree of monopoly a simple function of the discrepancy between marginal cost and price, quite independent of the level of average cost, profitability, or any other consideration. Indeed, on the assumption of profit maximization, it is but the corollary of Mrs. Robinson's $\dfrac{E\text{-}1}{E.}$ Her formula isolates the share received by the factors on the restricted assumptions that make elasticity decisive. Lerner's formula isolates the "profit" share on the same assumptions.

Yet Scitovsky, who at other places stresses entry, finds the principal defect of Lerner's measure to be the lack of a specific value for simple monopoly.[10] He also lauds Kalecki's use of the degree of monopoly as the best effort to develop a theory of income distribution under restricted competition.[11]

[9] Abba P. Lerner, "The Concept of Monopoly and the Measurement of Monopoly Power," *Review of Economic Studies,* I, No. 3 (June 1934). Kalecki's work appears in "The Distribution of Income," *Readings in Income Distribution* (Homewood, Ill.: Irwin, 1951; formerly published by Philadelphia: Blakiston, 1946); *Essays in the Theory of Economic Fluctuations* (London: George Allen and Unwin, Ltd., 1939); *Studies in Economic Dynamics* (London: Allen and Unwin, Ltd., 1943); and *Theory of Economic Dynamics* (New York: Rinehart, 1954). The first and last of these are used exclusively here.

[10] Scitovsky, *Welfare,* pp. 395-6.

[11] *Ibid.,* p. 440n.

Kalecki's analysis is in line with the understandable predisposition following the acceptance of monopolistic competition reasoning to find all of the objectionable characteristics of simple monopoly, among them an unequal income distribution, present to some degree wherever a firm can influence its selling price. It builds upon the technical apparatus of the early 1930's which defined exploitation as payment of less than the value of the marginal product to the hired factors, and which tended to group payments to variable and hired factors together on one side and payments to fixed factors and entrepreneurial returns together on the other as gross profits.

Kalecki's analysis ostensibly finds the division of national income between wages and profits to be a function of the degree of monopoly, as defined by Lerner. Actually, however, it turns instead upon a classification of productive factors into two categories: substantially fixed, and substantially variable. The first of these is regarded as the source of entrepreneurial returns, and the second is identified with the payment of hired factors. In 1938 this point was subjected to some analysis, but in the 1954 treatment it is reached almost at once by the use of two assumptions: one, that the firm operates "below the point of practical capacity and that the prime costs per unit of output are stable over the relevant range of output," and, two, that *aggregate* overhead costs are about stable as output varies and therefore do not influence the point of profit maximization.[12] The logic followed is clearer in the 1938 version, an analysis of which will show the danger inherent in the easy assumptions made in 1954.

The components of cost are divided into four sections: E, the entrepreneurial return; O, the overhead return of interest, depreciation, etc.; W, the return to wages; and R (or M in 1954) the payments for raw materials. Each factor is classified as fixed or variable in a very special sense. The effect of the 1954 assumptions is to make the marginal cost *per unit of output* of W and R equal to their average cost *per unit of output*. Obviously, this relation is a function both of elasticities of supply of each factor and of their marginal productivities and implies competitive equilibrium in the labor and raw materials markets. Since Kalecki regards the typical firm as operating under monopolistic conditions and, therefore, with excess capacity, overhead costs are assigned a low, virtually zero, marginal cost per unit of output. The entrepreneurial element is regarded as entirely fixed and, therefore, a zero marginal

[12] *Theory of Economic Dynamics.* p. 12.

entrepreneurial return is implied, although no discussion of this point is made.

The key formula used in 1938 is $\Sigma xPd = \Sigma xe_a + \Sigma x(O_a - O_m) + \Sigma x(W_a - W_m) + \Sigma x(r_a - r_m)$ where x is output, P is price, d is the degree of monopoly, e is the entrepreneurial return, O the overhead return, W the wage return and r the cost of raw materials. The subscripts a and m indicate the average dollar cost per unit of output and the marginal dollar cost per unit of output respectively.[13]

Obviously, when average and marginal costs are equal, the term for that factor drops out of the equation. Under Kalecki's special assumptions this occurs for the wage and raw material components, leaving $xPd = E + O$, the aggregate entrepreneurial and overhead returns. Thus the gross entrepreneurial return is made equal to a proportion, d, of the national income, that proportion being the direct reflection of the discrepancy between marginal cost and price as cast up by the degree of monopoly. The 1954 version, although quite similar, looks quite different, the overhead-plus-profits share being defined as equal to $(k-1)$ $(W+M)$, where the ratio of proceeds to prime costs, k, is determined by the degree of monopoly. (M is used to denote the cost of raw materials.) A given elasticity yields a higher $E + O$ in this case.

With such a conclusion, it is odd to find in part of his 1938 analysis, and never denied, the suggestion that the division of income might be much the same whether or not monopoly exists. Kalecki recognizes that in fully competitive industries some part of income must go to $E + O$ as unavoidable real costs. Yet two sentences later he states, "The distribution of the product of industry is at every moment determined by the degree of monopoly . . . both in the short period and in the long run." But he sidesteps this problem by simply remarking that his theory is not applicable to free competition, an admission that would seem to be damaging to a theory that is attempting to show that the degree of monopoly is significant in determining the *degree* of exploitation, especially in an economy where some competitive industries do exist.[14]

It may be useful to illustrate Kalecki's dependence upon the division

---

[13] This equation was developed by defining average cost as equal to price $= e_a + O_a + W_a + r_a$. The marginal cost $= O_m + W_m + r_m$. Subtracting the second from the first equation, $P - M = e_a + (O_a - O_m) + (W_a - W_m) + (r_a - r_m)$. Dividing both sides by P, the degree of monopoly, d, is produced on the left side. Then multiplying both sides by Px, the total revenue is inserted for each firm. The national dividend produced by all firms is found by summation of the equations for each firm.

[14] Kalecki, *Essays*, p. 305.

of all factors into the two special groups with peculiar cost and productivity characteristics. Consider the following situation. Suppose that a world of monopolies exists, each with elasticities of demand of -3.0. Let all factors, including the entrepreneurial, be available to the firms at constant supply prices. Since the absence of all economies of scale is inconsistent with monopolistic structure, acccpt the concept of a long-run average cost curve which declines at an ever-decreasing rate. Since factor prices are constants, the decline of the average cost curve is due to economies of scale. Although marginal costs will always be below the average cost curve under these circumstances, the marginal cost function may be declining, constant, rising or U-shaped. This average total cost curve is one of the types envisaged by Kalecki for imperfect competition, but differs in that *all* of its components are hypothesized to have horizontal supply curves to the firm, rather than being divided into two groups of virtually opposite characteristics, and that *all* are regarded as variable inputs. Let us consider the partial productivity functions to be the same for each factor. This is quite realistic in the light of recent experience in regard to the expansion of entrepreneurial and overhead expense. Indeed, it is interesting that Kalecki remarks that excess capacity was no larger in 1929 than in 1923. Finally, suppose that the demand curve is tangent to the average cost curve at the relevant output.

If we apply the Kalecki equation we find $xPd = E/3 + 0/3 + W/3 + R/3$. In other words, a *productivity function* that produces a falling average cost curve produces a gap between the marginal and average factor costs per unit of output which is identical to the gap between price and marginal cost. By no stretch of the analysis can one show that the hired factors receive only one third to total receipts. On the contrary, they receive them all. There is no room for a residual between marginally-determined returns and total revenue in Kalecki's case where price is equal to average cost.

In other instances altered levels of production will produce a residual, positive or negative, which in most situations adds to or subtracts from the income of the entrepreneur, although it may be shared with hired factors. This residual is recognized as pure profit, the rest of the return to the entrepreneur as normal profit. The size of the residual, however, is unrelated to Kalecki's "degree of monopoly."

We find, then, no particular relation between the degree of monopoly and the distribution of income. $E + O$ can be any proportion of income regardless of the degree of monopoly. There is an important connection between the productivity functions of the various factors and their returns, as there is under pure competition. There is also an important relation between the persistence of pure profits and entry. But this also is without relevance to the "degree of monopoly."[15]

One more theory that relates monopoly to income distribution remains to be discussed here. It is put forward by Joseph Steindl and is related to the Marxian conception of the capitalist process.[16] Like Kalecki, he attempts to explain the share of value added in manufacturing industry going to wages by associating it with a coefficient of monopoly. But Steindl rejects all measures of monopoly power related to elasticity and therefore rejects Kalecki's use of "degree of monopoly." He uses, instead, the 1935 statistical coefficient of concentration of production by the four largest firms. Again, in distinction from Kalecki, Steindl does not argue that there is any long-run absolute proportion of wages to value added that results from any given degree of monopoly power. Rather, he believes that he has established the proposition that where the industry is "concentrated" or "highly concentrated," the share going

[15] Although monopsony and bilateral problems are neglected in this paper, it may be well to consider the effect of rising factor prices. If the elasticities of supply were everywhere the same, the only effect would be to give an upward bias to the average and the marginal cost curves of each firm so that efficiency would be impaired at the long-run equilibrium, because sharper rises in productivity as scale increased would be required to reach the given level of elasticity of average costs required to bring average cost into tangency with average revenue. There is no reason to suppose that in fact all do rise at the same rate, and, to the extent that they differ, Kalecki's formula suggests that those with sharply rising prices will make contributions to those with constant or falling prices, since their marginal cost per unit of output will tend to be higher than their average cost per unit of output. A priori, there is little reason to believe that labor or raw materials are more likely to display rising factor costs as compared to overhead or entrepreneurial components, since this depends upon relative mobility and variety of alternative employments.

But none of this is relevant to the division of the total product between the factors paid on the basis of productivity and pure profits. If entry is free, factor prices will be bid up on one hand, and the demand curves facing the individual firms will shift leftward (and perhaps become more elastic as well) until pure profits are eliminated.

While some would then say that the employed factors fail to get even their marginal revenue product, and are therefore paid less than their market values, it is evident that this argument is no more correct than the earlier one to the effect that failure to earn the value of the marginal product produced that result. In this case, it is clear that greater use of the factor increases the scarcity value of the resource. Thus the marginal outlay reflects not only the value of the additional resources employed, but also the increased values of the resources previously employed. It is, therefore, erroneous to insist that each unit of a factor receive "its" marginal revenue product when supply prices rise with quantity taken. The difference between average and marginal outlays, or, more properly, between net and gross marginal revenue products, measures the increasing need to economize them in all uses.

[16] *Maturity and Stagnation in American Capitalism* (Oxford; Blackwell, 1952).

to labor falls more or less continuously *as a trend*, whatever the relative share may have been, while it remains constant where "competitive" conditions prevail.[17]

Steindl's work supports the conclusions reached in this chapter in two ways, although its logic is very different. It denies the existence of any relationship between the elasticity of demand and the division of national product between wages and profits, and it looks to something akin to entry—cost differentials among firms—for the basis of monopoly power.[18] The larger the unit cost disadvantage of smaller firms, the greater the supposed "monopoly" power of the larger firms. This proposition is not altogether satisfactory for at least two reasons. First, it implies that all entry, including potential entry, is by relatively inefficient firms and, second, as Steindl states, the mere fact that existing firms using existing techniques have similar costs tells little about the degree of competition. Our example of the fisheries shows this. Restriction of entry yields monopolistic profits whether the active firms have the same or different costs.

But even in terms of its own frame of reference, Steindl's work suffers from the failure to show any sudden increase in the concentration just prior to 1923 although the decline in the share going to wages is alleged to have begun then. It suffers somewhat from a number of important exceptions to his generalization in each of his groups for which he introduces special arguments. More damaging are the calculations for the years since 1939, the last year of his data. The data for 1947 and 1953 reveal an increasing wage share both in "concentrated groups" and in the "competitive" sector as well. Explanations of these developments seem better sought in increased competition among industries for labor and increased labor mobility due in part to the high level of employment, rather than in a decline in concentration ratios on one hand, or on the other in an increased short-run competitive pressure in product markets which has forced prices down in the concentrated industries as the large firms moved to increase concentration ratios, the two major modes of explanation espoused by Steindl.

Finally, the effort to relate the degree of concentration *in specific industries* to the proportion going to wage payments in those industries is hard to reconcile with certain facts, notably the fact that the concen-

---

[17] "We have here what seems to be a fair illustration of the dictum that the 'ideal' pattern of competition works in competitive industries, but in industries with high concentration, or difficult entry, the share of profit shows a long run tendency to increase." *Ibid.*, p. 80.

[18] *Ibid.*, pp. 17 and 71.

trated industries pay wages at least as high as industry in general, and higher than nonindustrial firms, and that considerable mobility between industries exists. Bain recognizes that many industries typically compete for any given resource so that any monopolistic restriction in a specific industry would tend to have a *generally* depressing effect rather than an effect localized in the monopolized industry.[19] This criticism applies to Steindl although one might argue that the concentrated industries have been more progressive, so that the percentage of value added going to wages would fall in spite of the fact that they paid market wage rates or more. But Steindl specifically rejects this interpretation.

It is true that an *overall* depressing effect might be felt even if the actual wage rates paid were, as they actually seem to be, as high or higher in the concentrated industries. This would be true if, at the higher rates, the concentrated industries produced less, pushing a larger number of workers into other employment and holding them there by employment policies or union restrictions. But American data reveal no tendency toward a declining wages share.[20]

We conclude, then, that there is little or no reason to expect to find either a close relationship between concentration in particular industries and the share of value added going to labor, or a declining trend in the share going to wages in those industries. Nor do we find a trend in the distribution of income unfavorable to hired factors that may be accounted for by growing oligopoly. If this indeed had been the case, examination of alternative explanations would be necessary here.

Although many individual instances of maldistribution due to monopoly no doubt exist, their aggregate importance in the national income is questionable and no trend is apparent.

On the basis of the analysis thus far, our tentative conclusion is that oligopoly, as compared to alternative industry structures, is not inimical to welfare when welfare is defined in terms of growth or income distribution, but that efficiency under oligopoly may be less than optimum.

D. Oligopoly and Misallocation Among Industries

Allocation among industries, the third dimension of the welfare criterion adopted for this chapter, remains to be discussed. The literature on this subect is extensive and a few econometric studies have attempted to measure the amount of misallocation. The present analysis finds the usual analytical models to be of questionable relevance and the statistical

[19] Bain, *Pricing*, p. 256.

[20] I. A. Kravis, "Relative Income Shares in Fact and Theory," *American Economic Review*, XLIX, No. 5 (December 1959), 917-49.

estimations to have important lacunae. Tentative support is found for Harberger's and Schwartzman's conclusions that the misallocation is small.

Professor Chamberlin and Mrs. Robinson found that with entry and large numbers, equilibrium is found on the downward sloping part of the long-run average cost curve under conditions of monopolistic competition. They assert, and textbook writers typically declare, that the same output can be obtained through fewer and larger firms operating where marginal (and average) cost equals price. Chamberlin also makes a good deal of the tendency, noted in Chapter VII, for firms to build up selling costs until pure profits are eliminated. In such cases, profits are reduced or eliminated by rising costs. Functional and personal income distribution is little affected, but efficiency is said to be impaired because fewer and larger firms operating at the low point of their average cost curves could produce the same output at lower cost. Selling costs are viewed as waste effort that adds little or nothing to consumer satisfaction.

One can question the appropriateness of this conclusion especially when related to a set of differentiated products. Donald Dewey in particular has made this point.[21] He notes that *all* costs, including transport and selling costs, need to be taken into account and argues that product differences recognized by consumers must be respected by theorists. Thus "the demand curve" for a firm that sells in more than one locality is a conglomerate thing made up of many submarkets—the demand at location *A* plus that at *B*. at *C,* and so on, each location involving additional, and presumably progressively higher, transport and/or selling costs. Dewey pointedly disavows a graphical approach, but one may observe that the (net) demand curve, as seen from the factory, displays downward slope—partly because the curve appropriate to each market has downward slope, but equally because of the additional cost of reaching additional markets if one adopts Dewey's point of view. Transport costs to new markets are partial substitutes for greater selling efforts in existing localities designed to reach additional classes of customers or to develop new uses for the product within the market area presently served. But when additional costs are necessary if these submarkets are to be served, the price paid by the consumers in the new markets will be higher than the price in the original market. Pressures of entry that eliminate profits will then leave each firm in a position where aver-

[21] Donald Dewey, "Imperfect Competition No Bar to Efficient Production," *Journal of Political Economy,* LXVI, No. 1 (February 1958); also the appendix to ch. viii in his book, *Monopoly in Economics and Law* (Chicago: Rand McNally, 1959).

age production costs are falling, but average transport and selling costs are rising just enough to offset them, in relation to the conglomerate demand curve. If one wishes to subtract the latter costs from both the demand and cost functions the Chamberlinian tangency appears, but, as Dewey says, no finding of inefficiency is justified. In the absence of a complete canvass of alternatives, the presumption must indeed be the opposite, namely that efficiency is being served. Presumably, similar analysis is appropriate to all types of differentiation.

While this *may* be the case, it is hard to accept as a general rule. The calculating machine example, cited in Chapter II, provides a suitable illustration of a no-profit multiproduct equilibrium which may involve an inefficient allocation of resources. Several subproducts sell at substantially different prices. Total costs, including selling costs, are different for the different subproducts but may yield only normal profits to the firms. Research produces useful new features which further differentiate the product. Variety of product and choice of supplier are valued characteristics of the market from the buyer's point of view. Nevertheless, the alternative proposed by the production department is not put on the market for test, so one cannot know whether or not buyers of the simpler machines at a low price would have preferred a more highly featured machine at the same or slightly higher price. If they would have, customers' welfare is less than optimal in spite of the fact that each buyer enjoys a free choice of machines and (presumably) firms earn only normal profits. Thus inefficient allocation may be said to prevail.

Were a single product line produced by one firm or set of firms in competition with multiproduct lines of other companies, and should all survive, one could not assert inefficiency. Product variety would then be in tune with variety of desire, so that all that then can be required is that the various marginal conditions be satisfied on the production side. If "more calculators" could be produced with a given amount of resources, one can only say that "calculators" is too broad a category for analysis.

These considerations are neglected in statistical studies such as those examined below.

1. Harberger's and Schwartzman's Estimates of Welfare Loss Due to "Monopoly"

Arnold C. Harberger[22] and David Schwartzman[23] in separate studies

[22] A. C. Harberger, "Monopoly and Resource Allocation," *American Economic Review,* XLIV, No. 2 (May 1954), 77-87.

[23] David Schwartzman, "The Burden of Monopoly," *Journal of Political Economy,* LXVIII, No. 6 (December 1960), 627-30. The calculations are based

have attempted to measure the amount of misallocation of resources due to "monopoly."

Harberger uses profit rates both to classify industries as "competitive" or "monopolistic" and as a basis from which the misallocation of capital and welfare loss is calculated. Schwartzman uses concentration ratios for the former purpose and a calculated ratio between price and average variable cost for the latter. More specifically, Harberger uses Epstein's data on profit rates in seventy-three industry groups for the years 1924-1928, assumes constant costs, ubiquitous unit elasticity of demand, and a normal profit rate of 10 per cent in order to generate estimates of the shift of resources required to produce a competitive allocation of resources and an estimate of the money value of gains to consumers that would be forthcoming.

Schwartzman selects from 1954 Canadian and United States data for 4-digit manufacturing industries twenty-seven where those for both nations are considered unconcentrated, nineteen where the Canadian industry is concentrated and the United States' is not, and fifteen where industries are concentrated in both nations but the Canadian industries are the more so. He then calculates the difference between average variable cost and price for each industry in each nation in order to estimate the size of monopoly profits, applies Harberger's assumptions and model (although substituting a demand elasticity of -2.0 for Harberger's -1.0), and verifies Harberger's general conclusion. That conclusion is that the welfare loss may be valued at less than one tenth of 1 per cent of the national income.

Following Bain's finding that firms in industries with 8-firm concentration ratios above 70 per cent enjoy higher profits than those with lesser ratios, Schwartzman classifies industries characterized by a four-firm concentration ratio of 50 per cent or more as "monopolistic," or "concentrated," and those below this figure as "unconcentrated." He tests the validity of this classification by comparing the more and less highly concentrated industries and corroborates Bain's discovery of the dichotomy rather than the usually postulated functional relationship between concentration and profits.

A recent study by Stigler tends to support this dichotomy. After reviewing 1954 company data in seventeen industries he concludes, "In general, the data suggest that there is no relationship between

---

upon results published in an earlier article in the same *Journal*, "The Effect of Monopoly on Price," LXVII, No. 4 (August 1959), and were modified somewhat in a "Correction," LXIX, No. 5 (October 1961).

profitability and concentration if H is less than 0.250, or the share of the largest firms is less than 80."[24]

2. Criticisms of Harberger's Analysis

A considerable number of criticisms of Harberger's procedures and estimates have been made, but I find no critical apprasial of Schwartzman's work. The criticisms of Harberger's fall into three classes: (1) the appropriateness of using differential profits to identify monopoly; (2) the appropriateness of using differential profits as a basis for calculating the welfare loss due to monopoly; and (3) specific criticisms of the data, theory, assumptions, and procedures used. Our criticisms of Schwartzman's estimates fall in the same categories, except that the appropriateness of the use of concentration ratios to identify monopoly must be substituted for number one.

The following pages review the criticisms that have been made of Harberger's estimates, assess their relevance to Schwartzman's work, and offer some additional strictures that apply to both. The critical tone of the comments may seem misplaced because the general conclusions of the preceding chapters are in harmony with the findings of these authors; but there are possible sources of distortion that neither study considered. Some of them also qualify the conclusions reached earlier and this provides a convenient way to focus attention on them. Our procedure is to clarify the objections to Harberger's study without attempting to assess their merit at this time, but rather to observe how many of them are met by the procedure followed in Schwartzman's work. The remaining objections, plus some additional ones not broached, or only inferentially broached, by Mrs. Mack and Professor Stigler are then considered.

Mrs. Mack, the discussant assigned to Harberger's session at the 1954 American Economics Association meetings, offers the following criticisms: (1) The assumption of unit elasticity of demand is most ques-

---

[24] G. J. Stigler, "A Theory of Oligopoly," *Journal of Political Economy,* LXXII, No. 1 (February 1964), 44-61. H stands for the Herfindahl index of concentration. The index of 0.250 is identical to 2500 as expressed in Chapter VI. H is 0.250 for an industry composed of only four firms of equal size, or for an industry with approximately fifteen firms, the four largest of which enjoy 80 per cent of the market and have respectively, 42.6, 21.4, 10.7 and 5.3 per cent of the market. Stigler uses data for from two to nine firms in each industry where at least 35 per cent of industry output is accounted for by them. These firms are principally involved in the industry listed, and secure 50 per cent or more of their sales from their principal industry. Concentration at the 5-digit or 7-digit level is probably higher, although the products in this sample are rather narrowly defined.

tionable. (2) The horizontal long-term cost curve is vulnerable. (3) The Epstein data are "rather special." (4) Firm data are to be preferred to industry data for such a purpose. (5) A five-year period cannot substitute accurately for the long-run equilibrium. (6) Since total profits are a relatively small part of national income, a measure of monopolistic distortion based upon a portion of profits is bound to yield a small index of distortion. (7) In any case, the size of profits is a poor measure of maldistribution of capital. (8) Misallocation of factors other than capital may seriously elevate the costs of the monopolistic enterprise. (9) Monopoly may also lead to maldistribution of income, inflexibility, and other unfortunate results, in addition to malallocating capital.

Objections numbered 4, 5, 7, and 8 cast doubt on the appropriateness of profit as a criterion identifying monopoly. These objections also hold against the use of differential profit rates as an indicator of how much monopoly exists or of the welfare loss associated with it. Objections numbered 6 and 9 also count against the latter use, as may 2 and 4. The remaining points, 1 and 3, together with 2 and 4 may be regarded as technical objections.

George J. Stigler has also criticized Harberger's study.[25] He makes four criticisms: (1) The unit elasticity figure is illogical and too low since it requires monopolies to operate where marginal revenue is zero. (2) If monopoly profits are capitalized, only competitive rates of return will appear to be earned. While Harberger found that intangibles did not "hide" a significant amount of profits, other asset titles may; and in any case Stigler simply is not convinced that some industries Harberger found to be excessively competitive and others which he found to be monopolistic can be properly so classified. (3) There may be monopoly gains to some wage earners, material suppliers, executives, and others which inflate costs. And (4) the competitive rate of return should be found for the whole economy, which is probably lower than for the manufacturing sector. Stigler argues that adjustment to meet each of the criticisms would lead to a higher estimate of malallocation and welfare loss.

Stigler does not follow Mrs. Mack's attack on the assumption of a horizontal long-term cost curve, the use of Epstein's data, the use of industry rather than firm profits, the notion that the 1924-1928 period may not serve tolerably as long-run equilibrium for the economy as a whole, nor does he assert the importance of additional dimensions such as income distribution and flexibility. His first and third points pretty

[25] "The Statistics of Monopoly and Merger," *Journal of Political Economy*, LXIV, No. 1 (February 1956), 33-5.

much cover the remainder of Mrs. Mack's objections, and he adds the capitalization argument and the notion that manufacturing is, on the average, more monopolistic than business as a whole.

Stigler's first and fourth points are essentially technical in nature. His second and third points are equally critical of Harberger's use of profit rates to identify monopolistic industries and to measure the amount of monopoly profit and/or welfare loss due to the presence of monopoly in industries so identified.

3. Schwartzman's Estimate

As noted previously, Schwartzman provides an estimate of the social cost of monopoly and the dollar value of the welfare loss, using different data and a larger value for elasticity so as to avoid, as far as possible, the criticisms leveled against Harberger's estimates and procedures. It is useful to review his procedures more specifically at this point. As we have noted, he uses four-firm concentration ratios drawn from census 4-digit industry data in order to classify industries as concentrated or unconcentrated. Gross value product for the industry is taken as the measure of total revenue, but only direct costs as given by the census are included. These encompass cost of materials, fuel, purchased electricity, and production workers' wages. Capital costs, management, and sales office personnel's wages, legal and credit costs, and the like are omitted. The "competitive" profit rate is not an average profit rate which includes the monopolies, but is based only on the earnings of the unconcentrated industries. While elasticity of demand is considered to be identical for each industry group, -2.0 rather than -1.0 is used, and the formulation is constructed so as to enable the reader to insert any elasticity he wishes. The nature of possible bias due to non-constant cost curves and cost curves which differ in height because of monopoly are discussed, but no adjustment is made. Industry data are used. A single year, 1954, is used rather than the four-year average, 1924-1928, since 1954 is the only year for which both United States and Canadian data on concentration are available.

Schwartzman's study avoids objections 1 and 3 as voiced by Mrs. Mack and partially avoids her criticisms number 6, 7, and 8. It avoids Stigler's first criticism and partially avoids those numbered 2 and 3. From this it would seem that the principal objections remaining after Schwartzman's articles are: that asset titles other than profits or intangibles may hide monopoly gains, that factor prices may be inflated by monopoly gains made by suppliers, including labor, and that the profits shown by the "competitive" industries may include some monopoly gains, thereby understating the monopoly element in the return of the concentrated, or high profit industries. All of these objections hold against the use of profit differences both to identify monopoly and to measure the significance of monopoly. The use of profit differences in each case tends to produce an underestimate of the extent of and the loss due to monopoly.

Schwartzman's procedure provides a narrower basis for some of these objections because it rests on quasi rents rather than profits, providing fewer hiding places for capitalized profits and correspondingly fewer factor costs that may be inflated by monopoly at earlier stages. For that reason it is also somewhat less likely to overstate profits in the "competitive" sector. Nevertheless, opportunities for bias remain and may even be enhanced.

In his preliminary comments Schwartzman lists four criticisms that might be made of any effort to relate monopoly to profit rates. They are: (1) Although monopoly and economies of scale probably go together, monopoly profits may be small if the output is small relative to the technically most efficient point. Monopoly may also show small profits if there are diseconomies of scale, but in that case one would expect smaller firms to expand at the expense of the larger ones. This is the objection that Mrs. Mack raised against the horizontal long-run average cost curve. (2) Census industry groupings may submerge small monopolistic industries in heterogeneous industries and large competitive industries may be divided artificially into smaller sections that falsely appear to be monopolistic. (3) Capitalized monopoly profits may be included in the base from which profit rates are calculated. (4) Failure to adjust for profits reported as costs probably results in an understatement of the profits of competitive industries.

Taken together, his arguments imply understatement of both monopolistic and competitive profit, with monopolistic understatement perhaps less than competitive understatement. Still, to the extent that some true monopolies have small profits, and the profits of some other monopolies are either overlooked or hidden in heterogeneous industry classes called competitive, the existence of monopoly is missed by these studies. The size of such error is not known, but it is not likely to bulk large as a share of total production.

4. Additional Sources of Inaccuracies

a. Failure to Apply Standard Welfare Criteria

It is surprising that criticism has not been directed more forcefully to the failure of the basic models to conform to the standard welfare rule—namely, that marginal cost equal price. The relationship between average cost or average variable cost and price does not provide significant evidence about the existence or nonexistence of this equality. Perhaps authors and critics alike are convinced that neither external economies nor economies of scale are important. In that case long-run marginal cost equals average cost, and short-run marginal cost equals average variable cost. But it should be noted that should declining average-cost firms, such as public utility enterprises, price so as to achieve normal profits, monopolistic welfare loss will exist, since marginal cost is less than average cost. Output should be expanded, perhaps substantially.

Likewise, an industry may be characterized by many firms which differ greatly in size and which nevertheless have the same unit costs and still experience a downward shift of its unit cost curves as the industry expands. As in the case of utilities, efficient use of resources requires marginal cost pricing in this instance, which means pricing on the marginal to the long-run supply price of a competitive industry. This must lie below average cost.

Such cases are ruled out by the Harberger and by the Schwartzman techniques, for both measure output in terms of value, the unit of output being a dollar's worth of output. This device ingeniously permits aggregation of highly dissimilar products, but it also makes it impossible to distinguish between an increase of output sold at the same (competitive) price and a larger increase of output sold at a reduced price. Likewise the implied costs cannot distinguish among constant, rising and falling costs, although stability *requires* rising cost per dollar's worth of output. Manifestly, such techniques cannot catch those instances where welfare losses exist due to economies of scale.

The welfare losses due to external or internal economies are probably moderate as a proportion of the welfare loss which their studies do catch, but we have no way of knowing how much escapes. It is very much less than it would be if Chamberlin rather than Dewey were thought to be correct and the numerous monopolistically competitive situations were included.

Additional sources of error confronted by Harberger-Schwartzman type estimates remain to be discussed or elaborated. They relate to the identification of monopoly, the use of quasi-rents or of profits to measure the significance of monopoly, and certain technical matters related to these problems.

Nothing need be added at this point to the critical conclusions in earlier chapters relating to the use of concentration ratios to isolate monopoly power, except to urge that definitions of products defined more narrowly than the typical 4-digit industries used by Schwartzman, and the still more broadly defined groups used by Harberger, are needed for the problem at hand. Until such studies are made, sweeping policy recommendations cannot properly emanate from professional economists.

b. Quasi Rents

Even if 4-digit industries could be accurately identified as competitive or monopolistic, quasi rents provide an unreliable measure of the economic importance of monopoly and of the welfare loss.[26] In addition to the warnings related to profits, listed above, additional problems arise when quasi rents are substituted as in Schwartzman's work. His procedure runs the danger of identifying as "monopoly gains" any favorable difference in capital costs, sales costs, and other costs included in the quasi rents. Industries concentrated in Canada but unconcentrated in the United States may be expected to suffer a higher share of such costs because the smaller but geographically extensive Canadian economy can absorb relatively few firms large enough to be technically efficient in some lines. Because of the sparse population in much of Canada one would also expect sales and credit costs to be higher there in just those industries where concentration is high in Canada and lower in the United States. Efforts to widen and deepen markets may produce lower average total costs but require considerable outlays. But again Schwartzman counts these outlays among the quasi rents. Thus, exclusion of these asset titles which may indeed hide some profits in the guise of costs, nevertheless provides a source of error, particularly when reliance is placed upon comparisons between nations that differ in the way that Canada and the U.S.A. do. This point is elaborated in connection with the next point following.

The composition of Schwartzman's list of 19 industries concentrated in Canada but not in the U.S.A. is not reassuring on these points, including, as it does, such items as malt, narrow fabrics, cement, fountain pens, cotton yarn and cloth, synthetic textiles, petroleum products, slaughtering and meat packing, and aircraft, some of which may require relatively few firms to fill the Canadian market and may tend therefore to have relatively high capital and sales costs per unit of output.[27]

[26] Harold Hotelling, "The General Welfare in Relation to Problems of Taxation and of Railway and Utility Rates," *Econometrica*, VI, No. 3 (July 1938), 242-69. See Harberger "Monopoly and Resource Allocation," p. 81 note.

[27] It may be noted that two of these, petroleum and meat packing, are industries which Stigler, in commenting on Harberger's study, refused to believe to be "excessively competitive" in the United States.

c. Product Differentiation and "Dollars'-Worth of Output"

Another possible source of bias, and one that does not depend upon the possible differences between the Canadian and the United States market, is the degree of product differentiation. While only five or six of the nineteen industries used by Schwartzman can make much use of differentiation, the effect, as noted above, is to understate misallocation. This is closely related to the idea of quality. Suppose a company maximizes its monopoly profit by selling one million games of "Marble Polo," whose total costs are $16 million, at $20 each. The price-average variable cost ratio is 1.25. If in a subsequent year one million games are again produced but in three lines—say $40, $30, and $15—and if they sell approximately equal amounts, but only after substantial design changes and at higher unit costs because of smaller runs, the need to stock a wider variety of models and parts, and so on, total revenue may then rise to $27 million and total variable costs to, say $20 million. The Price/AVC ratio used by Schwartzman rises to 1.35, but the amount of "distortion" and the nature of the welfare effects are unclear.

The increase in sales (total revenue) is not accompanied by any increase in physical output. A large number of buyers get a model at a price lower than heretofore offered, although it is of somewhat inferior quality. The others get a nicer model at greater cost. If we accept the notion that the heterogeneous output of the firm can be homogenized into "dollars'-worth" of output, as both Harberger and Schwartzman do, output rises by $700,000 while costs rise only $400,000, and we may applaud the increased efficiency of resource use and look for entry to eliminate the monopoly profits in time. In time, differentiation may proceed and "dollars'-worth of output" rise further. But costs also rise and a ratio of 1.25 or less may result, indicating a fall in the welfare loss due to monopoly. But if one believes that the differences in price reflect the failure of the industry to offer the preferable alternative, single price pricing to the consumers, then not only is the $400,000 of added costs to be counted against the "monopoly" but the whole $700,000 increase in revenues may be so counted. Entry may or may not reduce prices but it will surely increase total costs and can at best reduce, not eliminate, this type of monopolistic distortion.

Aggregating the output of many firms into products and many products into industries does not average out such error. Schwartzman's model accepts gross receipts as the measure of production not merely for a firm or a product but for whole industries. It may, therefore, be subject to this criticism although few of his industry categories contain much differentiation. Other things being equal, no monopolistic distortion is indicated by Schwartzman's study unless higher sales cost per unit of sales is associated with higher concentration in the Canadian industry. But one of the fruits of large-scale nationwide organizations is access to mass communication on favorable terms. Moreover, a full monopoly has the least need to advertise and otherwise push its product, while a less monopolistic industry structure in the United States may include substantial sales costs among its quasi rents. For these reasons large quasi rents may characterize competitive smaller-scale merchandising rather than entrenched large-scale monopoly power.

In Schwartzman's study five of the nineteen concentrated-unconcentrated pairs do in fact show higher price-average variable cost ratios for the unconcentrated United States firm. The industries involved are excelsior, fountain pens and pencils, macaroni, aircraft, and abrasive products. All have moderate-to-high ratios in the United States, ranging from 132.2 (macaroni) to 183.8 (fountain pens and pencils); while the range for the whole group is from 101.9 (slaughtering and meat packing) to 194.5 (cement). While the last three of the five are declared to be exporting industries and thus more competitive than the concentration ratio may indicate, it seems obvious that the characteristic structure of local markets confronting specific Canadian firms producing the several products of these industries might well differ enough from the United States firms to produce different proportions of sales, capital and other costs per unit which would in no way reflect differential monopoly power.

Schwartzman recognizes the bias that may result from the very considerable conglomeration of unlike products found in many 4-digit industries but did not adjust his estimates to allow for it.[28] Mrs. Mack criticized Harberger for using industry rather than firm data. The arguments found in Chapters II and III of this book would go further and urge a product-centered approach because firms are usually multiproduct enterprises. The profit margins for different products differ considerably. Unless the 5-digit, and even the 7-digit, products are considered separately, one cannot tell whether a high price-average variable-cost ratio indicates monopoly gains, unusually high but competitive costs of the types excluded by Schwartzman, unusually high product differentiation of a non-monopolistic type, or some other condition such as an unusually high growth rate.

Harberger also considered the problem of conglomeration within a

---

[28] Schwartzman, *Effect of Monopoly on Price*, p. 352.

category and concluded that the understatement of distortion for this reason was not great. He calculated that if profit rates for three sub-industries were, say, 10 per cent, 20 per cent and 30 per cent rather than 20 per cent each as the overall figure would show, the welfare loss would be increased from 2 per cent of aggregate sales to 2-1/3 per cent.[29] But this does not meet the point that the 10 per cent "competitive" profit rate is too high because it may include costs as well as monopoly returns. Building up costs by non-price competition (which improves the functional distribution of income at the cost of a probable loss of efficiency) or capitalization of profit into executive compensation or rents may make the misallocation and welfare cost greater than that implied from the differential profit rates.

d. Vertical Industry Structure and Hotelling's Model[30]

There is another well-known relationship that has not been forthrightly expressed in criticism of the small welfare losses found by Harberger and Schwartzman when they applied Hotelling's model, although it is touched upon in a more or less elliptical way by both Mrs. Mack and Professor Stigler. The "marketing structure" of an industry can virtually obliterate the connection between the profits or quasi rents shown by an industry and the amount of misallocation appropriately related to it. The Hotelling model is then inapplicable to an aggregation of products (let alone industries) because of the fallacy of composition.

The Hotelling model may be applied to vertically integrated one-product industries of the classical type which are used in most theorizing. If industries of this type are monopolized at only one stage, output, prices, and profits are affected in the way postulated by Hotelling-Harberger-Schwartzman. But industries are rarely vertically integrated throughout, nor are the various stages of the production of input-output-input, etc., so neatly coextensive. Let us, nevertheless, drop only the assumption of complete vertical integration and hold to the assumption that each firm produces only for its own industry, selling its product entirely to firms at higher stages until the consumer market is finally reached. Let us suppose further that labor unions are also organized on this basis.

It has been shown that under these circumstances two or more layers of monopoly separated by competitive strata will yield smaller than monopoly profits to the industry while production falls *below the simple*

---

[29] Harberger, *Monopoly and Resource Allocation*, p. 84.
[30] Hotelling, "General Welfare," *Econometrica* (July 1938), pp. 242-69.

monopoly optimum and consumers pay *higher* than simple monopoly prices. The kernel of truth in the doctrine of countervailing power, considered in a static frame of reference, is that aggregate profits can be greater, output larger, and consumer price lower if monopolistic firms enjoying monopoly powers must bargain with monopolistic suppliers to reach mutually agreeable results, rather than dominating the supplier or being dominated by him. Equilibrium is thereby moved from a worse-than-simple-monopoly position to the simple monopoly optimum.[31]

[31] It may be helpful to review the standard, highly compressed graphical analysis that demonstrates this point. Figure 9-A follows the usual practice, letting the two monemporists (where each firm has both monopoly and monopsony power) be virtual brokers, each of which sells the product it buys with negligible

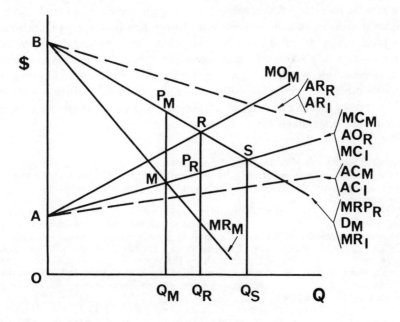

Figure 9-A

additional costs. Technically input is a fixed ratio of output, so that the marginal product of either firm is 1 throughout. The slopes of the demand curves reflect diminishing marginal utility, and of the supply curves reflect the increasing supply price of the basic factors. The marginal revenue for the "retailer," and for the industry as a whole, is line *BRS*, but it is the demand curve for the "manufacturer" whose marginal revenue is *BM*. The marginal cost for the industry and for the "manufacturer" is *AMS*, but it is the average outlay curve for the "retailer" whose

Where a competitive layer lies between the "bilateral" monopolists, worse-than-monopoly results may be enduring because of the remoteness of the potential bargainers.

Bilateralism cannot be expected to last very long when each stage of production fits so neatly into the next. But the neat coextension of the outputs at the various stages is uncommon. Even when it exists, two monemporists, separated by one or more competitive stages, can fail to see or negotiate their way to the improved, simple-monopoly position. Yet no analytical difference is raised because of the interposition of competitive stages.

In practice the various inputs needed almost always come from a variety of industries, so that monopoly at some earlier stage affects costs in several industries which are otherwise quite unrelated to each other. Some may be monopolistic, some not. Integration is scarcely practicable. A price policy designed to realize the private and public gains involved in moving to a position of simple monopoly where bilateral monempory or layers-of-monopoly exist, while holding to simple monopoly prices in the otherwise competitive sectors, would produce a price structure that smacks strongly of price discrimination and would surely be unlawful in the United States.[32]

---

marginal outlay curve is line AR. Thus the independent maximum for the "retailer" is OQ_R, who wants price Q_RP_R and who would thereby win profits equal to ARB leaving only AP_RR for the "manufacturer." Industry profits are reduced in this case should the "manufacturer" establish his preferred industry maximum at OQ_M with price Q_MP_M, but the "manufacturer" would enjoy profits of BMA leaving only BMP_M for the "retailer." But total profits may be increased to ASB by integration, since that is the simple monopoly profit. Price discrimination against consumers and suppliers may increase profits further. Division of the gain presents problems of the sort dealt with by the theory of games, but output and employment in the industry rise, and prices of the industry's product fall, as the consequence of integration and the dissolution of two layers of monempory into a single simple monempory.

[32] The possibility of monopoly gains is more restricted than often appears to be the case. The limitations are obscured because bilateral relationships usually start from a situation where one firm enjoys both monopoly and monopsony power, and the other has monopoly power. The usual conclusions could not follow were the "retail" firm selling in a competitive market and the "manufacturer" buying in competitive markets.

Imagine two such firms existing in long-run competitive equilibrium prior to achieving monopsony and monopoly powers, respectively. Let the retailer then discover that he may influence the price of his purchases by varying his sales provided that he concentrates them with a particular supplier, thus becoming a monopsonist. But nothing in this increases the efficiency of the supplier, and a lower price associated with lower purchases along the supplier's marginal cost curve will reduce total receipts below long-run total costs if the supplier buys from competitive markets. Hence, exercise of monopsony power leads to

If the analysis of oligopoly presented in this book is correct, the importance of structural distortion and the gain offered by bilateral negotiation or integration must be considered to be minor. The situation illustrated in footnote Figure A, for example, implies increasing marginal costs and huge profits. Under such conditions, entry is to be expected in the absence of restrictions enforced by government. Where legally free entry is associated with a reasonably well-developed capital market and moderately alert entrepreneurs, full monopoly is short lived. Oligopoly, on the other hand, when defined simply as few firms producing a rather well-defined product, is very common, as shown in Chapters III and IV. But if the difficulties and risks of coordination are as great as suggested there, the departure of the more typical oligopolistic price and output levels from competitive ones is not great when undifferentiated products are considered. Neither the restrictions associated with the layers of oligopoly (that undoubtedly exist) nor the possible gains that may be realized by their elimination would be so great as to invalidate the general order of Harberger's and Schwartzman's findings in spite of their shortcomings. This conclusion may not be appropriate where products are differentiated in such a way as to suggest first- or second-degree price discrimination. Nothing has been said so far, however, about the labor market.

e. The Labor Markets: Unions and Layers of Monopoly

The labor market is not the other side of the moon. The power to negotiate higher wages is restricted by competition from foreign sources, jurisdictional invasions by rival or tangential unions into more highly

---

exit and reestablishment of suppliers' prices, rather than to profits to the monopsonist.

Monopoly power on the part of the manufacturer against the retailer who is a typical competitor in his product markets runs into the same blind alley. If exercised, the supplier's monopoly power raises the retailer's costs above the market price, bankrupting him rather than yielding gain to the manufacturer.

In bilateral situations of this type, where the firms are otherwise in competitive markets, collusion offers higher aggregate profits than dominance by either one or the other of the parties. But in this case the only mutually viable collusive position is precisely the competitive one. If technical conditions are unchanged and neither firm starts with positive profits which can be shared, the integration of their structures offers neither economies nor power over the basic cost of materials or labor to the group, nor does it offer power over the sale prices of goods produced by the group.

We may conclude that there is no point in organizing a monopoly to offset the monopsonistic power of a firm selling in a competitive market at zero profit nor in organizing monopsony power against a competitive factor market unless the rival (and potential partner) can be expected, and perhaps assisted, to acquire a measure of monopoly power.

paid occupations when the discrepancy between skills and pay becomes too great, development and potential development of labor-saving capital improvements, growth of non-union enclaves, and other essentially market forces which shorten the reach and limit the aspirations of entrepreneurs of labor. Nevertheless, labor enters at every level into the structure of an industry from the raw materials to the sale to consumers. Moreover, a labor union, treated as an enterprise that "produces" labor, is not easily integrated into the industrial structure by merger with firms, although the bargaining and labor contract may be regarded as a collusive agreement. Nevertheless, if we think of the "manufacturer" in footnote Figure A as a union, it becomes more difficult to imagine the easy integration of the union and the "retailer"—even if their joint interests are served and some gains can be offered to the consumer to their mutual advantage. When such action does occur, as it apparently has in the bituminous coal fields of the Tennessee Valley, it is likely to be deprecated by union people and others as a betrayal in a holy war, and by some economists, at least, as a logical step but one that, for all of its virtues, smacks of a monopolistic conspiracy against the consumer, since the optimum position is monopolistic.

Moreover, the union movement has a pervasive tendency to produce —but little tendency to remove—layers of union monopoly at the various levels of production. Firms at each stage of production from raw materials to sales of final products deal with different unions, the leadership of which is constrained to work rather directly in the interest of its members. If one were to assume that the steel industry, the steelworkers' union, the automobile companies, and the United Automobile Workers were each a separate monopoly, mutual benefits to workers in steel and automobiles could follow cheaper steel and lower manufacturing costs for automobiles as a result of a combined union policy oriented toward simple monopoly rather than independent monopoly at each level. But this kind of coordination seems to be at least as remote a possibility as similar united action by the steel and automobile companies, in spite of the fact that unions enjoy a legal basis for coordination of policy that is denied business enterprises.

f. Unions and Differential Wages

The effect of labor organization upon wage discrimination is not clear. In principle, the same opportunities for second- and third-degree discrimination exist for unions as for firms as described in Chapter II and VII, although firms may be more rational. The benefits that go with length of tenure, in particular, spring to mind as possible violations of "equal pay for equal work." On the other hand union scales, worked out in negotiations with enterprises, are usually less complex and are judged by labor economists to be more rational than the scales usually found in non-union establishments of equivalent size and complexity. This suggests that wage discrimination which favors the employer may be replaced in part by wage discrimination that favors the workers. In that case, monopolistic distortion may as well be lessened as aggravated by union activity. But differing market positions yield vastly different degrees of influence to different unions with resulting unequal pay to people of similar aptitudes, skills, and efforts. These discrepancies persist indefinitely, although subject to the slow-acting persistent pressures mentioned at the beginning of this section.

Because the labor market equivalent to entry is weak, and because different unions are found at different levels in the industrial strata extending from raw materials to finished product, and also because the costs of union action are often borne by workers outside of the policy-making union or by the public generally, it follows inevitably on a priori grounds that "layers-of-monopoly" distortions are more likely to be associated with labor union activity in labor markets than with business activity in product markets. Econometric tests can, no doubt, be devised which can throw some light on the importance of this type of distortion. Neither Schwartzman's nor Harberger's studies are constructed in a way that can illuminate distortion in labor markets. From a formal point of view, estimates can be made using Hotelling's models if competitive earnings for particular skill and aptitude classes can be found and compared to actual rates, and some estimate of supply elasticity can be supported. This procedure would not allow for the shift of the functions involved with the removal of monopoly at earlier stages of production, and would therefore understate the loss. On the other hand, there is probably less putative distortion associated with second- and third-degree discrimination in the labor markets than there is in product markets, because the employers are more likely to be expert and the negotiating process less subject to Veblen-effects.

g. Long-run vs. Short-run Welfare Loss

It is surprising that Schwartzman (using 1954 data) should claim that his estimates provide close corroboration of Harberger's simply because the estimated dollar value of malallocation is similar. He finds monopoly profits to be $4.9 billion, while after adjusting 1924-1928 data for price and output changes, Harberger's estimate is $4.6 billions. But Harberger attempts to include all costs and to estimate the long-term loss due to monopoly while Schwartzman omits many costs and expressly attempts to find the short-term loss. Schwartzman's estimate should show a larger welfare loss for both reasons.

Short-term monopoly profits can be expected to exceed long-term profits by a considerable amount, for, as Harberger quite properly notes, his measure includes "not only monopoly misallocations but also misallocations coming out of the dynamics of economic growth and development and all the other elements which would cause divergent profit rates to persist for some time even in an effectively competitive economy."[33] These developments were surely present in both 1924-1928 and in 1954, but the longer time period should reduce their influence somewhat in Harberger's study.

Schwartzman's estimates should be still higher because quasi rents are larger than accounting profits. Thus Schwartzman's study does not provide corroboration except in the sense that both are smaller than commonly expected and that Harberger's estimate is somewhat lower than Schwartzman's.

5. Opposite Bias

Against the rather numerous reasons why Harberger's and Schwartzman's studies underestimate the welfare loss due to oligopoly, there are three ways of accounting for their statistical findings that do not involve oligopoly at all. The first of these is the multiproduct multi-industry nature of the large modern firm. The data summarized in Chapter VI and its appendix reveal that multiproduct firms also tend to be multiplant firms. Professor V. R. Fuchs finds that the extent to which firms are multiplant-multiproduct in their operations is more highly correlated with profit than is the degree of concentration.[34] While this finding can be interpreted in various ways, it tends to support the thesis presented in these chapters, namely that independent maximization (or quantity dominance) coupled with an active search for new subproducts or early entry into the production of variants of subproducts introduced by others is a satisfactory, perhaps a superior, road to high profits as compared to the monopolization of a product in the traditional sense of the word. Attempted monopolistic control or exclusion of entry involves special risks and may require costs out of proportion to the gain.

If this is true, attempts to isolate monopoly profits may instead be isolating industries dominated by aggressive innovating firms which

---

[33] Harberger, *Monopoly and Resource Allocation,* p. 84.

[34] Victor R. Fuchs, "Integration, Concentration and Profits in Manufacturing Industries," *Quarterly Journal of Economics,* LXXV, No. 2 (May 1961), 278-91.

have larger than normal profits because they have better than average representation in the newer markets and those which enjoy expanding prospects for growth. Their profits may reveal astuteness in finding wants and anticipating scarcities and reducing them, rather than revealing monopolistic restriction.

A second reason why the Harberger-Schwartzman findings may not relate to monopolistic restriction is that high growth rates, according to the proposition advanced in Chapter V, are associated with initial monopoly. One expects high concentration to exist during the period of entry and/or expansion by the innovator. Any industry, new or not, that is growing tends to have high profits. The fact, alluded to by Harberger, that small firms in profitable industries are typically as profitable as the larger firms in those industries is consistent with this thesis, because firms of all sizes innovate and invade profitable new lines. Neither concentration, nor anything more than the short-run profits needed to call for the desirable equilibrating response, may be involved in the small "monopoly" gains found by Harberger and Schwartzman. Indeed they appear too modest to perform that function unless some profits are hidden.

The third reason that may falsely relate concentration to profits rests upon the statistical work such as Weiss' cited in Chapter V, that shows the smaller firms in many industries to be suboptimal. Highly concentrated industries tend to have a disproportionate proportion of total output produced by the optimal sizes of firm. Small firms in most industries have lower profit rates while the larger firms in most industries have higher rates; the average profit rate will be higher in the more concentrated, especially the very highly concentrated, industries. But the average profit rates will reflect the composition of the industry, not monopoly profits by the large firms in one industry as against competitive profits by the large firms in the other industries.

These arguments suggest that the evidence relating monopolistic or oligopolistic structure to misallocation of resources is rather weak. Those factors, "layers of monopoly" and discrimination, whose effects are not measured, might reverse this judgment if their effects could be ascertained. But the welfare case against monopoly in modern America stands unproven.

E. Welfare and Size of Establishment

The traditional welfare economics is couched in terms of satisfaction of economic wants. It is quite possible for such wants to be satisfied in approximately an optimal manner while ideals of political and social organization are violated. For that reason, studies, even if irrefutably documented, showing the economic innocuousness of monopoly may diminish concern over the "monopoly problem" but little.

There is no evidence that the number of firms is declining, but the nature of the distinction sought can be clearly seen if one were to imagine the enterprise of the nation concentrated in 100 firms of equal size, all of which are equally active in the production of each product in each market. Suppose further that additional firms are prohibited by law, but that each existing firm is free to innovate new products and to match profitable new products introduced by the others. Concentration ratios and indexes of disparity would be low, and the ratios of marginal cost to price and of receipts of factors to alternative costs could be optimum. Nevertheless, the political power associated with the management of such enormous concerns would be considered a threat to the well-being of individuals, in that the independence offered by freedom to establish independent enterprises would be lost, and individuals at each job level, particularly those in management, would be dependent upon the continued good opinion of the controlling groups. The relationship between the management of such firms and government would always be suspect.

The data presented here, and conclusions drawn from them, would not lead one to suppose that enormous conglomerate firms would enjoy economies of scale, either as the output of a given product or as the total output of a multiproduct firm grows. If this is true, the political danger involved in large conglomerate firms yields small, perhaps zero, economic benefits.

A policy that limits the size of firms somewhat, promotes additional firms, and lowers indexes of disparity may safeguard those aspects of well-being that are associated with independence at small or even zero economic cost. But before any policy like this can be recommended, much more should be known about the competitive structure of the product and factor markets.

F. Summary

The welfare criteria developed from formal microeconomic theory are found to be paradoxical and too demanding to be applied directly. The effect of oligopoly upon output per head, functional distribution of income, and misallocation of resources is, therefore, substituted. Oligopoly is found to be no less compatible with growth than are other structures and not likely to worsen the distribution of income in spite of the analyses by Mrs. Robinson, Kalecki, Bain, Scitovsky and Steindl which lead to contrary conclusions. Differentiated oligopoly may result in significant misallocation of resources, however, if the analysis of Chapters II and VII is accepted.

The econometric studies of the welfare loss due to monopoly made by Harberger and Schwartzman are examined. While their conclusions are the same as those advanced in this book for homogeneous products, it is found that neither study would reveal misallocation that results from price discrimination—product differentiation if increased costs absorb the gains. Nor would either reveal the effects of layers of monopoly at multiple levels of the marketing structure of the industries. While merger or collusion can in principle reduce these to the simple monopoly level, this does not appear to be probable, particularly when it is remembered that rival unions may provide the monopolistic element. Nevertheless, while it is probable that these studies underestimate the amount of monopolistic distortion, it is possible that they overestimate it. The welfare case against the degree of monopoly that exists in the United States is not proven.

Finally, it is noted that from a social-political standpoint the sheer size of the larger enterprises may cause undesirable structural changes in American society even if the enterprises lack monopoly or oligopoly power.

Appendix A

Table 1

List of 5-Digit Products Included in This Study
for Which 7-Digit Data Were Also Available (Group 1)

Group Designation	Number	Description
A and B	28233	Regenerated celluolosic products, except rayon
	28523	Other inorganic pigments, including white extender
	37421	Passenger train cars, new
C	22413	Woven narrow fabrics, except elastic
	22522	Men's finished seamless hosiery
	23924	Other house furnishings
	23940	Canvas products
	24994	Other wood products
	27610	Lithographing
	34440	Sheet metal work
	34712	Incandescent portable lamps
	35993	All other machine shop products
	39711	Molded plastic products
	39714	Other fabricated plastics products

Table 1—Continued

Group Designation	Number	Description
D	28231	Cellulose plastic materials
	28421	Synthetic organic detergents, packaged
	28521	White opaque pigments
	28620	Softwood distillation
	32311	Laminated glass, including safety glass and wire glass. (Integrated producers only.)
	32720	Gypsum products
	32925	Asbestos-cement sheets and wallboard
	32926	Other asbestos and asbestos-cement products
	34920	Safes and vaults
	36131	Integrating instruments, electric
	36152	Power and distribution transformers
	36912	Storage batteries, except SLI type
	36920	Primary batteries
	36991	Lamp components
	37230	Aircraft propellers
E	22741	Linoleum
	28232	Vulcanized fiber
	37413	Locomotives, industrial and mining type

Additional Product Classes Used Where Comparison of
5- and 7-Digit Data is not Necessary (Group 2)

Group Designation	Number	Description
A	28253	Non-cellulosic synthetic fibers, except glass
	35831	Household sewing machines
	38712	Watches, domestic movements, jeweled type
	38713	Watches, domestic movements, pin lever type
	35112*	Steam, hydraulic and gas generator set units and parts

* 5-digit data are missing

Table 1—Continued

Additional Product Classes Used Where Comparison of 5- and 7-Digit is not Necessary (Group 2)

Group Designation	Number	Description
B	28251	Acetate yarn
C	34950	Screw machine products
D	33521	Aluminum plate and sheet
	34240	Files and rasps
	34293	Vacuum and insulated bottles and jugs
	36510	Electric lamps
	38615	Photographic film and plates, silver halide type
E	22231	Thread for use in home

Table 2

Number of Industry Groups, Product Groups, and Products
in Sample Taken from 1954 Census of Manufactures, by
Major Analytical Group

Group Designation	2-Digit (21 possible)	5-Digit[a] (1,023 possible)	7-Digit (7,000 possible)
I.			
1. Concentrated (8 firms or less produce 99%)			
A. (Expanding)	3	5 ⎫ (3)	⎫ 24
B. (Stable or contracting)	2	3 ⎭	⎭
2. Concentrated (20 firms or less produce 99%)			
D. (Expanding)	7	20 (15)	102
E. (Contracting)	3	4 (3)	15
II. Unconcentrated			
C. (Expanding)	7	12 (11)	151
Different 2-digit groups	13 [65%]	—	—
Totals	—	44 (32) [4.3%]	292 [4.2%]

[a] Where both 5- and 7-digit data are available, the number of classes is shown in parentheses.

Index

Sylos postulate, 94

Temporary National Economic
 Committee, 64
Thorp, W. L., 53, 67
Transportation costs, 139, 209, 210
Triffin, Robert, 50
Turner, Donald F. (*see* Kaysen)

Unions (*see* Labor unions)
Utility frontier:
 effects of independent maximization, 155
 effects of subproduct generation,
  19-23, 41
 in isolating generic products, 19,
  42

Variants, 21, 37
 as "centers" in identifying generic
  products, 24-25
Veblen effects, 225
Vertical integration:
 analyzed, 220-223
 related to research, 163
Vesper, Howard G., 97
Villard, H. H., 160

Wages:
 discrimination due to labor unions,
  224-225

effect on one-price policy, 21
share, under monopoly, 206-208
Watkins, M. W., 30
Weintraub, Sidney, 50
Weiss, Leonard, 86, 227
Welfare economics:
 criteria, 150, 195-197, 215-216,
  228, 229
 optimum industry policy, 228
Welfare effects:
 criteria for, 150, 195-197, 215-217
 loss due to concentration, 60, 195-
  229
  not proved, for U.S., 229
  understated, by Harberger,
   Schwartzman, 226, 229
 of oligopoly:
  on growth, 197-199
  on income distribution, 199-
   208
  on resource allocation, 208-
   227
Weston, J. Fred, 53, 62
Wilcox, Clair, 64
Williams, B. R., 157, 159, 171, 173,
 174, 192
Worcester, D. A., Jr., viii, 87, 104
World War II, 36, 125
Worley, J. S., 167, 168

Yule distributions, 85